# The Muselmann at the Water Cooler

ACADEMIC
STUDIES
PRESS

# The Muselmann at the Water Cooler

Eli Pfefferkorn

BOSTON

2 0 1 1

Library of Congress Cataloging-in-Publication Data:
A catalog record for this title is available from the Library of Congress.

ISBN 978-1-936235-66-7 (cloth)
ISBN 9781618111579 (paper)

Book design by *Ivan Grave*
On the cover: *Stefan Wegner, "Auschwitz". 1946*

Published by Academic Studies Press in 2011
28 Montfern Avenue
Brighton, MA 02135, USA
press@academicstudiespress.com
www. academicstudiespress.com

*This memoir is dedicated
to Medical Science and its practitioners
who have kept me alive to the distress of my foes
and to the delight of my friends;*

*And to Dieter Hartmann and Leon Elmaleh
who stood by me at critical junctions in my life;*

*And to Izzy Beigel, Vivian Felsen, Jon Geist,
Malkah and Harry Rosenbaum
who expressed faith in me, each according to his or her disposition.
Many thanks;*

*And to Lily Poritz Miller and Eli Honig
who weeded the solecisms out of the text;*

*And to Marcel Kedem, my pro bono lawyer,
who has shielded me from the evil eye of the law;*

*And to Sharona Vedol, my copy-editor,
who has scanned the manuscript with an eagle eye
and listened to its speech cadences with an eager ear;*

*And to all my well-wishers.*

*In memory
of David Hirsch,
who saw the skull beneath the skin before so many others.*

# Table of Contents

# Foreword

I started to read *The Muselmann at the Water Cooler* as a courtesy to an acquaintance I had known for some three decades. As a rule, I read survivors' memoirs because they bring me, an outsider, closer to an event that I study.

I was intrigued by this memoir because while from the time we first met I knew Eli Pfefferkorn was a survivor, he was quite reticent about sharing his own experience. The fragments of his story that I learned over the years did not cohere. From his age, I knew that he was a child survivor of the Holocaust; from his self-presentation, I knew that he was an Israeli; from his Bar-Ilan pedigree — for Bar Ilan is Israel's *only* Orthodox University, quite akin to Yeshiva University — I presumed that he had come from a traditional background. But his Jewish journey was far from traditional. And his academic background, a Ph.D. from Brown University in English literature, promised that unlike many survivors' memoirs, this work would be self-written and well-written.

I was not disappointed: within the very first page of this important work, reading it became imperative, intellectually and emotionally. I soon recognized that Pfefferkorn was a serious student of evil and could write brilliantly about it. His insights glisten throughout the work; there is no false heroism or self-aggrandizement, no simple story of cheap grace and miraculous escape from death, no simple affirmation of hope in humanity or trust in the noble efficacy of transmitting the story, of bearing witness. Rather, this is an honest and modest retelling by a man who spent a lifetime studying the evil once encountered, seeking to understand the human condition after the Shoah. His story was well worth waiting for, honed by time and life's disappointments as well as achievements. We are experiencing a first telling by a man now in the Biblical years of his strength; he has now lived more than four score years.

Eli's post-Holocaust story is fascinating. Rather than go to Palestine after the War, he went to England. His depiction of English society and of his host family is insightful and charming, with a touch of English reserve. He was still a very young man, with a long future ahead of him, and his restlessness and inability to settle down attracted him to the sea, where he sought training as a sailor, an odd job for a young Jewish boy. His maritime training attracted the attention of the Zionist activists, who were preparing for the inevitable War of Independence and sought his seamanship skills to defend the coastline. Drawn to Palestine by a sense of duty to the past rather than Zionist aspirations for the Jewish future, Eli ended up in land combat far from the sea, in the sands of the Negev. A member of MACHAL, volunteers from abroad, he refused an order to fight in Israel's one-day civil war to disarm the LECHI-Stern Gang, and ended up in prison. His depiction of the prison is cheerful — no prison memoir writes he!

Pfefferkorn slowly made his way into Israeli society from the outside in. As an outsider in Israel, a Jew among Canaanites, he provides insights into Israeli society of the 1950s and 60s that remind us of a bygone era, its aspirations and pretenses intellectual and otherwise. As an outsider in the USA later on, Pfefferkorn is a keen observer of American academic life in the tumultuous years when universities were defied, when students confronted their scholarly professors, who were unable to understand them or to transmit the classics to them.

Despite the seeming openness of this work, Pfefferkorn conceals almost as much as he reveals. We learn more about his girlfriends than about his wife and daughter, more about his scholarly life and academic politics than of family and community. His narrative is about his early quests for a Jewish, rather than an Israeli, identity, a quest that took him to Bar-Ilan University and the study of Jewish classics. These studies were instrumental in resolving the identity ambiguity he experienced during his life in the Diaspora, in contemporary Canada.

Pfefferkorn describes in depth his time at the United States Holocaust Memorial Council, where he was associated with Elie Wiesel, then the chairperson of the Council. Notwithstanding his recognition of Wiesel's contribution to bringing Holocaust awareness to the world, his criticism of Elie Wiesel is broad. Contrary to Wiesel's views, Pfefferkorn does not mystify survival. While Wiesel elevates suffering to mystical level, Pfefferkorn notes that

> Suffering is not necessarily a morally refining agent that turns apathy into compassion, greed into generosity, meanness into graciousness and ambition into humility. With few exceptions, the good did not become better and the bad might have become worse.

Few survived with the intention of bearing witness, he writes: "most merely wanted to live." Pfefferkorn's views further deviate from those of Wiesel on a series of issues, particularly pertaining to the obfuscation of the human forces at work in history. "After all, the concentration camps were invented and operated by humans, not monsters or Martians; and human depravity does not begin or end with the concentration camps", he asserts.

Sounding more like Primo Levi than Wiesel, Pfefferkorn points out that:

> Shocking as it may sound, the concentration camps demonstrate empirically that these mammoth human labs were essentially the microcosm of the human species and of the world at large; the predatory behavior of the inmates manifested in verbal and physical violence was a distorted reflection of the plots hatched at the water cooler, conspired in the Common Room, planned in the Boardroom and occasionally pillow-talked in the bedroom.

The core of this book is what happened to Pfefferkorn during the Shoah and its aftermath and the reflections he brings to bear on his experiences in his later life. Pfefferkorn knowingly walks us into the heart of darkness in a roundabout way and then pauses, inviting us to reflect upon it, changes the topic, only soon to return to that time and that place.. His weaving in and out from the narrative into ruminations requires the reader's attention and allows time to come closer to the core of the Shoah. If it is a hard journey, ultimately it is a rewarding one.

For a very long time, Pfefferkorn avoided sharing his Shoah experience publicly, concocting the story that he had spent the wartime years in England and had been part of the *Kindertransport*, the 1939 effort to bring German, Austrian and Czech Jewish children to England. His friends were not told, his professors were not told, his girlfriends were not told — even his wife was not told. Still, some surmised his true story from what he alluded to and wrote.

Still, for one who disguised his survivor identity for so long, Pfefferkorn insisted upon survivors' prerogatives. There is a distinction, he writes, between *knowing about it* and *knowing it*, the latter of which only comes as a direct encounter with the human instruments of evil.

Pfefferkorn's experience provided him with a direct encounter with the human instruments of evil. In the ghetto of Radzyń Podlaski in the German-occupied Poland, he worked as a sort of "gofer" for the Nazi Criminal Police. The Chief of Police, a fatherly figure, surreptitiously showed him kindness, a rare gesture of humanness.

In the Skarżysko Kamienna Forced Labour camp, he managed to get a job in the Mansion of the Camp *Kommandant*. From this vantage point, he was able to observe the dispensers of evil in their daily lives. He saw the perpetrators as men and women, inceptively made in God's image but disfigured in the service of the Nazi Dark Design. His portrayal of them is nuanced, and yet his revulsion at their deeds is no less intense.

Similarly to Primo Levi, who wrote of the concentration camp, "Here there is no *why*," Pfefferkorn notes that in that topsy-turvy reality there was no causal link between action and reaction. Survival required "quick adjustment, with ensuing traumatic effects." For others, the absence of *why*, the inability to recognize the reason for the absence of causality, endangered their survival. His own *modus operandi* for survival he describes in the following telling paragraph:

> Survival in this inhuman environment was driven by paradox. Exposure to rampant cruelty might intimidate you and dull your hunting instincts for extra food; a middle spot on the *Appell*; or a chance of getting into an *Arbeitskommando* overseen by a *Kapo* whose humanity had not yet been drained. Thus, to stay alert you had to shield yourself from the surroundings. But the protective shield that enabled you to keep the sight of terror at bay posed the risk of dulling your vigilance of your surroundings, a necessary condition while on the bread prowl. Darting back and forth between alertness and oblivion became my survival tactic.

It was true then, perhaps true of Pfefferkorn's entire life, and certainly true of *The Muselmann at the Water Cooler*. One had to dart back and forth.

In his closing paragraph, Pfefferkorn reminds us that the Warsaw ghetto Diarist Chaim Kaplan ended his *Scroll of Agony* with a question: "When my life ends, what will become of my Diary?" Pfefferkorn wonders: "And when mine ends, will my memoir survive to keep on telling the story? And has it been worth it?"

The answer to the first question, I am certain, is: *The Muselmann at the Water Cooler* is a major and enduring contribution not only to survivor literature but to our understanding of the evil that he studies. As to the second question, only Eli Pfefferkorn himself can answer. But I certainly hope that his answer is yes.

*Michael Berenbaum*
Los Angeles, California

*Written on Shushan Purim, 5771,*
*the festival when catastrophe was avoided and Jews were triumphant and joyous.*

# Preface

I was nurtured by oblivion. My nurturers had my best interest at heart, as well as their own. In conversation, they would gently steer me away from the ordeals I had experienced on the Continent (as they referred to mainland Europe), across the British channel. Of course, they would ask in amazement how I had managed to hold out for such a long time in such a Godforsaken environment and at such a tender age. Their pain was visible. Haltingly, stumbling on my freshly acquired English phonemes and vowels, I started to splutter bits and pieces of my experience. But these nurturers of my oblivion gently piloted my fragmented tale in another direction, distancing me from my recent past and nudging me toward a prospective future. And I readily submitted to silence. I needed space and time to draw a line of separation between the encircling barbed wires of the Majdanek concentration camp and the sprawling landscape of Hampstead Heath, where I sought peace of mind — and eventually achieved a separation of sorts, at least in my waking hours.

Shortly after Liberation, Leonard Montefiori secured permits from the Home Office to bring a few hundred survivors under the age of sixteen to England. The members of the Jewish community generously gave of themselves, shepherding us, with the guidance of a professional team, back into civilization. The community's members were urbane, woven into the fabric of English society's upper-middle class, and they maintained their ethnic identity through a variety of cultural and religious institutions, an identity whose native contours became more discernable in the wake of the war. They knew that it was only by the grace of God, or a quirk of history, depending on their viewpoint, that they were spared the fate of their European co-religionists. The Gestapo had lists of the Jewish communities earmarked for the *aktion* as soon as the invading German army landed on the British island. Undoubtedly, this fact was lingering at the backs of our hosts' minds. They saw the cinema reels showing mountainous piles of corpses being shoveled into mass graves and watched wide-eyed skeleton-like figures hobbling across the grounds of the recently liberated concentration camps. These images sent tremours through the social and mental equilibrium they had attained over the ages in some difficult trials.

Still, they refused to recognize the capacity of humans for evil, preferring to anchor their faith in the humanistic values of Western culture. This was no less true of the non-Jewish English population. Though painfully aware of the atrocities committed by their perennial enemy, going back to the Great War, the English too preferred to stay swaddled in the comforting perception of Man's rational image, a product of the Enlightenment philosophy. But all this I thought of only years later, in my nightly ruminations, when my memories persisted in demanding my attention.

Even before the dust of the war had settled, a curtain of silence descended on the bloody European theatre. Ironically, the survivors became willing participants in this silence. The world wanted to forget, people wanted to go on with their daily lives, and the survivors were inhibited from talking about their experiences. To be sure, there were those survivors of the Coleridge Ancient Mariner type, few and far between, who were driven to talk about their ordeals. Whenever the climate was conducive, they would freely roll up their sleeves, pointing to the number tattooed on their arm and accompanying the showing with a tale of horror. But on the whole, a kind of consenting silence was struck between the parties. The resistance fighter and poet, Abba Kovner, portraying a young Jewish girl in search of asylum in a convent, put it starkly in *My Little Sister*: "The world saw/ and withdrew."

In the Haifa University faculty lounge A.B. Yehoshua, a renowned Israeli novelist, engaged a group of professors in a discussion about the inimical relationship between the *Shoa* and Israeli society. In his habitually impassioned style, he questioned the reason for the manifested lack of sympathy towards Holocaust victims and the cool reception given to the survivor–immigrants. He posited that the catastrophe that had befallen the Jewish people demonstrated the truth of the premise of the Zionist ideology, and that one would have expected Israel to appropriate it, making it part of the Israeli narrative. I sat at another table listening to the exchange. By then, I had looked into the matrix of this troubled relationship and could have shared with him and his discussants my thoughts on the reasons for the alienation that he was questioning. But at the time, in the seventies, I was still living in a camouflaged identity as an assimilated Israeli, so as to be "one of us," as required by the then-prevalent social etiquette, and chose not to take part in the discussion.

Israel's view of the *Shoa* looked back to the twenties and thirties when a new tribe of Jews was born into Zionism, to quote Berl Katzenelson's famous coinage. An iconic Labour leader, Katzenelson left an indelible imprint on the life of the mind experienced by the early pioneers and their children. In his lectures and essays, he altered the sum total of the Jewish Diaspora mentality, from which a new generation emerged, committed to the singular goal of restoring to the Jewish people the majesty of a sovereign nation.

Renouncing Isaiah's prophetic vision of an idyllic era, they held on to the sword with the same tenacity as to the plough, for both were instrumental in shaping the fundamental structures of the coming Jewish State. And in this defiant spirit, the newly forged semi-military forces were ready to confront Erwin Rommel's army, which threatened the invasion of Egypt and Palestine, in 1942. In his recent book *In Ishmael's House: a History of the Jews in Muslim Lands*, Martin Gilbert points out the impending fate that awaited the half-million Jewish residents in Palestine in the event of Rommel's breakthrough. In this state of mind, the new type of Jew in Palestine found itself a kindred spirit with the Jewish fighters in the ghettos and forests. He could not, however, identify with the Jewish masses who shadow-walked, arms locked, to slavery. Martyrdom was alien to the newly forged ethos in the Land of Israel.

Yehoshua was a friend whom I met socially on various occasions, and with whom I talked about a variety of subjects. He was an intellectually lively conversationalist who held his listeners' attention whether he talked about politics, literature or any other topic on earth. Should I ever be sentenced to serve time, Bullie, his childhood nickname, would be my first choice for a cellmate. In the course of our wide- ranging discussions the Holocaust came up in a number of different contexts, but he never asked me where I spent my time in the war years, and I did not feel comfortable enough to tell him, though this information might have added a stimulating aspect to our conversation, and probably would have coloured our relationship. Nor did I share my war experience with my closest friends or even my family. In the day, I was role-acting the *Sabra,* the newly minted Hebraic *Homo-Sapien,* and at night I retreated to my memory labyrinth.

Vered, my daughter, took an inordinate interest in the Holocaust at age seventeen, though she had no idea that I was a survivor. Her Holocaust awareness evolved in stages. First she became a vegetarian, and then followed that by becoming strictly Kosher and attending synagogue Friday nights. When I asked her whether she believed in God's existence, she retorted that that was an irrelevant question. Keeping the Jewish tradition was her response to Hitler's Final Solution, she told me. The full extent of her emotional involvement in the Holocaust, however, I only found out after we saw the film *Pawnbroker*.

The film features Sol Nazerman, a concentration camp survivor who sets up a pawnshop in Harlem, hardly an obvious choice of occupation for a former university professor. Vered took the pawnshop to be a metaphor for the concentration camp warehouses in which the belongings of new arrivals were kept. She was most troubled by Nazerman's alienation from his social surroundings and particularly by his outright rejection of the overtures of friendship shown to him by his pawnshop employee and particularly by a neighbourly social worker. She wondered whether his sense of displacement was symptomatic of survivors. After a rather long pause, she said that she looked around in the audience and she could not see a single classmate of hers. "They should make viewing this compulsory," she blurted out.

I'm relating this episode to illustrate the discomfort I felt in exposing my own past. In my relationship with Yehoshua and more poignantly with my daughter, I held back. This reticence also explains why I came to tell my story so late in life.

Many years later, while taking walks in Toronto's expansive parks, I began hearing incoherent voices coming from a far-off past, jumbled up with those from a nearer past.

It took a while to sort them out. Many of them came from the London stage, where I had watched Jacobean matinees and plays of The Theatre of the Absurd performed in the evenings. They had held me in a magic thrall, and I was fascinated to find that although the plays were written two hundred years apart, their respective characters did not vary very much from each other, except in language and outward appearance.

Others of the voices I recognized from my former concentration camp life; they were my fellow inmates. It was as if the actors had walked off of their stages and merged into the mass of the wearers of white-and-blue striped pyjamas. Among them was the *Muselmann* who gave up on life and shuffled at the end of the soup line but never made it to the vat. I avoided contact with him.

Still others were characters I recognized from places closer to home, to my present life. They were my office buddies. I whiled time away with them at the water cooler, and yet when I defied the powers that be, my water cooler companions unceremoniously dropped me. No more buddying at the water cooler — what would the offended CEO say if he saw it?

Even as I was in the midst of writing this memoir, I received a telephone call from Germany; the caller identified himself as Hans. He had read a hundred pages of my memoir (which I had previously sent to a friend in Germany) in one sitting, and wanted to translate the memoir into German with a view to finding a publisher. He spoke in a faultless American English, acquired at a North Carolina high school. Hans had a few queries that he would like to put to me, if I did not mind. The tone of his voice was reverent. From what he could tell, the manuscript had been written with an immediate urgency, so, he wondered, why had I not told my story earlier?

How to explain my reasons? The first difficulty was in finding a voice that would at the same time embody the many voices in my head and retain their respective individuality. Once I had sorted out the voices, I contemplated how to resolve the contradiction between the claim that the Holocaust was a unique historical phenomenon and the commonplace reaction of the concentration camp inmates to the extreme situation that they confronted. In these forbiddingly brutal circumstances, evil was rampant and goodness timidly manifested. Here, survival was the determinant factor that guided human behaviour. How was I to convey the paradox of a world that had no laws and yet was reigned over by rigid rules that required absolute obedience? And there was the nagging question of who would want to listen to such a harrowing story of a world that came off the Judeo-Christian hinges on which it had swung for thousands of years? What language could I use to convince my prospective readers that the employees at the water cooler who gave a wide berth to their fellow employee when he became a pariah were the moral equivalent of the concentration camp inmates who turned a blind eye to the *Muselmann* in the soup line? Moreover, the pariah and the *Muselmann* are interchangeable at some level. And I, who have lived in both worlds, have been on both sides of the divide.

Judging by the behaviour of human beings in extreme situations, one must come to the conclusion that human nature is plastic and that it transforms itself to meet the changing conditions of its environment, its primary impulse being Darwinian. In the final analysis, what we are rests on where we are at a particular time and at a particular life's crossroad.

# Glossary

*A dasz* — Put out (Hebrew)
*Aktion* — Deportation (German)
*Aliyah* — Immigration to the Land of Israel (Hebrew)
*An Amerikaner* — An American (Yiddish)
*Anus Mundi* — Anus of the world (Latin)
*Appell* — The roll call in concentration camps (German)
*Apellplatz* — Roll call ground (German)
*Arbeitskommando* — Labour detail (German)
*Aussteigen* — Get out (German)

Bar-Kochba — Leader of the 132 CE war against the Roman Empire (Aramaic)
*Blockaelteste* — An inmate supervisor of a barrack (Camp slang German)
*Brith* — Circumcision (Hebrew)

*Chevre* — Chaps (Hebrew slang)
*Cholent* — A traditional Sabbath stew (Yiddish)
*Cockney* — A dialect spoken in the London East End

Dachau — The first concentration camp, outside Munich, established in 1933
*Die Juden sind unser unglück* — The Jews are our misfortune (German)

*Einsatzgruppen* — Special Aktion Squads (German)
*Es muss klappen* — It must tally (German)
*Eved Adonai* — Servant of God (Hebrew)

*Feld III* — Majdanek was divided into five "Fields" — each "Field" was called Feld (German)

*Feldafing* — The Displaced Person camp where I stayed (Displaced Person Camp, DP)
*Führer* — Leader Hitler's official title (German)

*d`Golus* — Of the Diaspora (Yiddish)
*Gemainde* — Official Jewish communal organization (Yiddish)
*Gleichschaltung* — A method applied with extreme rigour in the concentration camps, intended to flatten out the inmate's individuality and make him a one — dimensional being (German)
*Guleh* — Redemption, deriving from the Hebrew "Geula " (Yiddish)

*Haaretz* — A respected Israeli newspaper (Hebrew)
*Hasag* — A German ammunition conglomerate
*Haverim* — Comrades (Hebrew)
*Hester Panim* — The concealment of God's face (Hebrew)
*Hitlerjugend* — The Nazi youth movement (German)
*Hosanna* — Redemption (Hebrew)

*Iberlebn* — To outlive the enemy (German, also Yiddish)
*Iberlebn di soinem Israel* — To survive the enemy of the Jews (Yiddish)

*Jedem das Seine* — Each to his own (German)
Jonathan Balter — Son of the Balter family, who became my foster parents In the course of the years, a relationship evolved that lasted for a long time
*Judenrat* — Jewish Council set up by the Gestapo to organize all facets of Jewish life in the ghetto (German)
*Judenrein* — Cleansed of Jews (German)

*Kaelnik/Kaelanka* — A sobriquet for inmates who had received their initiation in concentration camps and were transferred to labour camps (Polish)
*Kak dela, patsan?* — How're you doing, lad? (Russian)
*Kapo* — An inmate who has been appointed as block leader (Camp slang German)
*Khleb* — Bread (Russian)
*Kesselmeister* — In charge of transporting the soup vats from the kitchen to the Block (Camp slang German)
Kielce — Name of town in Poland
*Kharoshi Yevereiski Malchik* — Good Jewish boy (Russian)

*Kippa* — Skullcap worn by Orthodox Jews (Hebrew)

Knesset — Israeli Parliament (Hebrew)

*Krakowiaks* — The group of inmates that arrived from the Plaszòw camp, which was adjacent to the city of Kraków, Poland (Polish)

*Kriminal Polizei* (Kripo) — Criminal Police (German)

*Kristallnacht* — The night of Broken Glass (German)

*Kupiec* — My mother's maiden name, by which I went in the camps


*L`univers concentrationnaire* — The universe of the concentration camp (French)

*Lager* — Camp (German)

*Lagerältester* — An inmate in charge of a concentration camp In this case in charge of Feld III in Majdanek (Camp slang German)

*Lagerkapo* — An inmate in charge of a concentration camp (German)

*Lebensraum* — Living space (German)

LECHI — An acronym for Fighters for the Freedom of Israel (Hebrew)


MAHAL — An acronym: volunteers who joined the IDF during the War of Independence (Hebrew)

Majdanek — Name of a Concentration camp

*Malina* — A hideout

*Mały żydek* — Little Jew (Polish)

MAPAI — An acronym: Israeli Labour Party (Hebrew)

MAPAM — An acronym: The United Labour Party (Hebrew)

*Mezzuzot* — Traditional scrolls encased in holders nailed to doorframes in Jewish homes (Hebrew)

*Mikvah* — Ritual bath in which it is customary for a bride to immerse herself prior to her wedding (Hebrew)

*Minyan* — Ten Jews needed for public prayer (Hebrew)

*Mischling* — Product of an intermarriage between Aryan and Jew (German)

*Muselmann* — I have checked out the etymological origins of this term, but they are vague. What I am suggesting is as follow: Islam is a submissive religion, and the believer surrendering his will to Allah is not unlike the Muselmann who gave up on his life, surrendering it to be puffed to heaven through the crematoria chimney (Camp slang German)

*Mütze an/ mütze ap* — Cap on/cap off (German)


*Napoleonchiks* — Gold coins minted during the Napoleon reign (Yiddish)

*Naqba* — The Catastrophe, a word used by Arab leaders to describe the founding of Israel (Arabic)

*Nurenberg Laws* — Restrictive anti-Jewish legislation (Laws promulgated in the city of Nurenberg)

*Oberammergau* — A German town famous for its production of a Passion Play
*Oberscharfuhrer* — rank equivalent to staff sergeant (German)
*Palmach* — An acronym: Jewish Commando in Palestine (Hebrew)
*Picryners* — Worked in the factory that produces underwater mines made of picric acid Their longevity was about six to seven weeks (Camp slang Polish)
*Prominante* — Privileged inmates (Camp slang German)

*Quo Vadis* — Where to? (Latin)

*Rączka* — diminutive word for hand (Polish)
*Rapportführer* — A non-comissioned SS officer (German)
*Rateve zik* — Save yourself (Yiddish)
*Rause-rause-schneller-schneller* — Out-out-quickly-quickly (German)
*Rehmsdorf* — A camp satellite of Buchenwald

*Sabra* — A native — born Israeli Jew (Hebrew)
*Shoah* — Holocaust (Hebrew)
*Shtetl* — Jewish village in the Pale of Eastern Europe (Yiddish)
*Sieg Heil* — Nazi Salute (German)
*Skarżyko Kamienna* — A Hasag ammunition factory in Poland made of three slave camps: A, B, and C
Stanislawski Method — A unique theatre style of performance in Russia
*Stubendienst* — A person in charge of a number of bunks (Camp slang German)
*Sukkah* — A small booth built for the holiday of Sukkot, to commemorate the wanderings for the Israelites in the desert (Hebrew)
*Szmalcownik* — Polish thugs who blackmailed Jews living under Aryan identities (Polish)

Terezin — Theresienstadt in German A model showcase ghetto in Czechoslovakia
*Todesmarsch* — Death March (German)
*Tommies* — A sobriquet for British soldiers who served in Palestine to denote the Tommy —guns they carried (English)
*Totenkopf* — Skull sign emblazed on the hat (German)

Treblinka — Death Camp located in Poland
*Trzymaj się, Edek, trzymaj się* — Hold out, Edek, hold out (Polish)

*Überkapo* — Senior Kapo (Camp slang German)
*Übermensch* — Superman (German)

*Vernichtung durch Arbeit* — Destruction through work (German)
*Volksdeutch* — A German living outside Germany during the Third Reich
    (German)

*Waffen SS* — Military units composed of many nationalities (German)
*Wehrmacht* — German army (German)
*Wehrmacht Stabsunteroffizier* — An army corporal (German)
*Wenn das Judenblut vom Messer Spritzen* — When Jewish blood from knives
    spurts (German)
*Werk C* — The third camp of the Hasag ammunition factory (German)
*Werkschutz* — Factory police — made up of Volksdeutch (German)
Whitechapel — An area in East London
*Wiedergutmachen* — Restitution for Holocaust survivors (German)
Wintershill Hall — A beautiful old house in Southampton, England, which
    housed surviving boys and girls from Germany
*Wo ist der bursche?* — Where's the lad? (German)

*Yad Vashem* — The Holocaust Museum in Jerusalem (Hebrew)
*Yediot Acharonot* — A popular tabloid newspaper (Hebrew)
*Yishuv* — The Jewish community in Palestine before the establishment of the
    state of Israel (Hebrew)

*Zicharon* — Memory (Hebrew)
*Zurück* — Return (German)
*Żydy* — Jews (Polish)

# The Muselmann
# at the Water Cooler

Out of the crooked timber of humanity no straight
thing can ever be made.
*Emmanuel Kant,*
*Proposition 6*


I am Lazarus, come from the dead
Come back to tell you all, I shall tell you all.
*John 1:1 to 2:2*


## In the Beginning there was Bread and Freedom and Apathy

A walk through London's Hampstead Heath on a late, drizzly afternoon is
hardly a fitting scene with which to start telling my life's saga. Nor is it less
odd to undertake the task of bearing witness to the European Manquake in
the closing chapter of my life, seventy years after its first rumblings. But as the
intimation of mortality is becoming more tangible, I thought that I should try
to put down the experience of a boy, eleven years old during those incendiary
times that engulfed Europe, leaving behind them the smouldering pages
of the Enlightenment and its faith in the progressive refinement of human
nature. During those years, I was standing on the *Appell*, concentrating on
how to get into the most enviable spot of the soup line so as to increase my
chances of getting a ladleful of thicker soup. It did not occur to me to ask
myself why the new arrivals at the Majdanek concentration camp from the
West European countries, who often arrived in passenger carriages and had
been brought up in the spirit of the French Revolutionary Trinity — Liberty,
Fraternity, Equality — so readily fell sideways in the struggle for survival.
Primo Levi called them "the drowned." Only years later, assisted by hindsight
and literature on the subject of survival in extremity, did I learn that belief
in the lofty image of Man (in the generic meaning of the word) provided
a shortcut to the crematorium.

Where I begin my narrative, however, these thoughts aren't occupying
my mind. I am walking alongside Jonathan across the foggy patches dotting
Hampstead Heath's sprawling lawns. Jonathan is taking me for high tea to
his family, the Balters, whose role is to provide me with the personal care of
a foster family while I live with a group of other boys in my situation. Sensing
my anxiety about the coming visit, he is telling me about some members

of his family: his father, who came to England from Austria and is now a medical consultant on Harley Street, and his brother Richard, a lieutenant in the British army. Jonathan himself attends medical school, hoping to follow in his father's footsteps. And even as he is trying to ease me into the family landscape, he is feeling his way toward finding the right moment to coax even a tidbit of my own story from me. Ever so careful not to be invasive, he drops his voice to a murmur that trails off with a question mark. His curiosity rivals his intent to instil in me a level of comfort for the high tea occasion. The whole situation is awkward. Jonathan is much taller than I am and my ears are not yet attuned to the English inflections; I have to crane my neck to catch the meaning of his words. But apart from the physical communication difficulties, I have a mental difficulty in talking about my immediate past experience.

At 833 Finchley Road in the Northwest of London, just a short stroll from the Golders Green underground station, about fifteen boys resided under the tutelage of counsellors who were themselves refugees from Nazi Germany and who still mismatched the "th" consonant, that bane of English-language novices, with its succeeding vowel. If memory serves me, five of us shared a bedroom: Witek, Kurt, Hans, Julius and I. Surprisingly, our childhood and our parents lost to the Nazi *Judenrein* rage never came up in conversation. Usually before bedtime we would talk about films we had seen and gossip about the love affairs the staff was carrying on. The senior staff member, a strictly religious person, had reportedly been spotted frolicking with an atheist colleague in a closet. This affair was particularly titillating because of the theological incompatibility of the couple. Apparently persuasion was no match for passion; eroticism outweighed faith.

We engaged in the usual prattle and horsing around that could have taken place in any young male dorm after lights-out. Kurt, the most garrulous among us, flaunting his knowledge of German, mentioned that he was from Bielsko, a town in western Poland; Julius, prominent in his boxer's physique, declared his pugilistic ambitions; Witek, serious, often brooding, envious of Kurt and contemptuous of everyone else; Hans standing out in his Aryan appearance, a seeming poster boy of racial purity, blond, blue-eyed and tall. There was, however, one flaw in his genetics. Hans was a *Mischlinge*. Because he was fathered by a Jew, the Aryan blood his mother gave him was tainted and consequently landed him in a concentration camp. That was all we knew about each other. It was not that we sat around a table and formulated a code of silence. It happened of its own volition. I was still hovering in psychic numbness and fit neatly into this blank silence. It was as though we triggered a reverse homing device to steer clear of the ineffable images in our waking hours, only to make them appear in our nightmares. But the nightmares were also cloaked in silence. Psychologists might define our behaviour as denial. Rather, I believe it must have been an instinctive choice to mask death with life. Joy had ways of overwhelming sadness.

Even if I had the psychological vocabulary and the English linguistic skills, I could not break my silence to Jonathan. Now as we're drawing closer to the Balter home, I'm rehearsing the high tea etiquette I was gently tutored in by the hostel staff. "Don't forget to say 'please' and 'thank you' and keep in mind not to make noises when drinking your tea or munching on sandwiches." Thankfully, Jonathan has stopped talking. And I know that one day I'll be ready to respond to him.

## One or Two?

As we enter the anteroom of the house, Mrs. Balter, whom I have already met at the hostel, greets us. She hangs up my damp coat and leads me into the living room. The room is dimly lit. Around a blazing fireplace sit Richard and Mrs. Rubin, the grandmother. I'm dumbfounded. I've not seen a family sitting together in a cozy atmosphere in about four years. Richard, in full lieutenant uniform, gets up from his chair to greet me and I walk over to Mrs. Rubin, who clasps my hand. Her grip transfuses a warmth that makes me want to stay there forever. For a brief moment she brings back memories of my own granny's hugs. Talk is not coming easily, but we fall back on chatting about the weather and I manage to express my views in a way that surprises everyone. I like the misty blankets that often hang over the Heath, and the fine drizzle is also to my liking. To show off my English skills, I add, "as long as it's not raining cats and dogs," making sure that I have the animals in the right order. They smile. Our UNRRA instructors in Germany have taken into account the fact that the weather is the lingua franca of English daily conversation and thus have equipped us with the appropriate phrases.

When Dr. Balter arrives we all sit around the fireplace and Mrs. Balter tinkles a tiny bell. A door opens and a maid wearing an apron and cap appears, pushing a cart with the provisions for high tea. I'm tempted to go to the cart to check out its contents, but I hold back. These things are not done. I settle for a sneaked glance. Holding a white jug in her hand, Mrs. Balter asks me, "Eli, with or without?" even as she is pouring tea into a cup. I hesitate for a fraction of a moment, considering my options, but experience tells me that whenever food is involved, 'with' is always better than 'without.'

I watch a thin stream of milk flow into my cup. While still holding the cup, Mrs. Balter addresses me again "One or two?" This time I answer without hesitation. "Two, please." Two lumps of sugar plunge into my cup, which makes its rounds until it reaches me. I hold it in my hand. I watch in amazement as others balance their cups on their laps, and carefully imitate them.

I am getting ready for the next question, concerning the tray that lies on the grid, holding crustless cucumber sandwiches, arranged in symmetrical order, which I consider the prize of the high tea gathering. They are tasty but tiny, and after my first helping I would very much like some more. I am trying to figure out whether there are enough of these miniatures for another round. I count them and divide the number into the seven high tea revellers, but lose count. When asked whether I'd like another sandwich, my answer is a steady "No, thank you." I surprised myself with my canapé restraint.

Whenever I reflect on my post-war experiences this high tea encounter stands out in my memory: the grand lady, Mrs. Rubin, clasping my hand, her dark penetrating eyes like a scope into my psyche; the serenity permeating the living room; and my hope that I could be part of this, even for a brief time.

Viewed from a rational perspective, relief should have ensued after our liberation, but it did not. Once the threat of physical extinction was gone, we were shocked into confronting our loss. Our families had vanished into the blue smoke; our homes were occupied by strangers or, worse, by former neighbours. This irreparable loss overshadowed our joy in freedom. Consequently, the pent-up sadness erupted into our consciousness.

## A Journey Back in Time

On a train journey I take back to my hometown in search of family and friends who might have eluded death, I meet liberated forced-labour Poles who are heading back home to their villages and towns, to their families. I crouch in a corner, my eyes seeking hints of another Jewish face. I'm looking around to see whether someone my age is sitting, like me, shrunk in a corner. As the train crosses the German border into Poland, a host of eagle-emblazoned, fluttering, white and red flags greet us. The young Poles rise to their feet and break into song, singing the national anthem. I'm alone and lonely amidst joyful celebration. I also stand up.

This train journey from Germany to Poland, acid-etched in my memory, evoked the same kind of sensation that had been my constant companion in the camps, albeit without the alienation. Alienation connotes ruptures of intimate friendships, distancing from familiar surroundings. Friendships, familiarity: these were alien to the camp ethos. Those inmates who put trust in friendship, who clung to the past, were brutally disabused of those notions.

I was travelling to a country from which I was estranged. The sight of the celebrating returnees on their ways to their homes filled me with envy. I felt a deepening abyss of emptiness inside of me. Notwithstanding their suffering and deprivation in Nazi bondage, they were travelling to their future, while I was going to a funeral. Ironically, we were travelling on the same train in the same direction but with two opposing destinations. There was no one waiting for me, nothing to look forward to.

I got into town early in the morning and began looking for the Soviet military headquarters. There, I would feel safe from Jew-baiting Polish vagabonds. My instincts led me to the building that had formerly housed the *Kriminal Polizei* (*kripo*) offices for which I had worked in the year of 1942 until my deportation to the Międzyzec Podlaski ghetto. My provenance, so to speak, being unmistakeable, the guard greeted me with "*Kak dela, patsan?*" His fatherly tone was heartening. My too-large clothes hanging loose on me, the rucksack strapped onto my shoulders, the worn-out sneakers showing parts of my toes, the gaunt appearance — my entire presence resembled that of a scarecrow, albeit a speaking scarecrow. In today's parlance, I made a perfect poster boy for a liberated concentration camp prisoner.

Using the rudimentary Russian that I had picked up in Majdanek and in other camps, I asked the guard whether there were any Jewish people in town, "*Ivrei Tcholoviak su da?*" He didn't know but asked me to wait. I sat on the stony stairs, lightly leaning on my rucksack, careful not to squash the bread and the marmalade inside it.

Images, grainy and fuzzy, slowly etching into the contours of vignettes, forced themselves into the present. The stairs I was sitting on now had a familiar touch. I had sat on them many times waiting for the arrival of my Gestapo masters, so I could carry their valises to their quarters on the second floor. Just a few yards from these very stairs S.D. Hoffmann had slapped me, sending me rolling on the cobblestones amidst the pealing laughter of his *Wehrmacht* companions. Across the street, I saw familiar faces, people I knew who had appropriated the house of a Jewish family. The streets were coming alive with people ambling to their work. The guard's voice jerked me back to reality.

A female officer approached and gently pulled me from the stairs. She led me across a yard to a parallel street. I gathered from her that there was only one Jewish family in town. "You've no family," she said.

"No!" I answered. She spoke German with a strong Russian accent. I knew the family that had lived in this home before the deportation. The entrance door was ajar, and the officer slowly opened it and the way she was greeted indicated familiarity.

I stood behind her rather expansive frame. She moved sidewise, and I stood facing the mother of a former school-mate of mine. "Oy, you saved yourself," she murmured, omitting my name. Uttered in a voice of a lament, a kind that I had never heard before or since. In the Sulejów labour camp, I had heard heart-wrenching woe on *Tisha B'av*,[1] commemorating the destruction of the First and Second Temple in Jerusalem. I had heard wailings in cemeteries. Nothing I had ever heard resembled this "Oy, you saved yourself." The "Oy" has been reverberating in my ears with a question mark till this very day. She and her two daughters had hidden with a Polish peasant for two years and were liberated by the Red Army. Her husband and son also hid, but with another peasant in a different village. Just before liberation they were betrayed and shot. All this she told me in a nonchalant and tired voice, periodically interrupted by a sigh, while intermittently turning her head to the window as if expecting someone. I was not surprised by the detachment of her narration.

On my first trip to Germany, perhaps two to three weeks after having been discharged from a Russian military hospital in Prague, a friend — of whom more later — and I traveled together. On the way, we stopped in Lódź and sought out a makeshift hospice set up by international relief organizations for post-Holocaust migrants. There we hoped to find lodgings for a couple of nights before resuming our travels. As we got off the train at the railway station, three well-dressed men approached us. Seeing middle-aged Jews in such robust physical condition was rare mere weeks after liberation. They did not even vaguely resemble concentration camp survivors. Indeed, they had lived disguised as Poles during the war, they told us, apparently to explain their unusual appearance. "Where do you come from?" the question was addressed to me. I knew that the man was not interested in finding out my hometown. What he meant was our more immediate provenance.

"Both of us ended in Terezin from Rehmsdorf," I answered.

"Either of you been in Skarżysko Kamienna?"

"I was in *Werk C.*"

---

[1]    Tisha B'av, a fast day.

A flicker showed on his face. "Did you know — " (he mentioned a name)? I had shared a bunk with him. A few years older than I, he had become my buddy, briefed me on the camp mechanism and its personalities, and comforted me when I came down with fever. After I got a privileged job at the Mansion, the Hasag administrative quarters, I was able to secure some extra food for him and shared rumours with him that I picked up at work. It suddenly occurred to me that I had not seen him at the deportation assembly in the camp. I assumed at the time that he had escaped the night before. Now, facing his father, my gut told me otherwise. With a hint of a tremor in his voice, he said, "He hid in a crucible to wait out the deportation and got shot." His sentence, spoken in a seemingly calm voice, belied a deep pain, echoing the voice of my classmate's mother.

The liberated of Paris, Oslo and other Nazi-occupied cities greeted the liberators with flowers and cheers. I do not think that we in the camps gave voice to outbursts of jubilation. Of course, there was a natural sense of relief, and there was undying gratitude, and there was bread to dull the twitching hunger. And there was a sense of resignation. At the time, this father's story about his son's death and my hostess's story about her son's and husband's deaths, told in tones of acceptance, had not sounded odd. It was only years later that I thought of it as strange behaviour. Apparently, human absorptive capacity of sorrow is limited, and on reaching a critical point, it shuts off. This is exactly what happened to the mother, the father and myself.

But now, back to Poland and my friend's mother's house. After a day's rest, I walked down to the river-bank. It was here that I had first learned how to swim. In the summers, my playmates and I would go down to the river to frolic in the water, play soccer and play pranks on our girl classmates, who tended to keep to themselves, soak in the sun and pursue their fantasies. The domineering presence of the older boys did not spoil our fun activities as long as we showed a certain degree of obsequiousness. Free from parental oversight, they indulged in Epicurean delicacies. They had voracious appetites for ham and pickles but would not dare to go into town themselves to buy the ham, for fear of being seen by a member of the Jewish community. We, the younger boys, became their "mules" hiking back and forth between town and the riverbank. "What if someone notices me and tells my Mother?" I tried to protest when asked to hike to town. "All the other boys do it, why, you scared or something?" This question explicitly accused me of cowardice. This I could not allow. On my way to town to purchase the non-kosher goods, I felt resentment. It was neither my piety nor the four-kilometre round trip that upset me, it was that they bullied me into this venture. After all, it was summer and I was away from school, an institution where I was expected to listen and obey. Now it was my time to do what I fancied, although Mother's summer guidelines were something else. I took the matter up with my friends. Though they shared my annoyance they nevertheless thought that the deal was fair: "The older boys teach us how to swim, allow us to play soccer with them and protect us, if need be." These seemed to be wise words. After the unclean goods were delivered, they would sit in a circle in the shade of an old oak tree and enjoy the feast in a communitarian spirit. During one of these rituals, the meanest of the bullies called me over and offered me a slice of ham. I refused to eat it. "What, you've had dairy," he mocked me, "and aren't allowed to eat meat?" I stood there wavering between being made a laughing stock and suffering the combination of God's wrath and mother's punishment. The fear of God and of Mum prevailed — or perhaps it was of Mum and of God?

This was all far in the past now. When I returned, summer had not arrived yet. The place was quiet. Here my mental childhood landscape had been shaped. Triggered by my encounter with this place in the present, scenes of the past began slowly rolling forward: at this spot I swam across the river for the first time; further up in the field, the girls huddled under the shadow of a tree, the same huge oak tree that gave shade to the older boys, who sprawled all over the place enjoying their Torah-forbidden food; here was Hochman, my classmate who surreptitiously dropped food for me in Majdanek, and there was Reuven, my chief accomplice in mischief at school, vying for the soccer ball — these memories came uncoiling from a world at once familiar and yet alien.

As I returned to my hostess's house, peals of laughter wafted through the open window. I was surprised. When I had arrived in the early morning, the house had been shrouded in silent mourning. Its contents were stuffed in suitcases, except for the functional daily items. It was a house in transit. The family was waiting for some valuables hidden with a peasant to be returned. The laughter I heard was incongruous with the sombre environment of the house. On entering, I came upon the older daughter in what looked like an intimate chat with a young man to whom I was introduced. We kept up an informative conversation, mostly about our immediate plans. Like other young couples, they had eyes only for each other. In this charnel house, new life showed its first budding.

Before leaving town, I thought I would go back to take leave of my interrupted childhood. In late morning on the following day, I set out to see what had become of the Jewish neighbourhood. Again I went back to places that were an integral part of me. Have you ever walked through a cemetery whose graves are open and empty, the names of the absent corpses chiselled on the headstones? As I walked along the street, the images of gaping graves loomed up in long lines before my eyes. Each house used to be home to a family that I knew: the bakery where Mother used to rush late on Friday to buy *challa* for the Sabbath; the ice cream and soda store, an essential stopover on the way back from the river; the school, where play was sought more than learning — each spot recalled a moment in longing. Much as I wanted to, I could not bring myself to visit our former home. It was another house now. There was a void. I returned to Germany.

### *Quo Vadis?*

The good people of the United Nations Relief and Rehabilitation Administration (UNRRA) registered the children in Feldafing, the Displaced Person Camp, for repatriation and immigration. These were savvy people who knew we had no place to return to, yet they had to go through the formalities. The Feldafing children's unit housed about 150 girls and boys ranging from twelve to sixteen years old. We were waiting… waiting for something to happen. The place was humming with rumours. A mere visit to the camp by an UNRRA high official sufficed to arouse new expectations. Soon, we whispered, we would be going to the United States or England, the preferred destinations. A medium choice was Australia; the last fallback was France. The rumours took on a life of their own. So when the news came, officially confirming that we were scheduled to fly to England, excitement swept across the camp. Two obstacles impeded our way to redemption.

One appeared in the form of a new contender. The Zionist activists in Feldafing vied for us with the intention of influencing us to immigrate to Palestine. In the year 1945 the Jewish community in Palestine, known as the *Yishuv*, launched an intensive series of actions to establish a sovereign Jewish state. To reach this objective, it geared up its intellectual and emotional energies as well as its manpower. But since Jewish manpower was limited in Palestine, its activists sought to recruit young people from the Displaced Persons Camps. They resolved to prevent our departure for England by putting psychological pressure on us.

Radical ideologies (irrespective of their origin, rationale or motivation) in their political implementation are zealously pursued by their adherents, who are usually oblivious to the cost in human suffering. The end justifies the means, sloganeered the Bolsheviks. Zionism was no exception, notwithstanding its noble aim.

Happily, we made it through their obstruction, only to meet with the other impediment: the English fog. After having waited for three hours at the Munich airport we were turned back because of foggy conditions. Naturally, we were disappointed, but the disappointment did not pickle into resentment thanks to a convent, our last refuge before take-off to England. There the nuns took care of us. Compassionate yet not overindulgent, they gave us a feeling of welcome. If the convent suffered from the short food supplies endemic in 1945 Germany, we did not feel its effects. The nuns made sure that we got fed and had enough sleep. The UNRRA staff kept us busy, teaching us commonly-used English phrases and folk songs that we sang in unison. The melody of "My Bonnie lies over the ocean/ my Bonnie lies over the sea/ my Bonnie lies over the ocean/ oh bring back my Bonnie to me," lingered in my musical repertoire for a long time. We waited for the English fog to scatter and, quite unexpectedly, while touring the countryside courtesy of the GIs, we detoured to the Munich airport. The fog had lifted. The RAF planes landed and waited for us to board.

On arrival at the Air Force base, we were greeted by the gracious Women's Royal Air Force (WRAF), who, after serving us a hearty supper, tucked us into crisp white sheets, curbing our freedom of movement during the tossing and turning occasioned by our nightmares. The following morning buses took us to a beautiful mansion in the countryside, Wintershill Hall near Southampton, where we would stay for the next few months. A huge backyard boasted a number of huts, apparently erected to accommodate the new arrivals. The mansion comprised a spacious kitchen, a large dining room and recreation rooms. It was there that our rite of passage into civilization began. But it was to be a long haul.

As we were led into a huge dining room by our solicitous hosts, my eyes met rectangular tables laden with an assortment of food: fruits, steaming pots of soup, and loaves of sliced white bread. It was like the end of times, the white bread ushering in a new millennium. Obviously, the staff had been apprised of the acquisitive food impulses induced by tormenting starvation over a period of three to five years. Upon encountering this bountiful display of food and the white bread, the centrepiece of the bounty, the boys charged the tables in a bull-like stampede. It was not as if we were hungry. Since liberation, we had been provided with plenty of food by a series of agencies. Only four to five hours earlier we had enjoyed a sumptuous breakfast at the Air Force base. Then why this wild food rush? It was a Pavlovian response to the sight of food. As concentration camp inmates, satisfying the monster relentlessly clawing at our entrails had occupied our entire beings. The monster had been particularly demanding of a growing thirteen-year-old boy. In all my waking hours I had been mentally focused on food, scavenging extra crumbs of bread and scurrying across the kitchen area in search of a soup vat which might have remaining morsels stuck to its walls, susceptible to scraping, and devising other tactics. Given this background, I should have been poised to join the stampede. My survival instincts urged me to go for it; my body was taut, rearing for the spring, and yet my mind would not give the command. I stood there zombie-like, watching my fellow survivors landing on the tables. Subsequently, I found a quiet place behind some stairs where I lay down on the rucksack bulging with my worldly possessions. Prominent among them were chunks of bread spread with marmalade that I had stored from breakfast at the British Air Force base. I soon fell asleep.

In the camps, food had become my daily hallucination and my nightmare realization. No wonder this fixation on it spilled over into my post-liberation life. It morphed from obsession with food to observing the way people ate. Weddings, wakes, parties and other feasting occasions were my prime fields of study. The velocity of the spoon, from the dip into the bowl to its arrival at the orifice; the angle of delivery; the amount of food heaped on the fork; the visible gratification spreading over the consumer's face as the food reached its target, the ensuing gastronomic epiphany — all these visuals were a feast to my eyes.

At the high school where I later taught, lunch hour assumed a kind of ritual which combined eating, gossiping and whining. The boys and girls sat on the floor in small semi-circles in order to eat their lunches. I was fascinated by the way they went about performing the ritual. The boys wolfed down multi-layered sandwiches and cheese-dripping pizzas; the girls delicately munched their vegetable sushi (presumably counting the intake calories embedded in each munch), sucking every bit of its essence. To a sociologist this would be an ideal scene for studying the comparative eating habits of the two genders. I too engaged in comparison, but of a totally different nature. I likened a thirteen-year-old boy obsessively focused on diluting the acidic fluids in his entrails to his modern counterparts indulging in their feasting spree. And as if by reflex, I speculated on who among them would have had a better chance of survival in extreme environments.

The six months of freedom I had experienced by the time we landed in England had not brought the sense of emotional equilibrium which would allow my inner turmoil to settle. It was not so much the harrowing ordeals of the immediate past that preyed on my psyche as their ramifications. My journey back home and return to Germany, the shuttling from place to place and the ensuing restlessness, were hardly conducive to achieving a secure state of mind. Cumulative exhaustion spread through every particle of my being.

I recall with deep fondness my stay at Wintershill Hall. From the day of our arrival the staff took in our vulnerabilities, the sense of loss, the confusion. A telling example of their thoughtfulness was the way they handled our food habits. Notwithstanding the variety of staples supplied by the British government at a time when austerity measures were in force, some boys were still hiding bread under their mattresses. The staff showed tact that stemmed from an understanding of our neuroses. To wean the boys from the food habits acquired under siege, the staff simply ignored the storage beneath the mattresses. Eventually the boys came to see the absurdity of their actions. If staff members wanted to know about our ordeals, they never succumbed to curiosity. The task at hand was to treat children who had been wrenched away from their natural habitat and subjected to a dehumanizing machine. They sought to restore our lost childhood, or to enact a virtual restoration of the loss. Alert to our traumas, the program director Dr. Max Friedman, known by the endearing name of Dr. Ginger because of his ruddy complexion, instructed the staff to be liberal about our class attendance. Basically, the program was designed to provide therapeutic treatment and to prepare us for relocation to permanent hostels.

As is customary in this kind of social interaction between guidance counsellors and their charges, affinities developed. I myself gravitated to Mrs. Doris Katz, who unobtrusively began engaging me in conversation in the recreation room. Her composed demeanour, expressed in a soft South African accent, somewhat calmed my restlessness. At that time I was plagued by two impediments. The Death March — the barefoot, fifty-kilometre *Totenmarsch* through Moravia to Theresienstadt — had left me with enlarged flat feet resembling amphibious creatures. My feet would not fit into any shoe, and I had to wear sneakers. This prevented me from playing soccer, relegating me to picking up the stray balls. The other impediment was my voice. It would not crack into adulthood; it ranged from a soprano to an alto. I would try to lower my voice but it would not cooperate. This caused me a great deal of anguish, particularly when my roommates attained low-pitched voices.

Mrs. Katz's husband, Shmuel, would come to Wintershill Hall on weekends. He particularly liked talking to a scrawny boy who had survived the Northeastern Lithuanian forests, serving as a gofer for the partisans. The contrast between the boy's diminutive physique and his impressive mental abilities must have intrigued Mr. Katz. Lithuanian Jews, from whom the partisan boy and Mr. Katz were both descended, were known for their keen Talmudic minds. Sometimes I would eavesdrop on their conversations. The boy's age was indeterminate. In conversation his eyes radiated brightness heightened by a shaft of irony; in silence the sadness in them became prominent.

I sought his company because we both craved solitude and avoided boyish rowdiness. And according to the undeclared code, we skirted our recently-endured ordeals. Eventually, our ways parted. He went to a hostel somewhere north and I went to London. In recent years I have conjured him up from the recess of my memory, trying to imagine him in his old age. But my memory simply flicks back to him in his corner of the recreation room, in conversation with Mr. Katz, his eyes illuminated, his brow furrowed. He left an indelible impression on me. His absence from my life is a great loss to me, but I cannot even recall his name.

## The Amphibian Feet and the Soprano Voice

The house at 833 Finchley Road in North West London was owned by Mr. Frischwasser, who had taken the English name Freshwater. A refugee from Nazi Germany who had escaped in the nick of time, he used his resourceful mind to prosper in real estate and paid tribute to his good luck by making the Finchley house available to accommodate the boys "…till they ready to go out into the real world," as he put it in his own inimitable way. It was a three-story house comprising spacious bedrooms and a small backyard. Its close location to the Golders Green underground station and within walking distance of Hampstead Heath enabled us to tour London, and, when hit by bouts of claustrophobia, to walk them off on the Heath. My own preference was the East End, where I found tranquility for my restlessness. The Hostel's congenial atmosphere was punctuated by Friday evenings before the Sabbath candle lightning which would usher in the holy day.

At Freshwater's instructions, Herbert Luster, the senior counsellor, implemented the Sabbath laws, which impinged on our regular activities. Table tennis games had to stop, the radio in the recreation room was shut and a series of intrusive restrictions were introduced. At the beginning, we balked at them, but subsequently we gave in. However, we took a firm stand when prodded to attend the Friday night synagogue services. The hostel housed about fifteen boys, out of whom only four followed the Orthodox laws. It astounded me how they could keep on praising the Almighty after having stood by while Jewish civilization virtually went up in smoke. I asked one of the Orthodox boys whether he did not feel odd when reciting God's glory. He confessed that he tended to skip lines incongruous with his experience. "… I do this because my parents would have wanted me to do so," he mused aloud. It is not that Mr. Freshwater meant ill. Himself a strictly observant Jew, he hoped to awaken in us religious sentiments from back home.

Rumour had it that one Friday night on his return from synagogue, Mr. Freshwater found his home enveloped in darkness. Surmising that the Sabbath clock — which was supposed to have kicked in the electricity — malfunctioned, and precluded by the Sabbath law from switching on the light — he came up with an ingenious plan. He hurried up to the Golders Green station and found a bobby on duty, to whom he said in trepidation that he suspected burglars had broken into his house. With the bobby in tow, Freshwater hastily led the way into the house, upon which the bobby methodically flipped the lights on in every room. No burglar in sight. Freshwater profusely thanked the bobby for his effort, and quietly blessed the Holy One for being less exacting with other religions.

What stands out in my memory of my two-year residency in the hostel is our trip to the Yiddish theatre in Whitechapel. The night's play was *King Lear*. Since we boys were ignorant of both Elizabethan English and the Lithuanian Yiddish used in the translation, we could hardly appreciate the majesty of the text. Painfully bored, I looked around the sparsely occupied red-covered seats where most of the boys were sprawled out dozing, only to be woken up by an *Oi vai* lament uttered by an old man carrying a young woman off stage. Lear's lament over Cordelia's death was symbolic of the demise of European Yiddish culture. An added ironic poignancy was that the very people who witnessed the demise watched this play. However, this realization only came to me many years later, when I came of intellectual age. After the play we were taken to Bloom's, where we indulged in Jewish dishes bringing back sensuous memories from a vanished past.

Unlike Wintershill Hall, the Freshwater Hostel was goal-oriented. By then it was assumed that we had bounced back to optimal levels of social norms and that the remaining psychological and other handicaps would straighten themselves out in the course of time. The hostel counsellors had a plan aimed at steering us to eventually become contributing members of society. After catching up on his elementary curriculum, my roommate Kurt Klappholz was among the first of us to attend high school. Other boys took up intensive studies guided by the hostel or attended vocational schools, and a few among us lingered in a twilight zone. I belonged to the last group.

I was still suffering from the injuries to my feet, and my childish voice refused to change into adolescence, despite my routine vocal exercise in front of a mirror. One day a volunteer lady took me to the shoe shop around the corner from the Golders Green underground station. She presented me to the senior clerk as "a young gentleman with a foot problem, a result of unfortunate circumstances." The clerk did not inquire about the nature of "the unfortunate circumstances" for which I was grateful. However, when I removed my sneakers, he did a double take. After humming and sighing, the discreet clerk fit me with shoes of extra width, which were a balm to my feet.

The removal of my physical limitation allowed me to participate in sports and roam the streets of London, which gave me a feeling of freedom. But this other thing lurking in the dark mazes of my psyche still needed remedy. After examining my vocal chords and finding them intact, a specialist sent me to a speech therapist. Over the years I've engaged in a good amount of introspection, some of which has helped me untangle the mysteries of my Holocaust and post-Holocaust experiences, and yet my encounters with the therapist remain suffused in mystery.

The first time she met me at the door, the therapist had a captivating smile that flowed from a profound source. Her firm handshake elicited my trust, which would have been impossible to achieve before I had seen that smile only a moment earlier. By now, I could distinguish genuine sympathy from perfunctory behaviour, a skill that stood me in good stead in the years to come. My therapist would talk with me from across a cluttered desk, yet her presence overcame the physical barrier. Our conversations meandered from my hostel mates to my taste in movies, my impression of London and a vast range of topics, none of which related to my voice affliction. Still, her words resonated with trust. When I mentioned that my favourite place was the East End of London, she was taken aback. "What is it that attracts you to the East End?" I told her I was enamoured of the Cockney dialect and the frank manner of the speakers, whom I often mimicked. I would loiter in the marketplace, engrossed in the fruit vendors' calls to entice the shoppers. One of my favourites could be transcribed phonetically as: "La:idy ta:ik awa:y the ba:bie and let the strawberry see the peu:ple." The vendors enjoyed their own theatrics and found a responsive audience.

Just as I was charmed with the Cockney dialect, I felt biased against the BBC announcers, especially when they reported on the Nuremberg trials. Their precise elocution and starched voices brought to mind the commuters heading to the city. Shielded behind the London Times, wearing black bowlers, their pointed umbrellas upright between their legs, they oozed Puritan righteousness spiced with Capitalist avarice. Upon hearing what I thought of the BBC, my therapist chuckled approvingly. Perhaps she herself was a Cockney who had upgraded her vowels at university.

I cannot account for how my therapist brought about the desired change in my voice. I will never know whether it was her unique personality, her empathy, her professional techniques or a combination of all these factors that navigated my voice into adulthood. And there was the chance that it was a happy coincidence. Now, with my feet comfortably positioned in my new shoes and my birthright voice attained, I was ready to face life. At least, so I thought.

An official from the Home Office came to the hostel at around this time to find out how we were progressing in the new country. Over porridge, tea, and white bread spread with jam, he led a lively conversation, unobtrusively assessing our potential to integrate into society. At one point, he asked each one individually what his future plans were. The answers ranged from drafter to chemist to tradesman, and some were still undecided. When my turn came I said I wanted to attend a maritime school and become a sailor. My answer was met with titters from the other boys. "Why do you want to be a sailor?" the official asked, somewhat amused. I could not give him a satisfactory answer.

On routine walks on the Heath with Jonathan, I conveyed my wanderlust, which manifested itself in restlessness, lack of purpose and something I could not share with him: fear of facing the world. Jonathan had other expectations of me. At Friday night dinners with the family, we talked about my future. Their consensus was that I should first enrol in high school, and after graduation take it from there. Even as I was considering my options, debating between a secure life and the excitement of the open seas, something happened that could only be described as serendipity.

A disabled World War II destroyer anchored in King's Lynn harbour, East Anglia, was designated to become a naval school. The vessel was renamed "*Herz*" after the Chief Rabbi of England and was intended to train young people to become sailors. The boat was equipped with the basic instruments and manned by the necessary naval crew to school the boys for their profession. Here was my opportunity. It came as a total surprise when Hans and Julius, my hostel mates, told me that they would also be going to King's Lynn. It was comforting to learn that I was not the only romantic vagabond. On the train to the harbour we fantasized about the free life we would enjoy after completing the three-year program. Each one of us had a different vision of his future, but we all shared the promise of freedom.

On boarding the vessel, the First Mate introduced us to the earlier arrivals. They were a chequered crowd of young people from troubled homes who sought a way out of their turbulent lives. They brought with them a variety of dialects and cultures from all over England, far removed from those of the Hampstead Heath environment of Northwest London. I enjoyed talking with them during the breaks, and particularly when chipping and painting the rail rust — tedious chores made bearable thanks to their titillating tales about the mysteries of the female world. They were street smart, daring, and quick-witted, and shamelessly used these qualities in their dealings with the instructors. Their contempt for authority stirred my dormant rebellious impulses. The colourful yarns they spun were often interrupted by the bo'sun, who, in his Scottish-accented brogue, would mildly warn us to "stop hangin' around and git'n with it," to which we responded with a resounding, "Yes, sir!"

Our program included boat-rowing exercises, boat sailing, diving and formal classes related to the maritime art. I could not for the life of me get the hang of making knots, and what calculus is to a science student, knotting is to a sailor. On Sundays I would put on our navy uniform and, proud as a peacock, strut along the King's Lynn streets admired by the town girls. With a lean body draped in a blue uniform and a sailor's hat that covered a shock of auburn curly hair, matching a pair of mischievous eyes and underlined by a foreign-accented English, I cut a romantic figure. Our popularity was enhanced by the fact that we were the only maritime material in town since the King's Lynn harbour lost its commercial importance after World War I, consequently leaving the town bereft of sailors.

For a while I was taken with the adoring looks directed at me while I waited in the queue for the pictures with my date, and enjoyed getting an extra helping when I bought fish and chips, which were wrapped up in yesterday's tabloid paper. Though these weekends took a bite out of my meagre weekly allowance, they boosted my ego. The adoration of the King's Lynn girls and the generosity of the fish and chips vendors could not, however, compensate for the rigours of the school. From lights on until lights out each chore had to be done precisely and meticulously in accordance with the manual. Though our naval instructors had our best interests at heart, their strictures did not make it easier for me to fit into this rigid mould.

One day, while I was lying on my bunk, it dawned on me that I might not be able to stay in school. Yet, if I quit I would have to go back to the hostel admitting failure. The sea's pull still captivated me, but the journey demanded a price that I was psychologically reluctant to pay. It required that I submit my autonomy to the "*Herz*" crew for the duration of the program. Having been brutally robbed of my freedom under the Nazi regime, I was reluctant to follow orders blindly. Julius and Hans shared my distaste for many of the mindless tasks but felt the prize was worth the sacrifice.

Hans, Julius and I went to London to spend our furloughs in the hostel, where we were fussed over. After all, it was not common for Jewish boys to brave the mighty ocean. The year was 1948, a time in which portentous events were unfolding in Palestine. A year earlier, on November 29, the UN General Assembly had passed a resolution by which Palestine would be partitioned into two sovereign political entities, one Arab and one Jewish. The Arab countries rejected the resolution out of hand and vowed to thwart the establishment of a Jewish state.

Threatened with annihilation by six surrounding Arab states, the Jewish community of Palestine, called the *Yishuv*, sent out representatives across the European and American continents to awaken the world's conscience. They invested their energies in the Jewish Diaspora with the intention of enlisting its political and financial support as well as seeking experts in different fields of warfare. Anxiety was rife in the London Jewish community. A violent end to the Zionist dream would have had a particularly demoralizing effect on the Jewish people only three years after the Holocaust.

We went to a lecture given by a Jewish Agency emissary on the prospects and perils entailed in establishing a Jewish state. The audience comprised young people, mostly members of a Zionist youth club. After the lecture, I milled around talking to people, the ritualistic cup of tea rattling in the saucer, spilling drops on my half-eaten biscuit. From the corner of my eye I noticed the emissary gravitating towards my friends and me. Polite and circumspect, he showed a great interest in our maritime studies. Almost imperceptibly he broached the possibility of our coming over, careful not to use the phrase "making aliyah," which connotes immigration. The Yishuv needed our maritime skills to help defend the prospective Jewish state. I could not help noticing the inherent irony of the situation. Three years earlier, in the Displaced Persons Camp, his colleagues had tried to prevent us from departing for England. They wanted us in Palestine, "where we belonged," as they put it. Now this ardent pioneer called on our meagre skills to join the battle against the imminent Arab invasion of the *Yishuv*.

On the train back to school, I reviewed our conversation with the emissary and a sketchy outline loomed in my mind. I weighed the pros and cons entailed in going to Palestine. The advantages were taking a break from school without losing face, and gaining firsthand experience sailing in a real ship. In my inward eye, I saw myself standing on a deck, scouring the sea through binoculars, the way I had seen it done in Hollywood war films. There were also nagging doubts. I had experienced enough of war to know that it was not an afternoon's outing. Still, it offered an opportunity to escape the school's regimentation.

In time this idea developed from fantasy into reality. I did not share my metamorphosis with Julius and Hans. Jonathan, my confidant, was privy to my dilemmas. His reaction was puzzling. While opposing the idea of my going to Palestine, he firmly held that it was the duty of every Jew to contribute to the war effort. The stakes were high; Jewish existence was on the line. He insisted, however, that the "boys" who had come to England from Germany should wait out the war in England. His words, spoken in agitation, came as a surprise to me.

Jonathan was the proverbial English gentleman. Dispassionate in judgement, given to expressing himself in understatements laced with irony, he was an incorrigibly civil man who would not jump over a line unless his life depended on it. I felt that Jonathan seemed to have taken leave of all these admirable characteristics, which were still out of reach for me. What I noticed in him was an undercurrent of passion. Little did I know on that sunny afternoon on the Heath that Jonathan had himself been contemplating leaving medical school and going to Palestine to defend the fledgling Jewish state, for which he subsequently paid with his life. His enlistment in the Israeli Defence Force was motivated by idealism, out of a feeling of shared responsibility for the fate of the Jewish people.

Undoubtedly, his consciousness was largely shaped by the Holocaust. The newsreels screened at the cinemas, the Nuremberg trials reported in the press, and the snippets of stories I managed to relate to him — all these left deep grooves in his emotional being. He responded to this momentous turning point of Jewish fate with the sensitivity of an Aeolian harp.

I was still groping in the vast treasury of words to find a few compatible with the realities of the ghettos and concentration camps, and incapable of describing my ordeals in narrative patterns. Revisiting man's destructive handiwork of the twentieth century endangered my precarious psychological balance. I would draw vignettes usually incomprehensible to the uninitiated into the *anus mundi*, yet Jonathan could feel the undercurrents of the words, thanks to his intuitive sensitivity. His genuine efforts to sympathise with my ordeals made it easier to find words with which to describe moments that defy conventional vocabularies.

Back at Majdanek, there was a young, tall, handsome German *Kapo* who used to parade the *Feld III* grounds, always at the same hour, sinking his teeth into a long brown sausage. It was an exercise in psychological torment. Hidden behind the block, I would watch his measured bites in fascination, swallowing the rising acidic spit in my mouth. At night, I would fantasize about being the *Kapo* and the acid taste would come back. "You see, Jonathan, I knew the time of his walk and I had to hide and see him eat the sausage. Every day I did this." My verbal inadequacy frustrated me. I looked at him. Jonathan came as close as humanly possible to knowing the essence of the moment.

## Three Levels of Knowing

Now with the perspective of sixty years I have a wider view and can better articulate the pain. *Knowing of it* consists of general information obtained through films or recommended readings at high school, Elie Wiesel's *Night* for example. It is like having read a book's blurb without having read the book itself. In an elevator going up to the U.S. Holocaust Memorial Council offices where I worked, a lady, meticulously groomed from top to toe, noticed that I was carrying copies of *Night*. In a charming southern lilt she asked me whether I happened to know Mr. Wisel (*sic*) and was "he really a prophet with a beard like in the Bible?" I responded in like fashion: "Yes, a prophet of sorts, but without a beard." This did not dim the glow in her eyes. Had she known my close relationship with Wiesel, she surely would have touched me in an act of second-hand sanctification.

*Knowing about it* requires familiarity with the Holocaust, a certain degree of vulnerability, and intellectual curiosity; attributes buttressed by a moral dimension, a capacity to identify with the suffering of The Other — Others from far away, whom you have never met and have had no traffic with. It assumes a variety of facets manifested in different circumstances. Illustrative of my point is the following episode: in a gesture of reconciliation with Germany, President Ronald Reagan visited the Bitburg military cemetery in May of 1985, where a dozen SS troopers were buried. The visit and the President's statement that the dead SS soldiers were also victims of the Nazi regime raised a national debate. The U.S. Holocaust Memorial Council, a government agency mandated to commemorate the Holocaust, vehemently opposed the visit and its accompanying statement, and asked me to present its views to a high school in northern Virginia.

As the school was in a prosperous county populated by a large number of military personnel, I expected their children to be supporters of the President's policy, as affiliating Germany with NATO would boost the Alliance against the evil empire from the East. I was therefore surprised to find an audience sympathetic to the cause I advocated. Among the questions and comments was one I recorded verbatim in my notebook: "Only the victims have a right to forgive, not the President and no one else." This statement, made by a twelfth-grade student, was greeted with thunderous applause. At the end of the assembly, she made her way through the crowd to the podium. Somewhat shyly, she thanked me for the talk. Her grandfather had liberated Dachau and her father served in Germany, where she grew up in her early teens. Both father and son *know about it* and handed down this vicarious sensibility to their descendant.

While *knowing about it* can be acquired, *knowing it* is not an acquisition. It comes as a direct encounter with the human instruments of evil. Those hidden in *malinas*; the latter-day *Marranos* who lived in the shadow of the swastika with a transplanted Aryan identity; the plague-infested starving in the ghettos; the pyjama-clad ghost-like figures inching through bits of life — these are the survivors who *know it*. But even their knowing is circumscribed by each individual experience. The question is whether one can develop a language and a sensibility based on human commonality that approximates the *knowing about it* and the *knowing it*.

In due course, Jonathan Balter evolved into a vicarious survivor thanks to, among other attributes, his compassionate capacity to empathize with the victims. David Hirsch of Brown University, who eventually became my thesis advisor — more on him later — had a firm sense of Jewish ethnicity. His sense was further honed by his mother-in-law's survival stories and enhanced by a sensitive intellect and led to a passionate ratiocinative cast of mind about the Holocaust. Terrence De Pres, of Colgate University, acquired Holocaust consciousness because his humanity was offended by the manifestation of senseless evil. My current family doctor, William Wishinski, has a number of patients who are survivors. He's heard their stories of survival, feels their pain and mourns their deaths. I myself could not wish for a more caring physician or a more eloquent eulogist — in the ripeness of time.

These vicarious survivors were the first generation to recognize up close the destructive evil rampant on the European Continent. Thirty-six years after the Manquake, I had the opportunity of assisting a group of young people in their quest to transcend the *knowing about it* level, evolving into vicarious survivors of sorts. In this process, I learned as much from them as they learned from me.

## Getting High on Zinger Tea

In 1980, I was a guest lecturer at Brown University, where I taught courses on Holocaust literature and Biblical echoes in seventeenth-century poetry. The majority of the students in the Holocaust course came from upper middle-class homes. It was a mixed bag of Jewish students, mostly from the East Coast, and non-Jewish students, hailing from across the country, with a smattering of children of survivors. One of them was Sherry Wilzig. She must have felt a sense of affinity toward me and was among the first to visit me in my office. Her father, Siggy Wilzig, came from West Prussia, and was transported to Auschwitz at the age of sixteen. The tattooed number on his arm testified to his early arrival in the camp. He survived, and in 1947 arrived in a blizzard-stricken New York and got his first job, shovelling snow. From there he became a shirt presser, graduated to salesman and through a string of shrewd deals and successful investments acquired The Trust Company of New Jersey and subsequently the ownership of the Wilshire Oil Company. His survivorship was deeply ingrained in his consciousness. Sherry narrated her father's lore in a matter-of-fact tone with obvious pride. There was a sense of familiarity in our conversation not usually found in first meetings, and particularly not in first meetings between student and professor. It must have been the latent affinity between a survivor's daughter and a survivor that narrowed the distance between us. This latent affinity subsequently developed into a kind of protective friendship, to Siggy's delight. Typical of a parent survivor, he was overly concerned about Sherry's well-being. In the course of time I noticed that her fragile physique held a sturdy core, later manifested when she became the chief officer of the family's oil company.

I first met Siggy and his wife Naomi in Providence, Rhode Island, when they came to visit Sherry, but I became familiar with him at the Borscht Belt's Grossinger's hotel and later in Miami during the winter break, when Sarah, my wife, and I were his guests. Observing Siggy was a fascinating exercise. His compact physical build brimming with energy, head boasting a shock of curly hair, and overall meticulously dressed, Siggy circulated comfortably among the guests, engaged in lively repartee. He seemed to know everybody and everybody seemed to know him. While I could not picture him shovelling snow or pressing shirts, it was easy to imagine him plying his wares as a salesperson. A natural raconteur, he would engage me in conversations about his postwar life into the late hours of the night.

Whereas at Grossinger's and in Miami I got to know Siggy Wilzig the *shmoozer*, at the U.S. Memorial Council I came to know his multi-faceted personality, or to be more precise, his persona. He was a Presidential appointee to the Council whose judgement Elie Wiesel respected; Wiesel had invited him to look into the fiscal operation of the Council. Recognizing the urgency of the situation, he took time out from stewarding everyday business of his bank and came to Washington. The quality of steely resolve that undoubtedly navigated him to the ownership and the presidency of the bank also guided him in probing the Council's structure. Undaunted by the entrenched bureaucracy, he laid open the Council's operation, resulting in recommendations on how to streamline its management. He did not lose the charm displayed at Grossinger's and in Miami, but here the charm served as a persuasive tool, a means to an end. For the life of me I could not conjure up a scenario whereby this proud and fiercely independent person could have stood on the Auschwitz roll call grounds wrapped in white-and-blue striped pyjama-like garb and in an orchestrated manner followed the order, "*mütze an, mütze ab...*" bellowed by the chief *Kapo*. When I learned about Siggy's death, I felt much as I had when the radio had announced Moshe Dayan's death. Dayan was an organic part of the Israeli landscape, and it was as if a mighty wind had uprooted the oak tree in my backyard overnight, and the tree did not greet me that morning. When Siggy died, a tree in my interior garden was gone, leaving a gaping hole in the soul. I missed the autumnal turn of his life's leaves — and I was poorer for that.

During the semester I taught Sherry, I learned from my students that the topic of World War II was a frequent subject of conversation around their dinner tables — and of course central to World War II was the Holocaust. The late eighties and the nineties saw a flurry of publicity either directly or referentially on this topic. It received coverage in the mass media, novels written by known authors appeared, films and TV shows were produced. The academic community looked into this maze of darkness and found it intriguing. This is not the place to speculate on what factors aroused this interest in the subject. Still, it is worthwhile noting that the passage of congressional legislation designating a national Holocaust Remembrance Day attracted significant public attention. Odd as it may seem, I believe that the failure of the Vietnam War and its human ramifications brought Holocaust awareness closer to home.

●

Thus the students who signed up for my elective course at Brown University belonged to the knowing *about* the Holocaust. And as I found out later, it was the otherworldly subject that attracted them to the course — and probably to me, who "actually was there." I do not know whether they came across my name in publications or picked it up while chatting on the lawn, but by the time they came to class they knew, unbeknownst to me, that I was a survivor.

The class enjoyed energetic class discussions, its participants passionately examining the peculiar anatomy of evil. They questioned the factors that played into the emergence and flourishing of such an ideology of destruction in the country that had given the world Schiller and Beethoven. Hitler's *Table Talks*, spinning the Nazi philosophy, sounded like science fiction to them; Erich Kahler's book,[2] which describes the proceedings of the Nuremberg *Einsatzgruppen*-trials, struck the class with horror. From physicians to lawyers to university professors to clergy, the elite of German society stood in the dock accused of being accomplices to committing unprecedented atrocities. To emphasize the weirdness of it all, the accused called witnesses to testify to their good characters and deeds. How could people with such supposedly refined sensibilities and high moral standings descend into becoming killers? The students' probing questions touched the core of the human condition.

But at the time I had no rational answers to their questions. I resorted to an analogy to medical science: I asked them to consider "a cell that metastasizes and spreads to different parts of our organs, destroying the physical system. Something similar happened to the German body politics. Politically weak and psychologically bewildered in the aftermath of the military defeat in World War One, the Nazi cancerous cells penetrated into the judicial, scientific and legal cells of the German society." As we kept on studying the texts, further seeking answers to the radical metamorphosis of the German people, the discussions intensified. I must admit that I was proud of my pedagogic handiwork.

In fact, I was myself beset by the same questions that my students posed. Once, a long time later when we were cooperating on the creation of the Holocaust Museum in Washington, Elie Wiesel invited me to accompany him to Brooklyn, where he occasionally studied Talmud. Later we went to have coffee and his favourite brand of cake. Even as we were discussing some conceptual aspects of the Museum, he gave me his singularly other-

---

[2]    Erich Kahler, *From the Tower to the Abyss: An Inquiry in the Transformation of Man.* New York: Viking Press, 1967, p. 61.

worldly look, his coffee cup held at mouth level, and said, "…Perhaps… *it* did not really happen." This questioning of our own experiences lies in the fact that it emanated from a land of the grotesque where strange couplings of incoherence and rigidity reigned; a land suffused in a kind of haunted, nightmarish fog that refused to dissolve even when we awoke. Such unearthly images needed to be kneaded into coherent stories to make them credible and bring them as close as possible to an intimation of reality. In moments of grace it worked.

The class dynamics took on a different character in my office. The English department chair was my former thesis adviser, David Hirsch, and he gave me a spacious top floor office where I set up house, so to speak. In the absence of my wife, who had to stay back home to take care of her ailing mother, I was left to take care of myself. I set up a toaster and other valuable kitchen items in my office. This makeshift kitchenette enabled me to take breakfast and sometimes lunch there. For a fleeting moment I even entertained the idea of making the office a lodging for overnight stays, though I stopped just short of that. I had a kettle, which was particularly handy for boiling water for the little soirees I was giving my visiting students who dropped by to chat. Sometimes they would come in twos, but more often they appeared alone.

The conversations in the office, though personal and light-hearted, were nevertheless coloured by the bleakness that naturally pervaded the class discussions. My young interlocutors were in search of an intellectual and moral identity, a worldview still in the making. In this pursuit, they drew encouragement and, perhaps, solace from the literature of memory written by survivors under siege and after liberation. These memoirs and diaries yield stories of altruistic deeds, selfless acts, compassionate behaviour. In stark contrast to the destructive impulses of human nature, these spiritually uplifting stories break the darkness of those times. The class emotionally identified with the young women and men of the underground, close to their own age, who took up arms against their persecutors in the ghettos and forests. Facing overwhelming odds, the young resisters defied their oppressors, leaving behind them a legacy of triumph of the human spirit. And this high moral standing and physical daring, my protégées ardently believed, would have guided them in similar circumstances. They did not put it in these words, but their idealism came through in conversation. I did not disabuse them of these notions. And I wished that they would bring this Edenic naiveté of moral and physical courage with them to their real lives. Yet, what I knew of human nature told me otherwise. In extremis, self-preservation trumps idealism.

I conjured up an image: my charges are standing at the water cooler in their office hall leisurely sipping water from pointed paper cups while exchanging gossipy tidbits and making dinner arrangements. And Todd, a cerebral student with a flair for political science, has a falling out with the CEO, and relates the story of that falling out to his former classmates, now his fellow employees. Will they stand by him or give him a wide berth so as not to be seen as siding with him? Will he still be part of the water cooler crowd or become a pariah? I, who sipped from paper cups at the water cooler as well as gulped vesper soup from tin urns, saw two looming spectres in my inner eye: I remembered my fellow inmates missing the line-up for the eagerly-awaited ladle of soup and instantly knew that they had lost their hunger for life, that they had become what the camp lingo dubbed *Muselmänner*, to be avoided lest we be taken as their fellow travellers into the gassy blue clouds; and I saw Todd, in the future, at the water cooler among his former classmates. What about him: would he become a latter-day *Muselmann*, a casualty of the human self-preservation impulse, or would his friends stand up for him? But what about Beezie and Susan: how would they react to the water cooler situation?

Beezie and Susan were my regulars. We consumed gallons of Zinger tea amidst serious talk and banter in my office. On Sundays, they would trek to the Black Pearl in Newport to get me a serving of their famed chowder. It was Susan who shortened my name to the endearing "Pfeff." They were a study in complementary contrast. Susan was outgoing, curious, and expressed her curiosity in a string of informative questions disguised as rhetorical. Whether this was out of habit or was a designed investigative modus operandi was hard to tell. She introduced me to Matt, her boyfriend, who eventually became her spouse. Sarah and I happened to be in Washington, DC, when she married, and we enjoyed attending the wedding and meeting the families of both bride and groom. Beezie, on the other hand, was rather reticent, somewhat socially withdrawn, yet quite open with me. Despite their different temperaments, Susan and Beezie were inseparable. They had gone to the same grade and boarding schools. They were alike in many ways and yet different in others. I liked them both, and often thought about them. I wondered how their conversations were conducted. I assume that Susan did most of the talking and Beezie the listening, punctuating Susan's speech with her laconic comments.

Over the years, I kept in touch with Susan through an exchange of seasonal greetings and accidentally ran into her in Manhattan many years later. Well, not exactly ran into her. I had taken the bus across town from the East to the West Side. I sat down behind the driver facing the entrance doors, and from this vantage point watched, as was my habit, the passengers climbing into the bus. Unlike schools of fish that steer their tails in matching movements, choreographed by nature, and chorus girls who sway and quake their parts on the stage in harmony, passengers climb into the bus in ways very different from each other. From my own passenger-watching experience, I had never seen two identical climbs; each one had its own peculiarity, each ushered a unique temper onto the bus. Some passengers, as soon as they came aboard, surveyed their immediate surroundings and let their eyes roam further down the aisles; others grabbed the rail without much ado; still others nervously rummaged in their pocketbooks or wallets in an attempt to retrieve some coins to pay for the ride. Passenger-watching was fascinating, a study of people as they moved from one environmental plane to another.

And then a young woman, with a head of thick, curly blond hair, got on the bus, threw a quick look around her environs and settled her blue eyes on me, an activity that interrupted my passenger-watching. She stationed herself just across from me, ignoring the driver's calls to "step back, please, step back, please." Her eager stare induced me to remove my summer hat so as to make myself more presentable. Without taking her eyes off of me, she stepped forward to my seat, leaned slightly down toward me, and exclaimed in a wondering tone, "Aren't you Pfeff? I'm Susan Holmes, I had you at Brown."

We went for coffee, and sat over it, indulging in nostalgia galore. I told her about meeting Todd at the airport. He was working for Senator Claiborne Pell of Rhode Island on Capitol Hill. Another classmate, Michael Pollack, was a writer for NBC, and Chapin Carpenter, who sang dark lullabies in the class, was climbing the songwriter-cum-singer charts. She had told the class about her visits to William Styron's home at the time he was writing *Sophie's Choice* in his secluded hut. Beezie too had gotten a job on Capitol Hill, and she came to have dinner with us. Susan and I casually recalled other names and episodes with an immediacy that suggested we'd been in class yesterday. It felt like reminiscing about family.

When I had taught at Brown, my office had been situated at the top of the Horace Mann building, which accommodated the English department. The building was groaning under the weight of its age, and its stairs creaked when stepped on. So when my students made their way to my office, the squeaking sounds reached the occupants of all the other offices. Good-heartedly chiding me, they would comment, "They're climbing the stairs like they're going on a pilgrimage to Zion. What's the draw, Eli?"

And in the same light spirit, imitating a Rabbi's intonation, I retorted: "And Zinger, do you offer them?"

What I deduced from my encounters with Brown students was that human beings had the emotional capacity to identify with the Other's suffering, and that in the face of evil visited on their fellow-creatures, their own human dignity was offended. Whether they would be offended to the point of defending others in extremis at the risk of their own well-being was a question I could not answer. I would have wanted to believe that my Brown students would live up to their moral outrage when meeting evil, as they said they would in class and in conversations with me. I hoped that I at least made them aware of the human dilemma involved.

Teaching is not unlike farming. You sow the seeds, but you cannot predict whether they will yield the expected crops. This is especially true about teaching the Holocaust. Though I could tell the difference I made in raising my students' awareness of the human condition, I did not realize its effects till many years later — thanks to the correspondence I kept up with them. Michael, the future NBC writer who was a frequent visitor to my soirees at Horace Mann in 1981, wrote me seven years later how in his work "as well as (his) personal writings, I draw from your teachings, your scholarship and your gentle inspiration." At my farewell party, Michael dipped the pen into his satirical inkwell (this was in the B.C., Before Computer, era), portraying me in verse. Here is the opening stanza:

> There was once a man from the Mid East
> Who came to Rhode Island to teach
> His head was balding
> His humour scalding
> An accent pervaded his speech.

I was aware of my brand of humour but had been oblivious to the balding process that, at that time, was only beginning, baring merely the dome at the top of my skull. I thanked Michael for pointing it out to me.

About seven years later, Beezie wrote me from Maine in longhand, recalling the dynamics of the class, which prompted the students to "interact and learn from each other. It's not an easy thing to do with such a personal and such a sensitive topic."

In the course of developing my interest in Holocaust research and teaching, I occasionally have had second thoughts about whether it was a wise career move to shift from drama teaching to Holocaust teaching. Apart from the mental anguish it involved, the demands that teaching made required a level of dedication and honesty not always compatible with the moral values of the institutions where I was employed, which looked very much askance at Holocaust studies in general. My work challenged Israel's glorification of physical heroism and spiritual defiance — and at times, I've paid a high price in academia and in society at large for my stubbornness.[3] But the letters I've received from my students over the years have compensated me for the hardships and losses. Thanks to these frank exchanges, I have found out how my persona was perceived by the people who mattered most: the students. Measured by academically conventional conduct, and my alluded-to irreverence for authority, I was somewhat of an eccentric. Add to that my multi-layered accents, a reflection of my sojourns in a variety of countries, and my then-current dwelling in a country from which the First Coming originated and the Second Coming was looming on the horizon. With all of these underscored by my background, I took on an oriental mystique. But I refrained from nurturing it.

## Carrying the Armband *Jude*

About one year after the invasion of my hometown, Radzyń Podlaski, Poland, in 1939, the entire Jewish population was crammed into the Jewish quarter. It was left unfenced, though strict curfews were imposed. Soon segments of the poor and the disabled, followed by what the Gestapo deemed "the unproductive population," were deported. With each deportation the ghetto shrunk. Ingenious and clear-eyed, Mother sought a way to obtain for our extended family the enviable status of being in the productive category in the hopes of dodging deportation. She strongly advised me to look for a job with the *Kriminal Polizei,* a branch of the Gestapo. She had worked out a plan: first I was to ingratiate myself with the Polish girls who worked in the officers' households and in the offices, and from there I would somehow wriggle myself into the working detail.

Only a couple of hundred yards separated the ghetto from the Criminal Police compound. The Polish girls liked to have me around helping out with the domestic chores that kept me busy most of the day, but I had to will myself to go to work. While my friends played in the ghetto, I got up early in the morning to light the stoves in the offices and went up to the apartments to shine boots and help the housemaids.

The Chief of Police, Dr. Bekker, went out of his way to be nice to me. Realizing that the ghetto residents were deprived of food, he saw to it that

---

[3]  While Israelis did eventually accept and identify themselves with the Holocaust, this did not occur until the aftermath of the Yom Kippur War. See Eli Pfefferkorn, "Israel's Forgotten Legacy," Midstream, April 1983.

I took a food package back home at the end of my day's work. On my return to the ghetto, people waited in our congested apartment, which housed two families, and Mother would hand over the food to them. My family was well to do and bought food on the black market.

The distance from the workplace to the ghetto was short. My last job of the day was to shine boots and place them in front of their owners' doors. Sometimes I would finish work after the curfew came into effect, assuming that I was protected by the employment. One summer evening as I stepped out of the complex, my white armband off, and walked towards the ghetto, I encountered the SD officer Hoffmann, accompanied by three *Wehrmacht* soldiers. From across the street, he beckoned me over and without saying a single word, slapped me hard on the face, eliciting peals of laughter from the soldiers. The physical hurt was not as stinging as the psychological hurt. I ran home, tears streaming down my cheeks. I looked back and saw Dr. Bekker on the balcony watching me in my humiliation. The following day he looked at me in a way that showed he felt for me. But he would not say a word. This was my first lesson of helplessness.

It must have been soon after the High Holidays of *Rosh Hashanah* and *Yom Kippur*, in the fall of 1942, that news about the deportation of neighbouring *shtetls* reached our ghetto. The Nazis softened the news for the benefit of our non-Jewish countrymen, using a euphemism: *Judenrein*. Rumours about our own approaching deportation swirled around the ghetto. How long could our *Judenrat* Eldest, Mr. Lichtenstein, put off our fate? It was at about this time that my mother arranged a meeting with a gentile customer she had known for a long time. I accompanied her to the meeting, which was outside the ghetto. What I did not know was that earlier Mother had furtively visited his home in the village and handed over to him gold coins and other valuables. This meeting was a pretext for introducing me to this person. She said that she would send me to collect the coins and the valuables in due course. Later that same evening Mother showed me a sketch of the house that she had drawn, how to approach it from a nearby little bridge and what precautionary measures to take in case of emergency. At no time should I go into the village during the day.

Every afternoon when I returned from my job at the *Kriminal Polizei* she would pull out the sketch and make me study it. She also sewed bank notes of different denominations into my overcoat and instructed me in how to undo the stitches and then sew them up again. Whether Mother had a premonition that we would be separated or her actions were precautions alone, I will never know for certain. What I do know for certain is that rumours of children being separated from their parents were rife in the ghetto.

The unfenced ghetto allowed narrow lanes of commercial traffic between its residents and the general Polish population. Thanks to this contact, there was no widespread starvation of the kind that afflicted encircled ghettos. There were, of course, poor people who were taken care of by the *Gemainde*. *The ghetto eldest*, a towering figure with a remarkable presence, Mr. Lichtenstein hoped to "outlive the enemy," as the phrase went in the ghetto, without realizing that this enemy was an unprecedented foe. I remember him because of a sermon he gave at a *Brith* which my family attended. In a somewhat humorous vein that brought out the tragic, he provided a rationale for the circumcision even as the baby's wailing was dying down. The purpose of this painful procedure, he explained, was designed to initiate the newborn into the suffering that had been part of the Jewish people's experience since inception. Later, Mother explained to me the implication of Lichtenstein's sermon. In the camps in moments of despair, Mr. Lichtenstein's sermon came back to me. Its rationale was no consolation.

Mother's efforts to avoid deportation, equivalent to cheating death, were frustrated by the "Final Solution of the Jewish Question," as it was euphemistically coined at the Wannsee Conference of January 1942. On the cusp of autumn in 1942, the dwindling ghetto population of Radzyń Podlaski was herded to the front of the *Judenrat* office, put on horse-driven wagons manned by Polish peasants, and taken eastwards to Międzyrzec Podlaski, a way station to the death and concentration camps.

A long and winding column of wagons stretched along the road as far as the eye could see. From a bird's-eye view, the slow-moving column would have looked like a migrant tribe in search of new territory. No guards escorting it were in sight. The column trotted along the 50-kilometre road, watched by curious villagers neither gloating nor saddened — just indifferent.

By dusk we arrived at the ghetto gates where the Jewish police took over and started directing us toward the synagogue. My extended family, like other families, walked side by side, amidst dead silence. Everyone knew that the transfer of people from small ghettos to the central ghetto of Międzyrzec Podlaski boded ill. The local ghetto residents were scurrying to their prepared hideouts in anticipation of the *aktion*. I was holding my mother's hand when she abruptly unhooked hers from mine, gave me a look the way she used to at critical moments when she had to overcome my stubbornness, and said, "Run, save yourself." She didn't allow my bewilderment to linger for even an eyewink. Rephrasing her order with an icy edge, she added: "Go, go. With us you'll be lost." And I tore into the narrow alleys in search of a hideout.

The hideouts were carefully constructed to avoid detection and sized to hold only the tenants of the house. Food was in short supply and storing water and setting up hygienic facilities required space. Squeezing one more person into a confined space — small as I was — would upset the calculated ratio of space to person. In addition, no one could predict how many days the *aktion* might last — a fact that could strain the food and water supply. Ironically, while the Nazi Empire was gaining living space in the East, its victims' space was shrinking.

Finding a spot that would provide shelter from Hitler's racial onslaught was my first survival test. I saw people with small bundles under their arms rush into a door and leave it ajar. I followed. The rooms were in disarray: pots on kerosene lamps; clothes and shoes scattered across the floor. The chaos was staged to give the impression that the residents had left in a hurry. An eerie silence hovered over the place. I assumed that the people must have already crammed into their hideout either in the attic or in the cellar. I looked out into street. By now there were only a few people scurrying to their holes.

My eye caught an older person at the far end of an alley, hurrying, and I shadowed him into the house he was headed for. "I have nowhere to go," I told him, "and I need a place to hide." A tiny gap appeared in the ceiling and a makeshift ladder to the attic was lowered. Would he let me climb up the ladder into the hole or would he shut me out? It took him no more than a heartbeat to blurt out: "Come up." Was he taking pity on a thirteen-year-old boy, or was it rather a shrewd decision to conceal me from our persecutors so as not to endanger the safety of the hideout?

My eyes made out silhouettes of about a dozen people sitting shoulder-to-shoulder or back-to-back. One couple moved ever so slightly to make room for me. The man who let me into the hideout assumed authority over the place. He gave out instructions regarding the food and water distribution, the sleeping schedule and the need for silence even before the *aktion* began.

Squatting in a dark space among strangers, I should have given way to contemplation. Only one hour ago, Mother had torn herself away from me. Now, I was crouched in a corner, awaiting the men led by dogs who would ferret me out from my refuge. But should we fool — by an act of Divine grace — the mastiffs' sensitive noses, what would become of me?

These should have been my concerns. But instead of probing my emotional hurts and anxieties, I assumed a survival behavior, a psychological numbness that stood me in good stead in the days to come. I emptied my entire inner being. Thinking, feeling, memory, imagination: all were dulled into deadness. I had no idea in what state my fellow fugitives were existing. We did not talk. Only functional instructions were passed on relating to facilities, food and water distribution, and taking turns to stretch out for sleep. I was awaiting dawn.

What sounded like human voices mingled with the yapping of dogs punctured the silent early morning. The repeatedly barked-out words, *"Raus, Raus, Schneller, Schneller!"* punctuated the clomping on the cobblestones. The people positioned next to the wall facing the street peered through the cracks. I was sitting in the middle and had no access to the outer wall. The heavy footsteps and the yelping dogs were nearing the hideout. I could hear the canine barking and the human howls. They were the Ukranian henchmen recruited for the purpose of hounding Jews, and they were supervised by *Waffen SS* officers. They spoke in a gibberish of mixed German and Ukrainian. I could not tell how long they searched the house, but I felt a sense of relief when they left it. The self-induced dullness of the senses slowly gave way to a reawakening of emotional life. But hard on the heels of the reawakening, I experienced a painful longing to hold my mother's hand — perhaps it was a subconscious desire to be uncovered by my persecutors and driven to the assembly where the deportees waited to be carted off to their deaths.

## A Tom Sawyer Adventure

By the fall of 1942 all those willing to face reality knew that the postcards written by the deportees and sent back to the ghettos were forgeries or written under duress. Entire communities were vanishing from the earth. The Kraków underground newsletter "The Fighting Pioneer" repeatedly exposed the Nazis' dark design, as did other underground publications. Fugitives who managed to escape the massacres in the Russian-occupied territories and escapees from the death-bound trains confirmed the rumours filtering through the grapevine channels. The bells tolled, heralding "The Final Solution" across the beleaguered ghettos, and yet the besieged were holding onto life, making the best of the reprieve.

Soon after our annihilators left the house, I touched my sewed-up treasures — literally my life source. The following morning I crawled out of the hole. As soon as the lethal search party left, the ghetto sprang back to life. The houses, emptied of their previous tenants, were occupied by those who survived. Smuggling provided goods for those who could afford it; cultural activities began; and the *carpe diem* among the young people assumed Dionysian proportions. Age limitations and the dwindling of my financial resources barred me from taking part in this life-and-death orgy. Yet beneath this semblance of normalcy lurked a sense of imminent doom. The threat of *aktion* never ceased to hover over the ghetto. Some improved upon their hiding places; others tried to get Aryan identity papers or sought connections with Polish acquaintances to secure a sanctuary. In my innermost being, I consulted Mother. Since I'd emerged from my hideout, Mother's presence never left me. I sought to establish a connection with a person who knew the inner workings of the ghetto: how to get better housing, how to get access to a workplace sponsored by the *Wehrmacht*, which would grant one the illusory status of being indispensable to the war effort. Our distant family, residents of Międzyrzec Podlaski, had been deported by the time we arrived in the ghetto, so I was totally on my own, as many orphans were, although I was fortunate enough to have a certain sum of money. This would keep the wolf away from my doorstep, but would not keep the human beast away.

While roaming the streets of the ghetto, I happened to see a former schoolmate, Menachem, engaged in an animated conversation with a person who exuded an air of authority. Later he told me that the man was in charge of residency accommodations in the ghetto. Menachem was sharing a two-room apartment with two families and he needed a room of his own, especially to entertain his female visitors. Since coming out of the hideout, I had found various resting spots and had to sleep in makeshift places. Menachem offered to "buddy up" with me and share accommodations and perhaps use our street smarts to make our lives more tolerable. As far as street smarts went, Menachem had an edge over me. He and his family had been taken from our town in an earlier *aktion* and while he had managed to hoodwink death, his family ended up in a cattle car.

In the interim, between his deportation to the ghetto and mine, Menachem had acquired perseverance skills, which he kept on honing with the dedication of a Jesuit. That's how he accomplished the near impossible. Assisted by a supply of edible bribes, which he rustled up by his smuggling across the barbed wires, Menachem got a room from the Residency Commissioner. I knew Menachem from school, where he had been an upperclassman while I was in the lower grades. The hierarchical structure was strictly observed. The lower grades were kept in place and the upper grades dictated the schoolyard agenda. Notwithstanding this separation between the seniors and juniors, I had enjoyed a privileged status, thanks to an episode that in Tom Sawyer's parlance would be described as an adventure.

At the time, the boy whose desk was located next to mine was popular because of his generosity. Reuven shared his footballs, bicycle and the various creatures he bred in his backyard. One morning he shared his excitement with me: his beloved cat had littered a bunch of kittens. What would he do with so many kittens? I asked. He hoped that some of the girls would want them. I thought giving the kittens away in the schoolyard would be a good idea. They could be displayed there and the girls would choose from the fuzzy litter. But the give-away would have to wait until the kittens were weaned. By the time the day of the kitten display arrived, I had added a wrinkle to the operation. I suggested to Reuven that he have the kitten display not in the schoolyard but during Mr. Friedman's Bible class. The choice of Mr. Friedman's class was deliberate. He had a comic disposition that did not change even when teaching the saddest of stories. This disposition made him tolerant of his charges' marginal mischief.

Since Reuven lived near the school and also had a bicycle, he could time the kitten delivery to coincide with Mr. Friedman's class. The logistics were set, the timing co-ordinated. At the appointed hour, Reuven hauled over a small bag whose contents he released during class. Even as Mr. Friedman's outstretched arm was poised in mid-air, a litter of tiny creatures, looking dyed in a rainbow of colours, crawled all over the place, seeking a warm cuddle. What ensued can only be described as pandemonium. The girls jumped on their desks howling primal cries as if they had seen hungry wolves about to pounce on them. The cries alerted neighbouring classes, adding to the disarray. The principal burst into the classroom. He was not amused. Mr. Friedman pointed to Reuven, who was summarily marched into the principal's office. Even as the custodians were picking up God's creatures, I was summoned to the office to be confronted by a red-faced principal who, on the evidence of Reuven's story, accused me of being the architect of the kitten display. When I declined to confess, he directed me to follow him. The principal led the column, followed by me, while Reuven made up the rear. I was asked to apologize to Mr. Friedman and the class, and when I responded, "it wasn't me," he slapped me on the face in view of the entire class. This was a portentous slap, changing the course of events.

Humiliated and holding back from bursting into tears, the echo of the slap still ringing in my ears, I ran home, broke open my clay piggy bank, collected a few essential items, and hurried to the bus station where I boarded a bus that would take me to my grandparents' town, Parchew Podlaski, about thirty kilometres away. The bus driver knew me from my frequent trips to Parchew and was somewhat surprised to see me unaccompanied and in the middle of the school year. "My grandfather is not well," I boldly lied, "and I am going to visit him just for the day." This was my first white lie to cover up my subterfuge. My next one was a leap of the imagination. On my arrival at my grand parents' home, I was met with the anticipated question of what had happened, to which I replied, "A plague hit our town and all schools are shut till further notice." When Mother learned about the "kitten episode," which she rightly assumed had resulted in my abrupt departure, she cabled her in-laws asking them to send me back immediately. I had foreseen my mother's steps and for two days I intercepted her communications. But on the third day, I was lured away from my watch by a soccer game played by the neighbourhood boys. It was the third cable that undid me. Unceremoniously, I was escorted by my aunt (who was probably making sure that I would not take a detour) to the station and she packed me into on the bus.

Mother, to my utter surprise, was conciliatory. The reason that I had taken off in a huff was the fear of her wrath, but instead of berating me, she cajoled a promise out of the principal that no disciplinary measures would be taken against me. Neither would she punish me. "But what about the slap in front of the class?" I asked somewhat aggressively. "What about it?" she echoed my words. "This is it, you're going back to school tomorrow." Well, the slap could not be undone, but my defiant reaction to it had brought me prestige and name recognition at school. Now my former deeds were rewarded. My reputation stood me in good stead with Menachem. The scheme I had plotted, followed by my reaction to the principal's measures, proved to him that I had the necessary stuff to brave our shared fate.

The mistaken perception found in popular Holocaust literature and in films portrays the ghettos, and by corollary, the besieged, as a grey uniformity, the handiwork of the Nazi flattening machinery. A video camera filming from outside the ghetto, either a walled-in one like Warsaw or one surrounded by barbed wire like Kraków, would have shown such a reality. The camera would have recorded people milling about the streets with worn-out, oversized clothing hanging on their emaciated bodies; children leaning against a wall holding tin cans; others lying on the sidewalk with outstretched hands; humans pulling carts carrying bodies piled on each other; men in uniform, wielding billy clubs, striding the streets. This seeming mixture of grey humanity would have taken on a very different look had the camera been filming the ghetto from the inside.

It would have shown that the uniformed men wielding billy clubs were actually Jewish policemen; the microphone would have picked up the chant of lamentation prayers wafting from a back street house, and in other houses young adults debating issues of morality and art, matters unrelated to ghetto existence. Indeed, the ghetto could have given the impression of possessing a semblance of normality.

The Międzyrzec Podlaski ghetto in which Menachem and I found ourselves fell roughly into this category of "a semblance of normality." Both Menachem and I enjoyed considerable advantages over other ghetto residents, particularly those our own age. Through cleverly managed bribes, Menachem established connections. He got himself into a labour detail assigned to work in a tannery outside the ghetto. This position afforded extra food to the workers and provided the illusory status of being indispensable to the war effort. Menachem used his position as a ploy for smuggling goods into the ghetto, which he sold to the people who could still afford them. He invested the earnings from his smuggling to establish connections with the decision-making authorities in the ghetto and to enhance his living standard. This is how he secured a place for me in the tannery labour detail.

Menachem obtained the job for me not because I was in need of extra food portions. The bundle of money Mother sewed into my overcoat would last me for a long while. Still, each time a denomination came off the bundle, I felt bereft of my life insurance. The purpose of enlisting me into the labour detail was to obtain for me the ardently desired status of "indispensable." Working outside the ghetto also provided an escape hatch should I opt to leave the ghetto; slipping away from the tannery was easier than from our barbed-wire-encircled home. The perennial deportations, the capricious changings of rules, injected into ghetto life a volatility that required a kind of cat-and-mouse play, weighing the chance of survival in the ghetto against that of survival outside it. Hiding with Polish people, obtaining false identity papers, or trying to get linked with a partisan group in the forest were possibilities, but each one involved a deadly risk.

Menachem and I sometimes discussed these possibilities, painfully aware of the mortal consequences if any one of them failed. In addition to experiencing fear of the unknown, dilemmas of what to do next, and the searing pain of family loss, I dreaded losing Menachem. Though he was stealthy and careful with his food-smuggling operations, each entry into the ghetto involved a body search by the Jewish police under the surveillance of a Polish policeman and often an SS guard. Menachem had to figure out the days that the policemen whose palms had been greased guarded the gate, for if caught smuggling he could be pummelled into pulp, or shot. At best he could be taken off the list of the labour detail that was critical for his expeditions into the black market. When he did his business outside our gates, he had to hide his pronounced Semitic looks by wearing the clothes of a young Polish youth and adapting his way of walking and speaking. Menachem was not given to ruminations, but when in the mood, he would tell me that the eyes were the hardest to disguise. The sadness jutting out of them were a give-away, making him an object of prey for the *Szmalcovnik*, and avoiding them became increasingly difficult. I could not bear the thought of him getting caught during one of his forays into the black market buying food for the ghetto or because of a misstep at the ghetto gate. I did not share my anxieties with Menachem; I did not want him to know that I was worried about his smuggling operations. Imparting my worries to him might have blunted his smuggling skills, I feared. But I also had an ulterior motive, for my dependency on him grew as the days and weeks passed.

Through his connections and associations with the Jewish authorities, he could pick up signs about the next impending *aktion* and give us time to plan our next step. We often considered the possibility of escaping into the forest where we might link up with some fighting groups. To do this, we would have to find a weapon — this was the entrance pass to joining a partisan group — and such an undertaking was fraught with danger. Menachem's mere presence gave me a sense of hope that made my ghetto existence bearable.

My life of going to work in the tannery and returning to the ghetto, the brooding, the nagging dilemmas about what to do next, the pain of loss — all these were abruptly interrupted when I came down with typhus. One night I felt like a locomotive furnace, my aching body steamed up in a bath of sweat. Typhus was widespread in the congested conditions of the ghetto. While medical doctors were aplenty, medicine was scarce. It could, however, be obtained at exorbitant prices. Thanks to the bundle of money sewed into my overcoat, and Menachem's ingenuity, I got the necessary medication to pull me through my illness. Once the fever receded, a weakness permeated my body, a body that insatiably craved food. Even as I was regaining my strength, the money bundle was getting slimmer. Menachem was helpful in reducing my food costs through his smuggling ventures and his reassurance that I should not worry, but notwithstanding his generosity, I was becoming increasingly anxious at the sight of the diminishing bundle, intermittently touching the spot which held it. Reluctantly, I fell back on a plan that I casually mentioned to Menachem.

I reconstructed the map that Mother had made me learn by heart. It outlined the peasant's village and his house. The money and valuables entrusted to him would last us for a long while once I'd gotten hold of them. It was a risky undertaking, involving walking a distance of roughly forty kilometers in hostile territory, vulnerable to the prying eyes of peasants who would sell a Jew to the police for a food reward. What if avarice got the upper hand of the trustee and he did away with me so as to keep the valuables? The "whats" and the "ifs" seemed infinite. No matter how dangerous, the risk was worth taking, or so I argued in the face of Menachem's discouragement. I did not approach my prospective journey lightly, but the alternative looked grim. The typhus had eaten into my inheritance, and the thought that I might be left with no means to supplement my meagre rations from the tannery was horrifying. And for the first time, I shared with Menachem my fears that something could happen to him. Winter was approaching and the time to set out was now.

We were sitting at a table bent over a map that I reconstructed from memory, plotting the route of my journey to the village where the peasant lived. In other circumstances, we could have been seen as two scout instructors mapping out the route for an outing. I would walk along the rails and just before reaching Radzyń Podlaski, my hometown, I would leave the rail route and take a side road to the village. According to the reconstructed map, the peasant's house was situated past the small bridge on the left. There was just one more thing to be tackled: What story should I tell the peasant? Notwithstanding the trust Mother put in him, the times changed people, and he could easily get rid of me with no one the wiser. It was known that many Jews who came back to retrieve their hidden treasures simply disappeared. We had to come up with a convincing story, one that would leave no margin for hesitation to hand over the valuables. I still remember the words verbatim: "Mother is in the forest with the partisans and she sent me to get the money. They need the money to buy arms."

I rehearsed the lines till I knew them backwards and forwards. Menachem outfitted me with a new peasant overcoat and a big hat and food for two days, though the journey was calculated to last about twelve hours. I left the ghetto with the labour detail in the morning and at the tannery compound gates ripped off my white *Mogen Dovid* armband and stealthily broke away from the column.

I walked with a brisk but unhurried pace, not glancing sideways. On reaching the outskirts of the city, I took a side road that led to an open field running alongside the rail tracks, hitting the ground whenever I heard the rattling wheels of an approaching train. Slogging through the mud mixed with leaves and stubble, seeking bushes and trees to hide behind, I had a singular objective in mind: to reach the peasant's house undetected.

I stopped to gobble down some food and plodded on. I cut away from the rail tracks heading towards the village. As I approached it, relaxation gave way to tension. I had to spot the perfect time slot to sneak into the village: while the dogs were on their last barks, bidding each other good night, and just as the villagers were sitting down to their evening meal. At the tail end of the fading bays, I glided into the village, landing in front of a bare window. The family was assembled around the table on which lay a large loaf of bread and a huge pot. A dimly-lit gasoline lamp stood to the side of the table. I slid around the cottage to the door and knocked lightly. The man to whom Mother had entrusted the valuables appeared and stood before me, his face registering recognition. Putting a finger to his lips, he led me into a side alcove and closed the door. I plopped on to the floor and shut my eyes. "He's shoved me into the alcove because he does not want his children to see me. But what'll he do next?" These thoughts were racing through my mind. "I have to get my message out to him that Mother and the partisans are waiting in the forest for my return. But if he has already decided to dispose of me, what can I do?" When the door opened, I saw him carrying food and a tea jug. The family had gone to bed and the lamp wick was turned down. He thought I had come to ask for shelter and was relieved to hear that I only wanted to retrieve the valuables at Mother's request. He would let me stay for the night and I was to leave in the early morning.

When the time came, my benefactor walked me, equipped with food, a bottle of water and a small pouch laden with coins, to the little bridge that I had crossed ten hours earlier. The night was lifting its darkness. I hastened my steps, leaving the village behind me and retracing my route. In the three years that I was subjected to mind-boggling ordeals, some of which I can still touch and smell, this journey left little imprint on my recollection. The only primary experience I recall was my encounter with a woman walking in the opposite direction on the other side of the road. She was wearing peasants' baggy clothes, her head wrapped in a shawl that covered her face and showed a few wisps of red hair. There was something about her gait that seemed familiar. Without stopping, though slowing her pace, she uttered, "*Rateve zik.*" I immediately recognized the person. Her son was the captain of the Jewish soccer team, which regularly played the Polish team. The Polish opponents would hurl ethnic slurs at their Jewish rivals and sometimes resort to rough elbowing whenever it was losing the game. On these occasions her son led his team to confront the Polish bullies, who folded on encountering resistance. He was my idol-cum-model, from whom I drew courage when scuffling with my adversaries. His mother must have been out to seek shelter with a peasant or with the partisan groups in the forest. Though this had been a blink-of-the-eye meeting, her single utterance, *"Rateve zik,"* echoed in my mind through the twisted roads of survival on which I trudged for three years.

According to plan, I was to return to the tannery gates, wait till the workers filed out to return to the ghetto at the end of the day's work, and slip into the crowd, sidling up to Menachem. This was a relatively easy timing manoeuvre compared to the one I had exercised in the village. Still, one had to be alert. Peril was lying in wait at every corner, at each turn. Hiding behind a building, I saw the labour detail shuffling out of the gate and, to my great relief, Menachem was among them. Replacing my armband, I merged into the marching column. Menachem's eyes exuded joy at seeing me. He kept on squeezing my arm; presumably to make sure that it was not my ghost walking beside him. I had never seen Menachem so sentimental and proud of me.

I emptied the small pouch on the table and a string of golden coins, rings and earrings fell out. The coins, known as *Napoleonchiks*, were minted during the Emperor's reign and carried a high value. My acquired riches would free Menachem from his perilous smuggling. Now economically secure, we faced anew our perennial dilemma: whether to stay in the ghetto, putatively shielded by our jobs at the tannery, or try to purchase a weapon, the entry visa into a partisan group. On these occasions, I conjured up Mother to seek her advice. She duly told me what I wanted to hear. Winter was on the verge of breaking, making the forest an alien host, and there was the difficulty of purchasing a weapon, which was fraught with deadly risk.

The members of the *Judenrat* responsible for the orderly running of the ghetto, believed or made themselves believe in obedience and hard work as a way to outlive the enemy. While Menachem and I did not fall prey to the illusion of "outliving the enemy" and harboured plans of the forest alternative, we pretended that we still had some time left. Time did not, however, appear to be on our side. Learning from the rumours swirling around the ghetto, we were fully aware of the inevitable end and yet did not act. We succumbed to the creature comforts provided by my retrieved funds and the illusory security given by our employment in the tannery.

## Caught in the Web

As I sit committing memory to paper, I realize that Menachem and I were mostly immune to the ravages of ghetto life. The starvation and sickness that stalked most of the residents missed us like the plagues in Egypt passed over the Israelites' homes. Our lives assumed a perversely routine rhythm projecting a semblance of normality. Our days were taken up with light menial work in the tannery, then returning to the ghetto in the evening, where Menachem cooked a nutritious meal and we kept talking about our plans to go into the forest as soon as the leaf buds appeared on the trees. In the winter of 1943, rumours of obscure origins pervaded the ghetto. According to the bearers of the news, the Red Army was sweeping across the Ukrainian prairies, dogging the retreating *Wehrmacht* to the west. The faithful, whose ears had been trained to listen for the steps of the Messiah, instantly picked up the echoes of rattling tanks bursting through the ghetto gates. "The eternity of the Jewish people will never disappoint,"[4] ran the motto that circulated among us, and in the circumstances of that time it had an ironically hollow ring to it.

In contrast to the *Judenrat*, the Zionist and Socialist youth groups treated the news with a healthy dose of realism. Unhampered by the "Eternity of Israel" slogan, they had looked the enemy straight in the eye and saw a racially bred opponent different from its Christian progenitors of the Middle Ages. They had — as I later found out in my research — been connected with other underground groups from whom they received news about the Eastern and Western fronts, but knew that the Nazi enemy would not relent. On the contrary, the impending Nazi defeat would speed up the race between the hunter and the hunted. Unfortunately, the events that took place in March and April of 1943 vindicated the less optimistic soothsayers. On the surface the rhythm of ghetto life seemed unchanged. The labour details went to work, the Jewish police patrolled the streets, the poor went hungry and the sick kept on dying.

Though there were no tangible signs of an imminent *aktion*, disquiet seized the ghetto, a disquiet soon to morph into vacillating nervousness. The veteran ghetto dwellers, those who had managed to survive two to three *aktionen* and had subsequently developed an inner ear, were the first to pick up the signals.

---

[4]    Samuel I, 15:29: "The eternal one of Yisrael will not lie or change his mind." The modern interpretation is that God's protection of the Jewish people will never end.

Their reaction became contagious and swiftly spread through the entire ghetto. By now the hideout frenzy afflicted everyone. People were darting along the barbed wire, seeking escape hatches. Menachem's informants confirmed the ghetto's premonitions.

Light years later, my family and I visit the Bronx zoo. I am about to enter Brown University for graduate work, with my war ordeal tucked away deep in my subconscious and my eyes trained on the future. I believe that I have control of my memories, except when I'm asleep. But on watching the primates swinging back and forth in their caged cubicles, the suppressed past explodes into the present. I have a strong sense of déjà vu: humans rushing up and down along barbed wires, one image imposed upon the other. Time melds, but only for a split moment.

One morning in the ghetto, we gathered as usual at the gate to go to the tannery. The ranks of the labour detail had increased that day by large numbers. These newcomers had previous arrangements with the police. At the end of the day, we assembled at the camp gate to return to the ghetto. But that particular day was different from all other days. Instead of returning to the ghetto after the day's work, we were taken to an adjacent building occupied by the *Wehrmacht* and directed to climb the stairs to the loft. It was a huge loft, very different from the one in which I had hid less than a year ago. There was ample room in which to stretch out and there was no need to keep watch, since we were the wards of the *Wehrmacht*, so to speak. And yet it felt very much the same. The race against time was on and we were losing. There was not much talk that night. Menachem and I bundled together in silence.

Early the next morning, as the late March sun streaked through the narrow shutters, I peeked out. The streets leading to the railway station, the assembly place for transportations, were quiet. Ordinarily, on *aktion* days the *Einsatzgruppen* would march through the streets singing "*Wenn das Juden blut vom Messer Spritzt*," as a warm-up for the real thing. For a short while we thought that the panic was a false alarm, but we were disabused of that notion after a few hours. Through the shutters I watched a column of people walking, arms interlocked, in the direction of the railway station. The girls' heads were covered with white kerchiefs; the boys also wore peasant-like caps. These were people from Zionist organizations who had worked on agricultural estate farms that had supplied provisions for the German army. I recognized some of the faces from my hometown; others were familiar from the ghetto. One face stood out — a neighbour of mine who, at the early stage of the occupation, volunteered to work on the farms. I must have been five to six years younger than she was and I had fallen in love with her. Falling in love with older women, I later found out, was to be a theme in my life.

I watched the column moving in silent resignation to enslavement or death, escorted by Ukrainian, Estonian and Baltic henchmen, led by pureblood Teutonic SS officers. These young men and women accepted their fate as one would accept nature's seasons. It was this submission to fate that elicited Hannah Arendt's vitriolic attack against the *Judenrat* and the victims. Her pure analytical mind failed to grasp the victims' psyche, cunningly manipulated by an intricate puppetry contraption that strung the victim from hope to despair and then spun him back to hope in a pirouette, rendering him a docile marionette in a vast theatre of destruction. Had fortune reversed its course and enabled those young people to reach their ancestral land, they would have become fierce defenders of their settlements against Arab marauders and some would eventually have enlisted in the Jewish Brigade to fight our mortal enemy in the Monte Carlo fortress. In my mind's eye I still imagine my young neighbour, safely arrived in Israel, milking the cows of her Kibbutz during the day and armed with a Great War rifle, doing guard duty, at night. But on that sunny morning on March 1943, she shadow-walked to her death and I silently wept farewell.

That night, following the *aktion*, we stayed hidden in the *Wehrmacht* loft. Again Menachem and I bundled together for a night's sleep. Menachem calculated that we had about three to four months till the next *aktion*. During this respite we would establish contact with a partisan group in the forest, buy two guns and get out of the ghetto. Always the realist, Menachem saw the end coming. But the gods assigned us different roles. In the morning, instead of being brought to our routine work, we were marched to the tannery gate, from which we were taken to the ghetto. This did not bode well. I suggested half-heartedly that we might be needed in the ghetto to remove the recent deportees' belongings and sort them out.

As soon as we entered the ghetto the granite truth struck us. The *Einsatzgruppen* had virtually emptied the ghetto; it had sucked out the little life left in it. Scores of survivors of the *aktion* were busy removing the property of the vacant houses. The Jewish police station stood bereft of its occupants. An *Einsantzgruppen* contingent oversaw the work. The SS guards led us to the centre of the ghetto, where heaps of personal belongings were piled up. We silently sorted out life's remnants. If there were a few among us who might have deluded themselves that we still had a lease on life, they were brutally disabused of that idea at the end of that day's work. Escorted to the assembly *platz* and put up in vacated houses guarded by the SS, even the congenital illusionists realized that we were in line for the terminal walk to the railway station. We had run out of options. But not Menachem. He was determined not to clamber into the cattle car. The ghetto fences were heavily guarded, and that would make any attempted escape suicidal. The only possibility left was to break away from the column on its way to the railway station. Menachem spoke to me, breaking a long silence. He would try this escape route. He neither encouraged me nor discouraged me from joining him. I sensed, however, that he would rather not have me with him. Or did I imagine it? I will never know the answer.

We were taken along the same route on which the deportees had walked three days earlier, and as we passed the building from which we had watched them I wondered whether anyone had managed to hide and was peering through the shutters. The Poles looked at us, some perhaps with pity, others with relief: *the Żydy killed our Lord.* Menachem, alert, was timing his break away from the column. When the column left the city and reached the outskirts, he bolted like lightning into the sprawling bushes. A fusillade of shots followed him as he zigzagged toward a curve around a mound of earth. The column was prodded forward, the shots reverberating. We were herded into the cattle cars, the doors were slammed shut with a metallic clang, and each captive scrambled for a spot. The journey into the darkening heart of Evil began. The *Judenrein* program, purging Europe of the Jews, was still in its operational phase.

The time, Early April, 1943.

### From the Armband to the Yellow Triangle

Since that day in April, when I was first trapped in a four-walled narrow space trundling to an unknown destination, I have been forcibly taken on many other journeys in similar, though not identical, circumstances. The SS escorts put no restrictions on the amount of food or water we were allowed to take; no body search was conducted. They seemed to be in a hurry to pack us into the cars and send us off. The small convoy of cattle cars lurched into motion. I could see night descending through the cracks. Though the car was full, it was not jammed, as cars were in my later travels. I managed to secure a corner where I was able to crouch and take stock of the situation. Just as I was about to probe my mental wounds, reviewing in my mind's eye the bullets chasing Menachem's sprint to the curve, an unexpected stirring erupted in the car. Two sturdy young men made their way to the door. Penknives in hand, they peeled away the plank that held the bolt from outside the car. Their task was to drill an opening wide enough for a hand to reach the catch that held the bolt. After a few hours the door slid ajar. Cool air rushed into the wagon.

The psychology involved in jumping from a racing train, covered by machine-guns on rotating turrets, requires a single-mindedness that verges on insanity. The two men requested silence. They informed us that the train was not destined for Treblinka,[5] one of the terminal stations of European Jewry. However, they were not sure where it was headed. They suggested that people jump from the train when it chugged uphill or slowed on a curve. Willing your entire nervous system into the act, you would hurl your taut body away from the board into the dark emptiness. The sporadic shots from the guard towers, punctuating the train's rattling, indicated that people were jumping from the other cars. Soon the two men hurled themselves from the train. They had a few followers. I heard people murmur that those young men belonged to the underground.

### A World that Has to be Imagined to Make it Real

My recall of ghetto life is immediate. I can feel its texture; smell its odours; see the gate of the police chief and his lackeys; hear the Yiddish dialects of towns spanning from Galicia to the Latvian-Lithuanian regions. It is as if I watched a video on a television screen, the remote control in my hand, rewinding and fast-forwarding through the frames. But this dexterity of memory deserts me when I try to replay my actual arrival in Majdanek. Only after acrobatic mental efforts do images begin to loom in the foreground of my memory. Stripped of the clothes that held sewn-in golden coins, I stand in a four- or five-deep line formation. Most men and women are in their twenties; there are few children or elderly people. Each line goes through the selection one by one, and then dissolves. My line's turn comes; one step forward.

Four SS officers, one of them swirling a baton, review us. I look around and imitate my fellow travellers. I put my best foot forward: stand upright, chest bulging, eyes trained straight. The baton moves pointedly from one to the other; it pinpoints me, directing me to a group of men standing aside. The walk up to the showers, and then the shower heads drip-drop, drop-drip....

The entire event was carefully choreographed, affecting the appearance of a religious pageantry. Clad in black boots and starched uniforms, their skulls boasting hats set on at identical angles, their stilted walk purposely measured,

---

5    A death camp in Poland operated from 1942 to 1943.

the SS officers performed a rite of passage into the *anus mundi*. The tenuously saved among us went through baptism, head-shaving, being draped in white-and-blue striped pyjamas and shod in wooden shoes. The others, those for whom the baptism in water was replaced by one in seeping Zyklon B gas, endured only the first stage of the ritual. They did not make it out of the showers, and their spasm-twisted bodies were dumped into the burning fires, an offering to the Latter-Day Moloch.

A lifetime later, I came across a poem entitled "My Little Sister," by Abba Kovner, an underground fighter in the Vilna ghetto, who had whole skeletons to pick with God. Speaking tongue in cheek, Kovner expresses gratitude to God who

> …took his bread, bless God,
> forty years from one oven. He never imagined
> a whole people could rise in the ovens
> and the world, with God's help, goes on.

Designed to become part of the distorted mirror image of this new pseudo-religious order, we were immediately led to its initiation process. The formative vehicle of the initiation was the *Appell*.

From a bird's-eye view, the scene strikes an unworldly chord. Row upon row of scarecrows wearing identical blue berets, arranged in parallel lines, swaying sideways, at times doffing and donning their berets in unison, kneeling rhythmically — movement enacted in perfect coordination. At the far edges of the *Appellplatz* appear elongated barracks in identical geometric shapes. The entire complex is encircled by barbed wire and dotted with watchtowers, spaced out at regular intervals.

We were corralled into a barrack, and each of us was provided with a bunk, a blanket, a metal bowl and a spoon. The *Blockälteste*, a fellow prisoner who served as the senior functionary of the block, greeted us in pidgin German. His speech was designed to impress upon us the severe punishment should we disobey orders, try to escape or manipulate the system. My immediate superior was the *Stubendienst*, in charge of a line of bunks in the barracks. His routine was to supervise our dawn ritual: awaken us and ensure that before the summons to the *Appell* the bunks were identically made up, each blanket folded with hospital corners. After shoving down a piece of bread and coffee, we would be goaded to the *Appellplatz* for the morning count.

Twice daily we were lined up in the *Appellplatz* in military formation. After meticulous counting by badge number, the *Stubendienst* reported to the *Blockältester* who, in turn, reported to the *Kapo*, who then reported to the *Überkapo*, who reported to the *Lagerälteste*, who finally reported to the

*Rapportführer*, a non-commissioned SS officer in charge of the roll call. The Great Chain of Being was reduced to a series of human barks. Until every inmate was accounted for, the *Appell* was not dismissed. The fearsome mantra was "*Est muss klappen*" — the partially living, the dying and the dead must tally, just as the lines must correspond and the inmates' movements match.

During my first week at Majdanek, I would drift into the forming lines in whichever spot chanced my way. But I was soon to learn that notwithstanding its rigid uniformity there were choice spots that the veteran inmates hastily edged themselves into. Exposed to the elements and the unbridled torment of the inmate functionaries, also known as the *prominante*, in their show of fealty to the system, the front row was the inmates' nightmare, as was the back row. Then there was the question of the far sides, closing the rows. These spots could be advantageous in that they allowed marginal manoeuvring en route to the soup line. But they suffered from the same drawbacks as the front and the back rows. Because of the gnawing hunger and the relentless demand of a growing body for food, I opted for the side spots, strategically positioned to reach the optimal spot in the formation.

Picture this: the vesper *Appell* was in the making. I found a spot close to my barrack. The smell of soup wafted into my nostrils, quickening the acid cruising in my entrails. And just a fraction of an instant before dismissal or a fraction after, I must have stepped out of the line, incurring the wrath of an inmate functionary. The punishment came as quickly as lightning. Bruised and hurting, I shuffled to the barracks with the tail end of the column. My fellow inmates kept on slouching towards the soup vat, oblivious to what was happening around them: an ordinary occurrence in a day's existence. To view the beating of a boy endangered their fragile sanity. I learned this from my own encounter with the brutality inflicted on other inmates.

Survival in this inhuman environment was driven by a paradox. Exposure to rampant cruelty might intimidate you and dull your hunting instincts for extra food; a middle spot on the *Appell*; or a chance of getting into an *Arbeitskommando* overseen by a *Kapo* whose humanity had not yet been drained. Thus, to stay alert you had to shield yourself from the surroundings. But the protective shield that enabled you to keep the sight of terror at bay posed the risk of dulling your vigilance of your surroundings, a necessary condition while on the bread-prowl. Darting back and forth between alertness and oblivion became my survival tactic. My age and physical size compelled me to carefully calculate my forages so as to avoid rivalry with other inmates. I did not think of these survival measures as strategies at the time. These are reflections distilled from a myriad of erratic events that defy rationality. At that time, it was the primary survival instinct at work.

The lesson I learned from the beating was to lose myself into the striped pyjama mass, and I also learned how to make time tick in sync with the overarching built-in clock of *l'univers concentrationnaire*, as aptly defined by David Rousset, an Auschwitz survivor. Within this tight frame time I negotiated between the various Majdanek concentration camp realities.

Majdanek was chiefly a supply warehouse camp of manpower for the German industry. Periodically representatives of the industry would come to pick the physically fit inmates and cart them off. Getting on such a transport became my immediate goal. Rumour had it that in these forced labour camps the conditions were bearable, for the industry needed the inmates to do the work for the war effort from which it benefited. This was, as I later learned, an optimistically exaggerated rumour, grounded in wishful thinking and in logic, both lethally dangerous. But for now, what I wanted to know was how could one stay fit in an environment designed to be life-sucking?

A friendly inmate, who had arrived from Warsaw four months earlier and thus qualified for the veteran category, gave me life-saving advice. The key to getting on an industry *Arbeitskommando* was to keep clean and avoid confrontation with other inmates, no matter how unfairly one was treated. "Avoid jostling for desirable soup spots or *Appell* spots; step aside when shoved from the water taps or any other facility — that might cause friction with other inmates. Giving way to the stronger is essential for a young boy," he counselled. "This is not a place for schoolyard face-saving scuffles." He himself had tried twice to get picked for forced labour, but he didn't make the cut because of his age. The industry liked us young and physically fit to feed its machinery with our sweat. We were the machinery-fodder, and when the fodder gave out, the industry disposed of us, courtesy of the SS. In SS jargon this regime was called *Vernichtung durch Arbeit*. Since the industries paid the SS per capita, they bought and covered the transportation expenses. My benefactor's age apparently made him a bad investment. Still, he would try again next time. His tutored eye would pick up signs of an impending selection for the industry and then he would let me know.

The gnawing hunger never let up. All my endurance was rolled into it, as was probably true for the other inmates my age. Whether I was standing at attention on the *Appell* or working in a labour detail or dreaming nightmarish dreams, the beast never stopped clawing at my entrails. And then, as I have mentioned elsewhere, there was the young, slender *Kapo* of towering height, boasting a green badge designated for criminals, who had invented a role intended to torment us. Every afternoon shortly before the vespers *Appell*, he would strut through *Feld III* holding a huge brown sausage, devouring it in full sight of stalking, food-craving spectators. I became transfixed by this ritual. Lurking in a corner, I would eagerly await the sausage to appear and vicariously sink my teeth into it. The sausage transformed itself into a ghost shadowing me in my waking hours and haunting me in my nightmares. But the voracious beast within me would not be deluded. Delusion, under those circumstances, could have hampered my survival skills, with devastating effects.

Then, unexpectedly, help materialized in the form of a wagon harnessed to two people in front and two pushing it from behind, with a fifth one, exuding an authoritative air, leading the procession. None of them looked like inmates. They appeared more like people from the planet from which I had been exiled two years earlier. They wore civilian clothes and regular shoes and their bones were covered with flesh. This was a provision supply wagon for *Feld III*, an unapproachable Holy Ark making its way to the kitchen. And one of the two harnessed people was a former classmate of mine. He glanced at me in recognition. And thereby hangs a tale within a tale.

## A Mother Mourning her Children

The Hochman family deserves a brief diversion. Hochman was the eldest sibling in his family, with a younger brother and sister. About a year before the outbreak of war their mother went to Palestine, then ruled by Britain, to persuade her alienated husband to secure immigration certificates for the children, who had been left in the care of their grandmother. Then war intervened. The Hochman family must have been deported with the first wave in early 1942. That first wave comprised the poorest town residents, who were assigned for deportation to meet the quota prescribed by the Gestapo. I learned later that none of the Hochman children survived.

After the 1948 Israeli War of Independence, I remained in Israel in search of family photos and memorabilia from my hometown, in the hopes that some of my townspeople might have brought them along in their travels. In the course of my search, I met a woman who told me that Mrs. Hochman was eager to talk to me. When she had finally come to grips with her children's fate, she had put on a black dress and now wore black-tinted glasses. Her mourning was deep. I was torn between an obligation to share with her what I knew about her children and reluctance to do so.

What would I tell her about her two sons and daughter? I knew very little, except that when I'd last seen her eldest son, he looked healthy, either pushing or drawing a wagon of provisions, and that he dropped chunks of bread and margarine for me at a grave risk to himself. I did not know what had happened to her younger son and to her baby girl. What could I tell her? That if not for her son, I might not be standing here to tell the tale? I neither had the words nor the courage to face the grieving mother. It was not by any means a manifestation of the "survivor's guilt syndrome," sweepingly handed out from the perspective of the armchair psychologists; rather it was the emotionally jagged rawness entailed in such an encounter that I dreaded. After all, I made it to the finishing line in this unimaginable race against death, but I had not done so at his cost. I had not taken his place in the selection line that chose the inmates for work in the industry; I had not elbowed him out of the soup line; I had not sneaked into his customary *Appell* spot. Yet I could not bring myself to accede to Mrs. Hochman's request, and never did so. The image of this stillborn encounter has visited me many times over the years.

As I said, a couple of years before the outbreak of the war, Mrs. Hochman joined her husband in the British mandatory Palestine in the hope of having her three children brought over as soon as their immigration papers arrived. Meanwhile, the children were left in the care of their grandmother. The war upset the plan. The children and the grandmother were among the first deportees from town. The oldest son, Menachem, made it through the selection, but his siblings did not. Thanks to his relatively early arrival, he landed a job in the Supply Provision Block.

Nourished by the tidbits dropped by Hochman on the way out of *Feld III* and the tips from my fellow inmate, I held out. Slowly I honed my survival instincts and measured my steps, matching them with the tick-tock of the camp's clock. I would not dare, for example, to carry the soup vat from the kitchen to our block or back to the kitchen without the *Kesselmeister's* orders. He was Master of the Vat that contained our lifeblood, and the inmate who was lucky enough to be in his favour had a better chance of survival.

The vat was set in a stand from which four handles protruded. Twice a day it would be carried from our block to the kitchen and back: at daybreak for the ersatz coffee and at sunset for the watery soup. While the *Kapo's* sausage aroused my fantasies and the provision wagon my reveries, the vat was something to which I could relate. I soon developed a relationship with it. It was an intimate relationship. After all, I was in its presence about thirty seconds twice a day at matinee and vespers and followed the

*Kesselmeister's* ladle in silent prayer as he slopped the lifeblood into my tin. I sometimes got to carry the vat back to the kitchen and was rewarded with extras.

The inmate who occupied a bunk a couple of spaces away from mine enjoyed special privileges. Though not one of the block's *prominante,* he was always the first in the soup line. After *Appell* he returned to the barracks to perform cleaning chores, and he also had a secure place on the *Appell* formation. My quick inquiry as to the reasons for his privileged status pointed to his son. In the first or second week of my arrival in Majdanek, I noticed nearby a boy dressed in white clothes roaming through the camp compound with a bouncy gait reminiscent of the camp elite, who imitated the stride of the SS. I got a better peek at him when he came to see his father. He was roughly my age and bore a tan complexion that accentuated his well-cut white suit, pinned with a yellow star. His entrance to the block made quite a stir. The *Blockälteste,* his subordinates and hangers-on greeted the boy with the kind of servile flattery accorded to a *Kapo.*

The boy and his father came with one of the Warsaw transports immediately after the Ghetto Uprising, my benefactor told me, and as soon as they made it to *Feld III* after the selection, the boy was espoused by the *Lagerältester* and he became his "pupil," a euphemism for a sex slave. His authority derived from this status, which he exercised with a cruelty rivalling that of his master, a stocky figure with a huge head and a scarred face. In a show of fealty to the system and in sight of his master, the boy once whipped his own father for not making his bunk properly. Fear reigned when he made an appearance in the block. Once I saw the boy from nearby; he had brought food for his father and his father's bunkmate.

This erratic behaviour, swerving from cruelty to compassion, was not uncommon in the camp's ethos. The functionary who beat one up for not holding the broom properly while sweeping the dirty floor might throw his victim a piece of bread the next day. One could not foresee the conduct of those who held power over us. Within the inmates' society, two pecking orders prevailed — one in the confines of the camp and the other outside the camp, in the *Aussenkomando.* In the camp the *Lagerältester,* reigning supreme, pecked the *Blockälteste,* who in turn pecked at the *Stubendienst.* In the *Aussenkomando* details, the *Lagerkapo,* ruling supreme, pecked at the *Kapo,* who in turn pecked at his assistant, the *Vorarbeiter* — and it was open season on the inmates for all. There was no recourse for complaints.

While shadows of hunger still lurk in my visceral system, easily prompted to the surface, it is arbitrariness that has dogged my post-Holocaust life.

Those who have held power over me in my realistic life are in essence not different from those who exerted power over me in my surrealistic life. The stakes have changed, but not the impulse that drives ambition, vanity and self-interest — all propelled by the passion for domination. Those people who enjoy freedoms and rights accorded to them by a constitution often meet the whims of arbitrary power with a shrug — a luxury denied to concentration camp inmates.

After liberation, hunger vanished from my life, but the flaws of human nature persist. After all, the concentration camps were invented and operated by humans, not monsters or Martians; and human depravity does not begin or end with the concentration camps. Its antecedents go way back in history, or as my Christian friends would say, they hark back to the Fall of Man, and they might have added that they will persist until the Second Coming or the Coming of the veteran Messiah. Plato's cave allegory may be instrumental in illustrating my thinking.

## The Plasticity of Human Nature

Prisoners sit shackled in a cave facing a wall on which images are reflected from the outside world. Never having been outside the cave, they perceive the reflected images as their reality. Upon release from the cave, they encounter the true reality, and realize that the earlier images are just illusions. When I came out of the surreal world of the concentration camp and after many years integrated into the real world, I found, in contrast to the cave prisoners, that the human realities of the concentration camp bore a close resemblance to the real world. In a reversed image, a mirror image, both worlds stare at each other. "No straight thing can ever be formed from timber as crooked as that from which humanity is made." Kant's aphorism relates indirectly to Daniel J. Goldhagen's *Hitler's Willing Executioners*[6] and, in turn, has bearing on the underlying issues discussed here.

Close on the heels of the celebratory debut of Goldhagen's work, volumes of adversarial criticism appeared in academic journals, somewhat dampening its promotional hoopla. The critics laid bare the book's methodology, its prejudicial choice of sources, its absence of nuances, its redundancies and its sloppy style. The egregious lack of a comparative methodology essential to the author's argument, and his obtuseness in comprehending the meaning of

---

[6]   Daniel Jonah Goldhagen, *Hitler's Willing Executioners: Ordinary Germans and the Holocaust*. New York: Alfred A. Knopf, 1996, p. 32.

pedagogy, have been commented on by Ruth Bettina Birn in *A Nation on Trial* and widely discussed by Jacob Neusner in *Hyping the Holocaust: Scholars Answer Goldhagen.*[7] Thus, there is not much that one can add to this characterization of the book. And if I were not committing my life's experience to paper, I might not ever have come back to *Hitler's Willing Executioners*. However, Goldhagen's portrayal of the German people as uniquely evil, ironically, has the potentials of making a new brew of Holocaust Revisionism. His understanding of human behaviour is at odds with my own experience both under siege and after liberation. I feel, therefore, that I would be remiss if I did not point out some of the fallacies contained in his book.

In his introductory chapter, Goldhagen promises to show that

> much *positive* (sic) evidence exists that antisemitism, albeit an antisemitism evolving in content with the changing times, continued to be an axiom of German culture throughout the nineteenth and twentieth centuries, and that its regnant version in Germany during the Nazi period was but a more accentuated, intensified and elaborated form of an already broadly accepted basic model.

Implicit in this statement, as in many others, is an allegation that a straight line connects Heinrich Treitchke's nineteenth-century coinage, *Die Juden sind unser umglück*, for instance, with the Nuremberg Laws and the *Kristallnacht* pogrom, inexorably leading to the gas chambers. Since Goldhagen is interested in linking historically sequential constructs, it would be instructive to know whether Arthur Gobineau's racial ranting spawned the Dreyfus Affair that in turn presaged the Vichy regime, and whether French culture had bred the likes of the Parisian Police Commissioner René Bousquet, who dispatched 6,000 Jewish children to the Drancy camp, a way station to Auschwitz. Even a casual glance at *Vichy France and the Jews* by Michael R. Marrus and Robert O. Paxton shows that "Vichy's anti-Jewish program was not so blatantly foreign to the French political tradition that it could be rejected out of hand."[8] Furthermore, in the French war records, "…there are unmistakable signs of popular antipathy for the Jews,"[9] and indications "that Vichy's anti-Semitism had reflected

---

[7]    Franklin H. Littell, ed., *Hyping the Holocaust: Scholars Answer Goldhagen*. Pennsylvania: Merion Westfield Press International, 1997.

[8]    Michael R. Marrus and Robert O. Paxton, *Vichy France and the Jew*. New York: Basic Books, Inc., Publishers, 1981, p. 180.

[9]    Ibid, p. 179.

popular wishes." Vichy's legislation, the *Statut des Juifs* in 1940,[10] resembles in places the Nuremberg Laws of 1936. In short: France of 1941 looks at Germany of 1933-1939 through the rear-view mirror. Astute commentators have found that the virulent French anti-Semitism could easily have morphed into a Holocaust, had it been given enough time. "Social historians," writes George Steiner, a seasoned observer of cultural phenomena, "have shown how numerous were the signs of developing hysteria between the Dreyfus Affair and the 'Final Solution.'"[11] Equally enlightening would be a description of the Flemish Dutch collaboration with the SS in deporting their Jewish fellow citizens to "the East," as it was euphemistically dubbed by the Gestapo. The historically inclined reader might want to know whether the Flemish *SS Freiwillinger-Sturmbrigade Langamarc* was an extension of the traditional Flemish anti-Semitism whose environment had grown a Paul de Man. A cultural anti-Semite, de Mann wrote a column for the Fascist newspaper *Le Soir*, advocating the deportation of the European Jews to Madagascar.

Had Goldhagen compared the German anti-Semitic culture with those of its neighbours to the West and North, the entire premise of his thesis would have collapsed. It would have shown that the Passion Play has been acting upon the Christian psyche outside Oberammergau, notwithstanding the Second Vatican absolution of the Jewish people of their guilt for killing Jesus.

Goldhagen is not a naïf. He must have learned in Hebrew afternoon classes about Genesis 8:5 and the flood that once engulfed our planet with the purpose of eradicating the evil that stalked its residents — as epigrammatically put, "the tendency of man's nature is towards evil from his youth." He mentions a long list of barbaric acts carried out by humans against humans throughout history. Yet he finds the barbarism of the German people to have a uniquely noxious element that virtually banishes them from civilized society. The cumulative effect of reading the book inescapably leads the reader to the conclusion that the perpetrators, the representatives of the German people, as he has it, had no control of their actions. Driven by orgiastic impulses, they put to the sword six million Jewish women, men and children with either the acquiescence or the collaboration of their compatriots. Indeed, a nation possessed by demonic forces.

Ironically enough, Goldhagen shares common ground with what can best be described as Apologist Revisionism. Both agree that the bloody events

---

[10]   Ibid, p. 3.

[11]   George Steiner, *In Bluebeard's Castle*. London: Faber & Faber, 1971, p. 35.

perpetrated on the Jews were driven by uncontrollable impulses. They part ways when it comes to the culpability of the perpetrators and the German people. Ernest Nolte's earlier attempt to exculpate German guilt by claiming that the "Asian" hordes (namely the Bolsheviks) champing at the bit, ready to charge the German borders, were the decisive reason for the Holocaust, did not take hold (Frankfurt Algemeine Zeitung June 6, 1986). However, a plea that a moral outage, a kind of stay of sanity, had beset the German people, might have had a better chance of finding a responsive audience in this psychology-disposed culture. Furthermore, to bolster their argument, the revisionist may call on God's apologists who suggest "*Hester Panim*," namely God's veiled face in the Holocaust, as an explanation for His non-intervention. After all, they are mortals, ridden with human frailties. Thus, the plea for absolving the German people of their responsibility, and the perpetrators of their guilt, is both timely and proper. It was a Time of the Eclipse.

From what I can discern, Goldhagen considers himself to be a literary connoisseur. He quotes the opening verse from William Blake's *Divine Image*, "Cruelty has a Human Heart," a view of humanity that the poet bodies forth in animal metaphors in the poem "The Tyger." After presenting the frightening majesty of the tiger, Blake puts a defining question to him: "Did he who made the Lamb made thee?" Blake, like Shakespeare, whom Goldhagen also quotes in another context, saw the fundamentally opposing qualities comprising the human condition, but he missed or ignored them. In extreme situations, as in the concentration camps and on the Death Marches, these oppositions met at deathly crossroads. I was the recipient of both, the tiger-like ferocity more often than the lamb-like compassion. This was as true of what I received from the *prominante* inmates as from the SS guards. The convulsive nature of human behaviour constituted part of the concentration camp and Death March realities.

Pinchas Gutter's story is emblematic of the volatile nature of human beings' actions in extreme situations. The thirteen-year-old Pinchas was trudging from Colditz towards Theresienstadt in April of 1945. He was falling behind the column, which was moving at a snail's pace. The S.S. guards escorted the column on foot, except for the *Oberscharführer*. He rode back and forth on a bicycle, making sure that the column under his command was marching according to plan. *Es muss klappen*, it must tally, was the guiding motto. Stragglers cannot hold back the forward march; they must be pushed aside and shot. Hard as he tried, Pinchas couldn't keep up with the column. He was on his last legs. At these critical moments, the commanding angel of death appeared. He noticed Pinchas falling behind the column, got off his bicycle and slowly nudged him forward until he was once again in comparatively safe space. In the course of the 542-kilometer march, the same *Überkiller* snuck a bit of food to the sagging Jewish boy. Here and in some other places, cruelty and compassion met in a deathly life-embrace.

One cannot help speculating on Goldhagen's ruminations upon finishing his opus. After having imputed eliminationist characteristics to the German nation virtually from its inception, and consequently banning them from civilized society, Goldhagen finds himself in a bind: how can he explain the intensive process of Germany's post-war democratization? How did the anti-Semitic noxious substance become detoxified merely half a dozen years or so after the war ended? And how did a pacifist post-war generation emerge from a culture steeped in aggressive militarism? These challenging issues Goldhagen meets in a most ingenious way. He relegates them to the "Notes" on pages 593-4, and asserts that "essentially, after the war, the Germans were reeducated," a notion put to ridicule by Birn and Neusner. Pray, how did a people possessed of "demonological, racially based, eliminationist antisemitism"(p.442) go through an educational crash course and become a model of cultural liberalism and political democracy?

Had he taken the time to look at the educational effort made by the Zionist movement to transform the Diaspora-mentality Jew into an Israeli, Goldhagen would have appreciated the enormous difficulties involved in transforming a tradition. It took Zionism over eight decades to carve out from the Judean rocks a new Israeli Jew, one who would hold a plough in the day and a gun at night. Amnon Rubinstein called him "the mythological *Sabra*." Modeled on the Bar-Kochba type, this Hebrew Homo-Sapiens was initiated into *Sabra*-hood on the *Massada* Mountain, the embodiment of ancient Jewish bravery. Tapping into this heroic past, the Zionist leaders succeeded in bringing about a paradigm shift in Jewish consciousness, shunting from submission to self-assertion. It was a difficult hike from the Chagalian *Shtetl* setting to the gritty landscape of the Judean desert, but the journey reached its destination.

Employing a similar method, the leaders of the German Republic drew on the German liberal heritage to shape a new German ethos, an ethos that yielded a new political culture. To suggest that the inherent poisonous anti-Semitism of the German people transubstantiated into democracy thanks to the education efforts instituted by the Allies, as Goldhagen intimates, is to engage in pedagogic hocus-pocus. The glass rooftop imposed on the old Reichstag heralding political transparency is the emblem of the new Germany, an emblem resurrected from the German liberal tradition.

I have met the post-war generations in Israel, Germany, the United States and Canada. Those descended from Germans wear contrition on their sleeves and make amends for the criminal actions of their fathers and grandfathers. These are not children who issued from inherently poisonous loins. Yes, the loins had been infected by the massive Nazi propaganda machinery. But this infection spread through the entire European Continent.

The absence of a comparative framework in *Hitler's Willing Executioners*, and the way its author cavalierly resolves the corollary "re-education" issue of the German people, reveal the basic fallacy of the book. The source of this fallacy is an oversight about the human condition originating in the Exile of Adam and Eve from the Garden of Eden and their children's unceasing longing to return to the Edenic age. Similarly, according to the Satmar Rabbi, I was sentenced to exile in God-forsaken lands because of my sins.

## Dodging the Muselmann's Netherworld

Meanwhile I was tenuously holding on to shreds of life. Despite Hochman's extra food drops and the occasional scrapings off the vat walls, courtesy of the *Kesselmeister*, the reigning soup master, life was slowly slipping away. I needed to supplement the daily 1,000 calories with another 380 to avoid the slump into the untouchable *Muselmann* caste. Glazed of eye, stripped of flesh and dignity, and hollow of spirit, the *Muselmann* slouched from somewhere to nowhere, waiting for nothing, drifting toward the processing line of the gas chambers and the crematoria. He was a pathetic figure to be kept at arm's length, and yet at the same time somehow tempted one to team up with him on that last journey, to the great beyond, where clouds trail to Heaven. And in those crucial moments, Mother appeared in my mind, and the determined expression on her face and her steely eyes urged me to hold out. I knew she was, as always, right in these matters.

In a letter to Heinrich Himmler dated September 1943, SS *Obergruppenführer* Oswald Pohl, the lord of Nazi-created slavery, writes that the mortality rate in Majdanek was the highest among the concentration camps. Malnutrition, among other factors, was a major cause of the 300 daily deaths in the five Fields that made up Majdanek. Supplementing my daily intake of 1,000 calories had been my preoccupation since my arrival there. The *Kesselmeister* occasionally allowed me to carry the empty vats back to the kitchen, but the task of fetching the full vats from the kitchen to our block was kept exclusively for the members of his close circle, into which I tried unsuccessfully to wriggle myself. Hochman's food drops, the occasional trips to the kitchen that enabled me to scavenge through the dumps, and the nutritious diet acquired in the ghetto thanks to Mother's foresight — all these had sustained me till now. But for how long could they last? Getting out from Majdanek to a labour camp became increasingly critical to forestalling the plunge into the depth of the *Muselmann* netherworld.

News in Majdanek was hard to come by. Hermetically sealed from the outer world, it was out of reach of any contacts with it, except when new deportees arrived. Then, by summer of 1943, there were no newcomers to the camp. The Warsaw ghetto had been eliminated and only its last remnants survived to tell the tale. The residents of smaller ghettos, like mine, had been penned in the concentration camps or gassed. I noticed the supply provision wagon pulled by Hochman and his mates coming more often, a sign that transports were in the offing. My observation was confirmed by my veteran fellow inmate. What was required right now was to keep clean and make a good showing for the out-of-Majdanek selection, which was closer to being elected than selected. When summoned to an unscheduled *Appell*, I knew that in order to leave behind this Satan-inhabited place I had to give the impression of physical strength. On the way to the *Appellplatz*, I tried to put a bounce into my shuffling step, a dry run before the real thing. I was getting ready for an inspection by the industry representative to prove that I still had the energy to contribute to the war effort.

The senior officer wore a dark blue uniform and rimless glasses. He did not swing a baton, in striking contrast to the SS officers who had made the selection upon my arrival in Majdanek. His appearance was more like that of a school principal than a representative of a slave labour enterprise. When my turn came, he looked me over with a studious eye. After all, he could not be derelict in his responsibility; the industry paid the SS per head, and it also covered the cattle car travel expenses. It took the officer a mere second to point a commanding finger at me, upon which I was directed to the "elected" formation. I was salvaged for the time being.

The "elected" for the transport were immediately registered, counted and trundled into a separate block. For the first time in six or seven weeks, I was not prodded to that evening's *Appell*. Instead, we got double portions of soup and a larger-than-life slice of bread. Light seemed to be glimmering in the darkness.

We were roused from sleep early the following morning, though not at the customary crack of dawn. For the impending journey we were given a loaf of bread and a generous portion of jam and margarine. Manna was raining down open us, but not from heaven. Tempted though I was to wolf down the whole supply, I held back and hid it between my threadbare pyjamas and my dry skin. Counted and recounted to make sure no illegal had sneaked into our midst, we were marched to the gate. The walk through it evoked a surreal feeling, as though this was a nightmare. I dreaded the sudden order *Zurück* — the numbers might not have tallied or the train might not have arrived.

## Virtual Reality

When initially committing my Majdanek recollections to paper, I felt that I was out of touch with its primary experience. It was more like writing about it from an outside viewpoint than re-experiencing it. It had the feel of a legacy handed down. Of course I could recall the anatomy of *Feld III*, the one I was in. Its layout, the dehumanizing rituals, the regimented routine — all these wound their way from the recesses of remembrance. But I was missing the actual feeling of the place. The passage of time gave me perspective; consequently it distanced me from the heartbeat of the camp's daily functions. To regain the tactile sensation, I had to shorten the perspective. While writing about the other four camps where I was an inmate, I could simulate sensory reactions: smell, taste, and sound came back through a reconstructive process. Not so regarding Majdanek. The failure of recall might have derived from the fact that Majdanek was my initiation into the grotesque concentration camp world. It was a world devoid of a causal link between action and reaction; where the imposed rules did not comply with any familiar social standards, not even those that regulated ghetto life. In these circumstances survival required quick adjustment, with ensuing traumatic effects.

I believed that what blocked my recall of the primary experience was a combination of two interrelated factors: trauma and perspective. A return visit to Majdanek became a necessary condition to overcoming this twin obstacle. Notwithstanding the advice of my doctor and friends as well as my family, I set out to Poland in August of 2005. My own misgivings were acute.

Accompanied by Dominika, my Polish guide, I left Warsaw early in the morning and headed for Majdanek. On my first arrival there in April of 1943, the camp had been situated in the outskirts of Lublin. As far as the eye could see, sprawling fields encircled it on all sides. Now buildings and communities surrounded it. I looked around in an attempt to jog my memory, but nothing around me seemed familiar. Only later when I walked up the gravel path through the gate into *Feld III* did the shadows of the past gradually come over me. I took the incline on the side pavement right to the top of the *Feld*, where the kitchen used to be. The enormous *Appellplatz*, once paved with gravel stones, was now covered with grass. I positioned myself on the *Appellplatz* to the right of the barracks where I had found my nightly rest. The watchtowers were placed apart from each other in equal distance; the once-electrified barbed wires still had the conductors attached. And even as I surveyed this forbidding landscape a strange sensation overcame me. As if in a trance, the camp landscape transformed itself into a movie set and I was an actor about to perform a role. I came to Majdanek to retrace my footsteps so as to overcome the trauma of my endurance and establish a time passage between then and now, and I ended up further distancing myself from my traumatic experience. Unable to sustain the recollection of the brutalizing effects of the environment, memory resorted to imagining, making the memory of the past bearable.

The following day, we had a museum guide show us the elaborate system, from arrival to transportation either to gas chambers or to a forced labour camp where, short of a combination of Darwinian ingenuity and a favourable constellation of circumstances, life ended in starvation. Did I come back from visiting Majdanek with a deeper sense of the place, did I connect at the visceral level with my seven-week stay there in 1943? Or did I take a shortcut that separated me from my first arrival there, the way station to destruction, and led to my now walking through the gate a free man? Indeed, did I take a leap in time? I cannot give a definite answer to these questions. As I was walking out of the *Feld's* gate, the watchman in the booth waved to us. I remembered the last time I walked through this gate, bound to a slave labour ammunition factory in Skarżysko Kamienna.

The cattle cars were hitched to an idling locomotive; beside it lingered armed guards. Among a large group of grey-uniformed soldiers wearing ski hats, I noticed a number of SS officers. "*Absteigen, Absteigen, Schnell, Schnell*," they yelled in a dialect that echoed that of my persecutors during the first *aktion* in the ghetto. Later, I learned that those were Ukrainian *Werkschutz*.

Still clinging to my rations, I crouched in a corner of the car and nibbled on my bread, savouring every morsel, accompanying it with a generous lick of jam and margarine. Soon the nibbles gave way to bites. But I did not submit to my body's demands, and took my time with the diminishing loaf, the depleting jam and margarine, gleaning every last crumb from the ration on the advice of my benefactor, who did not make it through the selection. I fell asleep lulled by the clicking of the train wheels and my own exhaustion.

### Beware the Yellowish-Green Colour

As hard as I try to recall the walking stretch from the railway station to the camp, my memory does not respond. But the absence of two objects does stand out: no chimney with leaping flames and no booth at the camp gate. A group of sturdy Yiddish- and Polish-speaking men wearing round caps and carrying rubber truncheons met us. They led us into barracks that had many rows of two-tiered bunks. I plunked down on a lower bunk, which actually had a blanket.

I was roused from sleep by knocks on my wooden bunk, accompanied by ear-splitting shouts, not in the pidgin German or Polish that I had gotten used to in Majdanek but in authentic Yiddish and Polish. The shouts ordered us to a small place at the camp yard near the gate. These were the Jewish camp police who arranged us into a rather loose two-line formation that would never have passed muster in Majdanek. A brawny man wearing shiny black high boots, a star-studded police hat and elegant clothes appeared and was greeted by the police with a military salute. He held a whip in his hand and pointed it at us as he laid out the conditions for our survival: "Obey or be destroyed." It was an initiation speech delivered in Yiddish, interspersed with Polish phrases. His boorishness was immediately detected by the cultured among us. The Polish words coming out of his mouth sounded like snarls punctuated with barks. He was a *Kapo-lite*, who would hardly have qualified to be a *Kapo* proper had he happened to be in Majdanek.

The man who would determine my fate for the next thirteen months went by the name of Heniek Eisenberg. He was the Jewish *Kommandant* of the slave labour camp that supplied manpower for *Hasag*, but he was only the instrument of Mrs. Fela Markowiczowa, the Tzarina of the camp, who was in turn the instrument of the SS officer Kurt Schumann, and particularly of the *Wehrmacht* officer Friedrich Schulze. As the gods wanted it, I came in close contact with all these figures after my few months' apprenticeship in the factory.

The following stories I gleaned from veteran inmates, some of whom hailed from the same hometown as the Tzarina and the *Kommandant* did — Skarżysko Kamienna, near Kielce, situated in Southern Poland. Around August 1942, the Gestapo selected physically ablebodied men from the Skarżysko Kamienna ghetto and its surroundings and hauled them to the factory complex, where they built three camps named A, B and C adjacent to the factories. These workers were spared the ordeal of the concentration camp, and this enabled them to smuggle in valuables and money. According to my informants, Lady Markowiczowa came from a wealthy family and managed, by bribe and feminine wile, to bring into the camp her two small daughters and her elderly mother, Mrs. Gutman — an unheard-of feat. Her younger brother, Lolek, and her brother-in-law, Heniek Eisenberg, came along with her. The Markowiczowa clan became the administration of camp C, running it with a ruthless hand, assisted by the Jewish police contingents to the full satisfaction of their Masters. Any dereliction of duties was met with flogging or solitary confinement.

Unlike Majdanek, where ritual dominated a day's life, the operational governing of Camp C was pragmatic. There were mutual interests between the Hasag Board of Directors and Herr Himmler: the former wanted to suck as much work out of the inmates as possible and the latter wanted to dispose of them. Hard work, malnutrition and sickness achieved both goals. The destruction through work rather than outright gassing was the policy of the day. The SS henchmen had no interest in further regimentation, as Markowiczowa's reign fell in line with this policy faithfully executed by Eisenberg.

In the camp, the Markowiczowa-Eisenberg fiefdom, while being invisible, was the only way to insinuate myself into the *prominante*'s outer circle. The *carpe diem* court did not like inmates roaming the campgrounds. Understandably, they wanted "camp peace," and not to be bothered with misery: "Eat your rations, go to your bunk and get ready for your next shift," was the camp's mantra. Keeping a low profile protected the inmate from the wrath of Eisenberg and his henchmen, but it left the inmate uninformed of the camp's anatomy. Getting familiar with the camp layout and its functions might open a porthole of hope, or so I thought. The goal I was pursuing was to get some kind of gofer position in the camp. How to be present and absent at the same time was an exercise in contradiction whose resolution called for creative thinking.

The Majdanek transport was assigned the twelve-hour night shift the day following our arrival. As we gathered to go to the plant, I saw a group of about sixty to eighty people whose faces and hands were yellowish-green standing apart from the formation. They looked like Majdanek *Muselmänner*, except that from beneath the unearthly colour stared life-hungry eyes. We, the new arrivals, also stood out in our white-and-blue striped pyjamas; the veterans wore tattered civilian clothes. The yellowish-green people, I found out, were called *picryners*, and their task was producing underwater mines from picric acid sodium, which penetrated into their bodies, colouring their skin. The average life expectancy in this plant was about three months. The high death rate had to be filled from the general inmate population. I was seized with an uncontrollable dread whenever there was a selection for the "yellowish-green plant."

In Majdanek, I knew the selection rules: keep clean, make a strong showing and look straight ahead with steady eyes. Not so in the *Werk C* selection for the *picryners*. The healthier one looked, the greater the likelihood that one would be picked for the plant. But giving the impression of a weakling pegged one on a far lower survival rung. Eisenberg mentally registered malingerers and no one would want to end up in his black book. So one had to fall back on a paradoxical strategy: to be strongly weak or weakly strong, depending on the nature of the selection.

My first night shift was in a filling plant. Empty cannon shells sat on a row of carts, and were to be filled with liquid. When a particular cart was full it was wheeled to another hall and a new one, carrying empty shells, was wheeled in. A *Wehrmacht* officer, wearing a white coat and white gloves, would check every cannon shell, and then their caps were screwed on. The Polish supervisor assigned me the job of moving the carts and instructed me on how to use the manual forklift. "Slide it under the cart, raise the load, haul it to the next hall and then replace it with a new cart of empty shells." He told me to follow the way the other inmate, a veteran, was doing it. The production process clicked along like clockwork. In charge of the production process was an officer wearing a dark blue uniform, identical to the one worn by the officer who had selected us for Hasag in Majdanek. A white coat covered his uniform. In the course of that night shift, he swept into the hall, took stock of the process, and left just as swiftly. My inmate co-worker told me that he was the representative in charge of running the process and that he showed up a couple of times in a shift. During the first night shifts, I did not learn the human landscape of the plant. My immediate concern was to acquire the mechanics of my job and make it energy-efficient.

I resolved not to abide by the *Kommandant's* alternatives: hard work or destruction. Looming before my eyes was the "yellowish-green" contingent, the poison carriers, shunned by the inmate community and consigned to be the first on death row. Avoiding their fate required a complicated modus operandi. I needed to find favour in the eyes of the Polish supervisor and his overseers. That meant endless hauling of the carts, but at the same time I had to seek breaks in order to conserve my energy. It was, therefore, the plant that required my immediate attention. Should the supervisor find me "unfit for work," selection would follow. For I was a disposable item and the *Werkschutz* would do their master's bidding.

Encounters with the Polish employees were weird. As the three rows of slave-laborers, walking five abreast, slouched to the plant escorted by the *Werkschutz* and the Jewish police, the Polish workers streamed in for the night shift. They came in small groups, engaged in intimate conversation. Dressed in civilian clothes, the women wearing colourful kerchiefs, the men regular hats, they made their way to the various halls that made up the *Werk C* plant. What immediately caught my attention were the food bundles they carried under their arms. This stimulated fluids in my digestive system which the watery soup we were given could not dilute. The daily diet of 300 grams of bread, a recent increase of 100 grams, could hardly sustain a fourteen-year-old boy stuck with a twelve-hour shift of hauling heavy carts.

The plant was made up of two manpower contingents: the Polish workers and the Jewish slaves. These were as widely apart from each other as the Synod from the Synagogue. The Poles were waiting for Time's tide to rise; the Jews, however, were racing against that same Time. For the Jews, the sand in the hourglass was fast running out, but the Poles could coast along the events taking place, if they chose not to become active opponents of the Nazi regime. Undoubtedly, the Poles suffered humiliation at the hands of their racist masters: their patriotism was offended, their humanity was compromised, and yet, notwithstanding these indignities, they remained confident in their future and in their ultimate liberation as a national collective. This sense of confidence manifested itself in the plant. Their bearing, their talk, the way they dressed, their manner of speech — all these were in striking contrast to the haunted eyes of the Jewish inmates. The Polish employees filled the supervisory positions, from overseers to hall supervisors, and they parcelled out the less backbreaking work to their compatriots.

In truth, the overseers treated me kindly. I knew that they were anxious to meet the shift quota and I gave my utmost to maintaining the production process. Failing to fill the quota entailed dire consequences for them. During the short time I worked in the filling section, I was treated with benign indifference, alternating between apathy and a flicker of pity, more of the former than the latter. The female employees' maternal instincts might have been awakened as they watched the gaunt fourteen-year-old boy heaving and wheeling carts all night long while their own children slept soundly, tucked in the comfort of their beds. They called me by my Polish name, Edek, and also referred to me as *mały żydek*, a term of endearment. And after I was forgiven for being a descendant of the God-killer, I received gifts of bread spread with jam and bits of vegetables and fruits that grew in their gardens.

But not everyone was as lucky as I was. My fellow inmates told me that they had been beaten by the Polish overseers for the slightest infraction. Rumour had it that some veteran inmates had confided in the Polish co-workers about valuables hidden in their hometowns, and they had been cheated out of their possessions. These stories made me work even harder at the plant in appreciation of the tolerant treatment I received from my overseers. But during the last few hours of each shift, my aching back could not keep up with the production pace, particularly at the beginning of my time there, when I was on the night shift. I devised a method of recovering my strength by sitting down for five or six minutes between hauling the cartload of empty shells to the liquid filling hall and wheeling a load of filled shells to the inspection station. Obviously, the overseers saw me sit on the cart in the corner, sometimes sneaking an eye shut.

In one of these self-indulgent respites, I felt a slap across my face that made me reel off the cart. Above me stood a high-booted, dark-blue-uniformed officer in a white coat.

I glimpsed at him through tears. He was the inspector visitor who would hastily glide through the factory. His eyes were piercingly cold. In a commanding voice he ordered me to wash my bloodied face and wait for him at the entrance. Coming out of the washroom I glanced at the Polish workers talking amongst themselves. Soon he rushed through the entrance and I tagged along after him. If anything went through my mind, I cannot recall what it was. This was the last leg of the shift and I must have been too physically and emotionally drained to be afraid. I experienced a *Muselmann* moment. He came out of an office carrying a radio and handed it over to me. He then mounted a bicycle and ordered me to follow him. The radio had no handle that would enable me to hold onto it. I held the radio tight to my chest and trailed after the cycling *Übermensch* like an unhitched trailer.

From time to time the *Übermensch* would turn his head. Luckily, the road ran straight, so I did not lose sight of him. Finally, he came to a halt next to a mansion which was located on the far end of the factory grounds. My arms were numb, my legs were collapsing under me. I still had stairs to climb, but I could not make it. I sagged onto the stairs holding the radio. Then I heard a whistle and a soft voice urging me to come up. Somehow I made it up the stairs and staggered in. When I put the radio on the table in the inspector's room, he gave me a big chunk of cake and told me to hurry back to the plant before the end of the shift. Dawn was breaking. I was as grateful to him as a dog would be to his master.

Between the first slap I received in my hometown in the summer of 1942 and the one I was dealt in 1943 in *Werk C*, my psyche went through a metamorphosis. Back in 1942, when the SD officer Hoffmann slapped me for not wearing my white four-star armband, I nursed my wounded pride in resentment. My mother comforted me as only a mother can. When one year later, in August of 1943, the SA officer, the *Übermensch*, the master of races, slapped me, this slap did not humiliate me. I felt physical pain, but my feelings were suppressed.

In the ghetto my buddy Menachem and the money I retrieved from the Polish peasant cushioned my human dignity. In Majdanek I was put through the SS *Gleichschaltung*, turning me into a cipher and robbing me of everything human. The concentration camp was designed to condition the inmate into a being of Pavlovian responses, and it mostly achieved its goal. I myself was proof of its success. Animal-like instincts became the dominant survival skills; arm-twisting of the weaker inmates by the stronger ones was not uncommon. Savagery was rampant when conditions became inordinately rough, as it did on the *Todesmarsch*.

It was only decades later, when I was equipped with hindsight and seasoned by studies of human behaviour under siege, including my own reflections on my three-year journey into the thickening night, that I was able to put my ordeals into rational terms. My cunning, fawning, manipulation, rapacity — all these were instinctual responses to biological impulses to exist. Granted, there were inmates who were determined to act humanely and lived to tell the tale, but these were few and far between. Elie Wiesel tells about fellow inmates whose survival was motivated by the purpose of Remembrance. While undoubtedly there must have been people who had the moral stuff and mental strength to envision themselves as the tellers of the story, these were exceptions; the rest of us held on because we wanted to live.

While I was still heaving carts at the filling plant, two events took place, both of which changed my situation in *Werk C*, one inching me along to the privileged class, and one threatening to end my mortal coil.

### Irena — My Willowy Sister

One day in November of 1943, on my return from my night shift to the camp, I noticed through my weary eyes girls walking through the camp yard. What was arresting about them was how they carried their bodies. There was a bounce in their gait that I had not seen since my arrival in camp. At closer range, I saw fresh faces out of which peered life-seeking eyes, and the clothes they wore were very different from the ones worn by the so-called *kaelniks*. They brought with them a vibrancy that touched the entire camp. Even the most hardened *prominantes*, the Tzarina and her sidekicks, seemed to moderate their attitude when it came to the Krakowiak girls. Their youthful vibrancy projected hope, temporarily lifting the gloom that permeated the camp. Soon the police and inmates occupying prominent positions began gravitating towards them; relationships developed that assumed the odd euphemism of "cousin." Even in this *anus mundi* people engaged in social practices of nicknaming. Irony, apparently, afforded relief. Thus Mrs. Markowiczowa was dubbed "Tzarina" and her abode "The White House"; Lolek, her brother, in charge of clothing distribution, was called "*a dasz*" as he demanded sex from the girls in exchange for clothes or footwear; and the epithet "cousin" denoted a romantic relationship.

I met Irena in the queue outside the clothing hut waiting for my turn. I hoped, to secure a winter coat. During my four-month stay in Skarżysko Kamienna, I gradually shed my blue-and-white concentration camp pyjamas courtesy of Lolek, the wardrobe master. The Industry had a vested interest in giving its *kaelniks* civilian clothes that would allow them to work unhampered by the Majdanek wear, which was suitable for rituals but not for the productive work expected of its slaves.

It was a bitterly cold afternoon, and I gathered my limbs into a protective ball to fend off the biting wind. Though she was two or three people away from me in the line, Irena went out of her way to talk to me. She spoke in the aristocratic Polish prevalent among the Krakowiaks, to which I responded with my third-grade elementary-school Polish. She needed a pair of shoes; otherwise she had enough warm clothes, which she had brought from the Plaszòw camp, to see her through the winter. Because I was a visible *kaelnik*, she asked me whether I might have come across people from the Kraków ghetto. Her husband had been taken away from the ghetto in an earlier *aktion* and she was hoping to ascertain his whereabouts. I was surprised to hear that she had already been married. She was young, about three years older than I was, and her willowy appearance and chiselled facial bones made her look even younger. We took an instant liking to each other. She asked me to stop by her block, should I need her help. The words coming out of her mouth sounded like a fantasy, the hallucination of a lost desert traveller in search of an oasis.

In *Werk C*, as in other labour and concentration camps, raw Darwinism reigned in human relationships. In the forbidding situations of the Death

March, rapacious inmates used violence to gain the upper hand over their weaker fellow inmates. Relationships established in the daily routine dissolved when their usefulness ended. This is apparently a human trait that also manifests itself in normative society. It is expressed in a variety of idioms, one of them particularly apt: "What's in it for me?" Then, when there is nothing in it for me, "Why should I bother?" The equivalent of "rapacity" entailing a life-or-death situation is the metaphor "cut-throat." In the business world it is the frequently-used metaphor "out for a killing," and in sports the killing metaphor sometimes becomes a reality. Readers of eyewitness accounts — those people who bare their chests to the experience from the comforts of their reclining chairs — may be shocked at this revelation of human depravity. But an unvarnished glance at what is going on in the workplace — be it office, school, or virtually any other place in a social dynamics environment — should cushion the reader's shock.

The biological impulse that drove the inmate to resort to rapacious acts in the concentration and labour camps assumes a socio-economic drive in normative society. To move up in the pyramidal structure of the workplace, to get a reserved parking spot and a key to the company's private bathroom, may involve manipulative undermining and, if necessary, backstabbing of one's fellow worker, and yet the moral compromise may be worthwhile. And there is even a counterpart to the untouchable *Muselmann* of the concentration camp. Lingering helplessly in the soup line, his tin hanging at his side, the *Muselmann*'s image brings to mind the shunned office employee who fell out of favour with his boss, principal, or dean, and is now standing at the water cooler, empty paper cup in hand, waiting, turning his head both ways, but finding that no one is in sight.

By drawing comparative features between the doomed *Muselmann* in the soup line and the lonely office employee at the water cooler, I do not mean to equate the two. Indeed, they are in entirely different circumstances, but the impulse that drives self-preservation, propelled by a biological urge or by a socio-economic imperative, contingent on circumstances, is not dissimilar. The one has recourse, at worst; he or she may end up in the unemployment line, but the other will be in the line to the gas chamber. What I am implying is that ultimately human nature, at its deepest level of consciousness, has not changed significantly.

I've often wondered why the Holocaust began to be integrated into Western culture only about three decades after its end, despite the mother lode of insights it offers about Man and civilization. It seems to me that the tardiness in making the Holocaust a point of reference stems from reluctance to face the truth about the human condition. For example, Anne Frank's universal recognition should be attributed to her pollyannaish view of human nature. While in hiding she wrote in her diary: "In spite of everything, I still believe that people are good at heart." This declared faith in humanity by a child victim gives comfort to those who hold faith in the goodness of mankind; it alleviates the pain of self-recognition of Man's destructive impulses and lightens the burden of belonging to the *Homo Sapiens* species. Clarence Darrow, a connoisseur of human nature, doubted the accepted notion that "…man is the apex of creation." But if he is, the counsellor added ironically, "the apex is not very high."

In an interview, Carole Mac-Neil of the CBC asked Louise Arbour, the United Nation High Commissioner for Human Rights, whether she still had faith in human beings after having witnessed the horrendous atrocities committed in Serbia and Rwanda, to which she instantly replied, "Given the opportunity, human beings are fundamentally good." A simple fact-check of historical annals belies the Commissioner's assertion. What the historical documents show is that goodness or evil are functions of the circumstances. When the centre of the polity does not hold, evil triumphs and people are left to fend for themselves. In contrast, in times of political security and economic stability the good qualities of human beings come to the fore. Whether Irena would share Frank's and Arbour's faith in humanity I would only find out two and half years later, when we met in the Feldafing Displaced Persons Camp in Germany after Liberation.

But right now, I was standing in the freezing December wind of 1943, a supplicant waiting for my turn to get a coat. Irena's offer to help me, a total stranger, deeply touched me. In the environment of *Werk C,* where, as the Roman Plautus coined it, *"Homo Homini Lupus,"* Irena's benevolence was as rare as getting an extra ladleful of soup. And it was not just a flicker of compassion for a shrunken fourteen-year-old. A couple of days after our meeting, she called me out from my barrack. I was again struck by the youthful wellness of her face. "Edek," she chirped cheerfully, "I got you a job in the cannon-shell cleaning department," — the place she worked at, which was the dream of every inmate.

The following day, when I was on my day shift in the filling department, a man of rather bulky frame wearing blue overalls lumbered into the hall, followed by an inmate who, by his relatively healthy physique, appeared to be of the latest Plaszòw arrivals. He was to be my replacement. After a short exchange between the man in the blue overalls and the department supervisor, I was directed to my newly assigned hall. Irena greeted me with a big smile.

Seated on low stools were about half a dozen female inmates, most of them from the Plaszòw dispatch, cleaning debris from empty shells with long, pointed brushes. I realised then that I would be the only male in this labour detail. Irena pulled up a stool for me next to her own. The work was easy and our direct overseer pleasant. Unlike the shell-filling hall, where the production was based on the conveyer belt principle, in this department everyone worked independently of each other. Getting this kind of job in Skarżysko Kamienna without monetary bribes, sexual favours, or connections of some kind was a virtual impossibility. So how did Irena pull it off?

The huge man in the blue overalls, referred to as Master, had been the chief production manager of the plant before the war, and thus his skills in making bombs made him indispensable. Irena's personality must have caught his attention. The Master engaged her in conversation on a few occasions. In one of these conversations she told him about the boy, Edek, whom she had befriended, and asked whether he could switch him to the shell-cleaning department. And that was how I went from hauler of carts laden with bombshells to shell-cleaner. It was a shift that allowed me to increase my chances in the race against time.

I had many occasions to eavesdrop on the conversations that the Master had with Irena. It was an odd human relationship. He treated her with the grandfatherly fondness one bestowed on helpless children, surreptitiously providing her with food, some of which she saved for me. Bit by bit, I learned about him from Irena. He had been with the plant for many decades before the war and had raised a family that had produced scores of grandchildren, one of whom Irena particularly reminded him of. Instinctively we knew that the Master's kindness was not limited to our department. There was something about him that made him larger than life, something which he shared with many inmates at great risk to his status and even his freedom. We did not talk about it lest the sharing of our feelings might be a betrayal of trust; or perhaps talking about the Master might bring ill luck. In *Yad Vashem* terminology, he qualified to be named one of the "Righteous Among the Nations," though not in the strict terms defined by *Yad Vashem*.

Irena saw to it that I washed, she mended my clothes, and with the small food handouts that she received from the Master, she helped to extend my lease on life. The thought that my newly-acquired workplace might have come at the cost of another inmate's well-being never crossed my mind. As a matter of fact, I had not given any thought at all to this Godsent manna in the form of Irena. In this place, contemplation did not make for survival. Such was the existence of *Werk C*, a place where people appeared and disappeared at the nod of the powers that be. The vanished left behind a bent spoon, a battered food container and perhaps a half-burnt cigarette or a few cigarette butts, picked up in the gutters at the plant.

It's hard to tell, indeed, impossible to tell, how long I would have lasted in the circumstances of *Werk C* in the remaining months of 1943. Thanks to Irena and the Master I was much better off than most of my fellow inmates, but the daily drudgery, exacerbated by a sense of slowly clawing hunger, the penetrating cold, and the sight of death surrounding me, deeply affected me. No matter how hardhearted I willed myself to become, the sight of human devastation dug deep grooves into my psyche. Though my hunger for life did not wane, my physical strength did. Life was seeping out of me. It was at this critical point in my struggle to survive that an unexpected turn of events took place.

As was customary, we gathered at the gate for a snappy count before marching to the plant. I was standing next to Irena in our labour detail, when the Chief of the Police pointed at me and in an unwontedly mild voice called out "Kupiec, come out here!" He asked me in Polish if I had ever tended to animals. "Of course," I answered quickly, and the kitten incident back home at school flashed rapidly through my mind. I did not think, though, that this incident would be a commendable reference. So I quickly related my work with the *Kriminal Polizei* back home, fibbing, "I took care of these two big dogs, and I love animals." He then quizzed me in his special brand of German. Apparently my linguistic skills met with his approval. He smiled. Meanwhile, the labour details started moving toward the plant. From the corner of my eye, I saw Irena's puzzled look. The Chief of the Police ordered me to go to the clothing warehouse, where I would be outfitted for the new job.

Lolek was in charge of the clothing enterprise, and his position gave him virtual power over life and death. I had been waiting for winter clothes at his warehouse earlier in the year when I had met Irena. Surviving the harsh winter partially depended on his whim. With his combed-back black hair accentuated by a sharply pointed beak-like nose, he resembled a raven. Irena had told me that he preyed on the Krakowiak girls when they came to ask for warm clothing for the winter. He greeted me with a smile. This second smile in a row coming from the camp elite could only bode well. And my feeling was soon confirmed. "I must fit you into something special…you're going to work for Schumann and Schulze in the Mansion."

I had been to the Mansion the night that I'd lugged the *Hasag* official's radio across the plant. But at the time I knew little about it. Once I assumed my responsibilities there, I got to know the place.

The Mansion housed the entire German staff that ran the plant and was home to a *Volksdeutsch* family: the husband was a *Werkschutz* sergeant, and his spouse was in charge of managing the Mansion. As I was climbing the stairs I was drawn toward a place from which cooking smells were wafting into the corridor. A woman of obviously Slavic features met me at the kitchen door. Her foreign-sounding German further gave away her identity. She was of German descent, presumably the several-times-great granddaughter of people who immigrated to Russia in the eighteenth century, when Peter the Great had invited a large group with the intention of modernizing Russia. My regular chores, which she spelled out in Slavic-laced German, would be helping around the kitchen and working for the officers *Herren* Schumann and Schultze, but my major responsibility was to take care of the rabbits. About a dozen rabbits were penned in cages in the courtyard, voraciously nibbling carrots and an assortment of vegetables.

By now, I had developed sensory antennas that were able to pick up the natures and the changing moods of those on whom my welfare depended. While I was enviously watching the rabbits freely indulging in their feast, she looked at me with understanding kindness. After a while, she asked me to come up to the kitchen to get leftover vegetables for the rabbits, and it was there that she gave me a bowl of vegetable soup. Both the bowl and the soup were real. I ate the soup on the backyard porch, which eventually became the regular place of the *"Kharoshi Yevereiski Malchik,"* as she called me in Russian.

My new work place marked a turning point in my internment. That relentless food craving was satisfied. I even had surpluses, which I gave to Irena and to my bunkmate. Or, I should say, former bunkmate. Since my work performance pleased the authorities, I was moved from the common block, where I shared a bunk with a Częstochowa boy, to reside with Mrs. Markowiczowa senior, where I got my own bunk with plenty of blankets. The Tzarina's mother resided in a hut separate from the one that housed the camp police and other functionaries. Now, no longer starving, relatively well clothed, and sleeping in a clean bunk, I became part of the camp's elite circle, albeit still an outsider.

I gained weight, colour came back to my cheeks, and a light bounce accompanied my walk. Holding on to my newly-acquired position depended on a series of factors beyond my control, Irena kept reminding me. The fortunate circumstances that allowed me the position could be reversed at the whim of the Mansion Lords, or upon a sudden evacuation order. Obviously, Irena wanted to prepare me psychologically for a possible adverse occurrence. Abrupt changes could be emotionally upsetting.

## Protecting my *Lebensraum*

The winter of 1943-44 passed uneventfully, amidst rumours making their rounds in the plant about the German military setback on the Eastern front. In early spring of 1944, rumours filtering through the Polish plant workers increased and became more detailed. The Mansion continued with its routine beat; the *Volksdeutsch* lady of the Mansion kept on reigning with a firm but gentle hand. Sometimes, I would sneak a glance at Schulze's and Schumann's faces seeking signs of concern or worry, but I could not notice any change. As the rabbit population multiplied and my responsibilities widened, Schulze had another boy inmate come to help me out with the chores. The boy and his uncle had come to *Werk* C with the Kraków contingent. With blond curly hair and in good physical shape, his job was to pluck green vegetables from the fields for the rabbits and to see to their comfort. I considered him my junior and expected him to take instructions from me, which he reluctantly did. To exacerbate the situation, the Lady of the Mansion called him by the same endearing name as me, and he enjoyed the same kitchen privileges. Scared that this young Krakowiak might one day replace me in my job, I started picking on him, sometimes to the point of harassment. In the course of my yearlong survival struggle, particularly in Majdanek but also in *Werk C*, I had acquired the necessary dog-eat-dog mentality, and I put it into practice now. I dogged my perceived rival at every turn, tried to prevent him from reaching the kitchen, and saw to it that he spent most of the time in the field gathering greens for the rabbits. I had no rational basis for my behaviour, except the anxiety of replacement.

But before the Darwinian survival-of-the-fittest exercise was fully engaged, the boy's uncle approached me. Sheltered from the nipping spring wind by a nearby barrack, he gently touched on the relationship between his nephew and me. Rather than berating me, he spoke to my anxieties, explaining how a cooperative relationship between us boys would make life easier for both of us. "All we want is to *Iberlebn*; any day now the Red Army might rescue us; each day counts." In the midst of an environment where basic instincts guided behaviour, where cunning and force defined social standards, the uncle addressed my rationality. And while I recognized the wisdom of his words, I was not ashamed of the way I treated his nephew in protecting my territory. But somehow in my subconscious I must have felt uneasy, for I did not relate this episode to Irena, with whom I shared everything else. Subsequent to my talk with the uncle, my relationship with the nephew became amiable, although the boy never dropped his suspicion of me.

Spring melded into summer and life went on with its deadly routine. The inmates shuffled their shrinking bodies to the plant in rapidly diminishing numbers and I eagerly reported to work at the Mansion each morning. There was an ominous restlessness in the atmosphere. Returning from the plant, people talked about the Red Army approaching Warsaw, 200 kilometres from Skarżysko Kamienna, and the Polish uprising in the city aroused further expectations. I thought that I noticed a kind of grimness in the face of the lady of the Mansion; sometimes she would softly speak to her Ukrainian help in their native language, a behaviour heretofore unheard of. But I could not, as much as I longed to, see any changes in the behaviour of SS officer Kurt Schumann or *Wehrmacht* officer Schulze.

These two were an interesting pair. The SS *Gleichschaltung*, intended to ultimately develop in the German people a *"Heil Sieg"* Pavlovian response, failed in Schulze's case and was totally successful in Schumann's. Their personalities were a study in contrast.

Whereas Schumann wore a poker face further emphasized by speech patterns framed in monosyllabic sentences, Schulze carried his active features with a frankness matched by a rapid stream of successive sentences. Schumann's measured gait set off Schulze's scurried walk. Schulze's amputated arm, supplemented by a prosthesis, earned him the Polish sobriquet *rączka*. This handicap made his body, while walking, lean to his right, damaged, arm, forming the shape of an unfinished question mark against Schumann's exclamation mark. The lady of the Mansion liked Schulze's debonair manner and readily cooked his favourite dishes. Whenever he spoke directly to me, his breath smelled of liquor.

As I later learned from some camp survivors and from Felicja Karay's book, *Death Comes in Yellow*, Schulze's cavalier behaviour belied a conniving mind that made him rich thanks to the Tzarina, who had reportedly stashed away valuables and money. He was a master manipulator whose character rivalled the Tzarina's in its serpentine nature. In contemporary political terms, Schulze could have been a politician crossing the floor at the drop of a hat.

Unlike Schulze, Schumann was a dyed-in-the-wool ideologue who proudly wore his *Totenkopf*. Like his *Führer* he was a vegetarian, and like him, Schumann loved animals. Hitler's pet was the dog Blondie, a companion unto death; Schumann's pets were the rabbits. He was obsessed with them. He would come down every afternoon, ostensibly to check on their comfort, but in fact it was to spent time in their midst. He would delicately scoop up a rabbit from the cage and lovingly stroke it, his habitual grim-faced devotional demeanour softening as if in prayer. This man who coddled the rabbits with such deep affection shot inmates point blank at the slightest perceived infraction. The chief dispatcher of unproductive inmates to the shooting range without a twitch or a qualm handled the rabbits with loving kindness. The lady of the Mansion would watch Schumann fussing over his rabbits in amazement. He was obsessed with these tiny animals and it was this obsession that nearly cost me my life.

## Looking into the Pistol's Muzzle

The portentous year was 1944, and the season, summer. Rumours of German defeat soon morphed into news, validated by tangible signs of an imminent evacuation of the camp. The signs were noticed in the plant as well as in the camp, and I myself picked up bits of conversation in the kitchen. Emotionally conditioned to the signs of change, I thought one day that the lady of the Mansion was telling me to bring a butcher in from the camp to slaughter the rabbits. I rushed to the camp and asked the Chief of the Jewish Police, Eisenberg, to find a butcher for me. He too must have been affected by the news swirling around. "What do you want a butcher for?" he asked me in a wistful voice. "The Russian lady told me," I said, and he gave me what I thought was a knowing look. He hauled out a husky fellow still drowsy from the nightshift and ordered him to come with me. A huge knife was at the ready provided by the lady of the Mansion. After the bloody slaughter and the skinning of the rabbits, we lugged the tiny carcasses to the kitchen. Even as I was cleaning out the cages, a distraught Schumann came rushing down the stairs hatless, hair dishevelled, followed by the lady of the Mansion and her husband. He sputtered some incoherent sentences and then pulled out the pistol from his holster and aimed it at me. I still palpably remember my fourteen years of life flashing before my eyes in a wink of time, ending with my mother's image. Even as I stood numb, empty of feeling, my eyes riveted to the pistol's muzzle, blows came pounding on me. Shielding me from Schumann, the lady of the Mansion and her husband were simulating a beating accompanied by repeated cussing; with each blow they were pushing me farther away from the execution spot. I darted like a shot arrow right through the camp gates and hid under Irena's bunk.

The night shift was just stirring from its sleep, getting ready for work, and the day shift would not be back for another hour. I would have that window of time to come up with some kind of plan. But thinking would not come. Primeval instincts triggered my next moves.

I looked out. There was no one on the campgrounds. I slithered to the very edge of the camp and clambered up a tree until I got hold of a sturdy branch. Fidgeting, I managed to sit astride it. This position caused me increasing discomfort, and eventually I heaved myself up to the top of the tree. The wood inside the tree was decayed, and the trunk was wide enough to enable me to partially slide into the bark. It was an uncomfortable fit. Gradually, thinking came back, piloted by an underlying Darwinian instinct. Dusk fell. A warbling flock of birds flew over the tree back to their nest. I enviously watched their flight just as I had once watched the stars at a particularly painful night-time roll call in Majdanek. What should be my next move?

Earlier escape attempts from the camp through the surrounding barbed wires, heavily patrolled by the *Schutzwork*, had ended in failure. Particularly of late, since the rumours of the camp liquidation had intensified, the patrolling became even stricter; I could try to join the Polish workers on their return home from the plant, but I would stand out because of my age. Attempting to slip through the gate would be like running against the electrified wires, which had occasionally happened to prisoners in Majdanek. Squeezed into the bark, I weighed my options. Suddenly I heard my name being called out in a cacophony of voices; among them Eisenberg's stood out. Surprisingly, it did not carry its usual snarl. "Kupiec, Kupiec, come out, nothing will happen to you." Eisenberg's voice sounded somewhat more humane, or at least that is what I wanted to hear. At one point, I heard Schulze asking Eisenberg, "*Wo ist der bursche?*" The search went on for about an hour and then silence fell.

What I earlier considered a tolerable refuge for the night soon began to cramp my body. To ease the cramps, I hoisted myself intermittently from the bark to the branches and back to the bark. This exercise took on a routine by which I drowsed in the bark and loosened the cramps on the branches.

But where would all this take me? Soon the old voracious monster would be demanding its portion of the food supply, and the fear of thirst brought back intimations of the dry lips and parched mouth of the cattle car bound for Majdanek. Had I known what I found out later on, I might have overcome my fear of thirst, might have been able to calm down the looming monster inside me, might have waited out the ordeal. When I finally mustered the courage to face Eisenberg on the campgrounds in the morning, he did not carry his whip; his body language missed its angular pose; his imperial sweep was gone. Eisenberg's appearance seemed to have had a makeover, to use a current cliché. He looked at me with a bemused eye. "Kupiec," he asked me in a mild voice, "where have you been?"

I briefly recited the events that had taken place the day before. He must have been amazed at my ingenuity. "Don't worry, Kupiec," he said reassuringly. And at once I felt life reawakening in me. For the second time in the last twenty-four hours I had stopped life's mental pulse in preparation for death and for the second time I had eluded it. When I went back to my privileged bunk in Mrs. Gutman's hut, I found the Tzarina's mother in a despondent mood. There was a bundle lying in the corner. Surprisingly, she had not known what happened to me yesterday. "I heard your name called out, and I thought you had escaped."

The tone of her voice distinctly spelled resignation, the kind that echoed back to the ghetto a couple of years earlier. In the early 40's, people of Mrs. Gutman's economic status in the ghetto expressed their resignation in moaning tones. In the face of impending deportation an anguished sense of helplessness set in, subsequently ending in acceptance of the inevitable. In the camps, however, resignation manifested itself physically: the way the inmate carried his body, the pace of his walk, his general appearance — all these indicated how much life he still had in him. Thanks to her daughter, the Tzarina, Mrs. Gutman was not wanting in food and enjoyed a certain measure of security in the camp. Now sitting on the bunk, drowsily digesting the food given to me by Mrs. Gutman, I listened to her lament. It sounded eerily familiar. "In a few days we'll all be transported..." her voice trailed off, but I could easily have finished the sentence for her. She was old with greying hair, and without her daughter's protection she had no chance of making it past the selection. Eisenberg's benevolence toward me, I inferred, was a result of the imminent liquidation of the camp. Whether his behaviour was motivated by pangs of conscience, or fear of what might happen to him when stripped of his authority in a new camp, or weariness of life, I did not know at the time. On the day of the liquidation, which occurred about three days after the rabbit incident, the Markowiczowa clan was absent from the roll call grounds, as was, to my relief, SS officer Schumann. Also absent from the roll call was the young lad with whom I had bunked before being elevated to the outer circle of the privileged. He had been in the camp for a while before my arrival and he introduced me to the intricacies of camp structure. When working at the Mansion, I used to bring him bits of food that I had scrounged from the kitchen leftovers. Now I was looking for him in the crowd, but he was nowhere to be found. I sought out one of his co-workers in the plant, but he did not know his whereabouts either. Irena was there, huddled together with the female contingent, who would apparently go with a different transport from the males. Once more I felt bereft.

Prominently absent were the *picryners*. As if painted in yellowish-green from top to toe, this company of creatures looked weird even in the eyes of their fellow inmates. From their foreheads jutted a pair of glazed-like goggles. Each day they shuffled closer to the shooting range via the Picric Acid Hall. Now that their department was no longer productive, *Hasag* did not consider it fiscally profitable to invest money in their transportation and had them summarily executed — simply a bookkeeping calculation.

Between the rabbit incident and the liquidation day, Irena and I had met every day. We both knew that the chances of going to the same camp were slim. The Master, her protector, speculated upon the designated plants to which we might be transported. We did not talk much; it was a silence punctuated by speech. Wrapped up in our sadness, we sat, waiting for the imminent command to go to the roll call grounds. In these situations of helplessness, I would conjure up Mother and seek her advice. At night, while the mind meandered back home, she would appear and fix her grey eyes on me. Strangely enough, I would not share my séances with Irena; this was just between Mother and me.

There was so much to be said between Irena and me, and yet nothing was said. What could Irena have told me? I was a strong boy and would find my way around in the new camp. Or what could I have said to her? She was pretty and likeable and would somehow get through. But these words would have sounded hollow. On the last day, when the liquidation was palpably approaching, Irena and I sat on her bunk sipping tea that she'd boiled. She hugged me and urged me to hold out, muttering, "*Trzymaj się, Edek, trzymaj się.*"

## Mottos Reflecting the Shifting Situations

The term "*Iberlebn di soinem Israel*" gained currency in the ghetto, where there was still some leeway for manoeuvering. Drawn from the language of lamentation and sorrow of previous persecutions, the ghettoites wanted to believe that like their persecuted ancestors they too would outlive the enemy. My mother used her money and skills to circumvent a series of restrictions. The fact that she sent me to work for the *Kriminal Polizei*, hoping to secure our stay in the ghetto, and gave valuables to a Polish friend for safekeeping, indicated a measure of control over fate. These kinds of initiatives were made by other ghetto residents as well. As the initiative margins narrowed and the residents of the ghetto realized the inevitable approaching end, *"Rateve zik,"* became the prevalent phrase. My mother used this phrase when she forcefully pulled her hand from mine in the ghetto and pushed me away from the marching column to the assembly grounds. The phrase *"Halt sich ois,"* commonly used in the camps, reflects the narrow margins left for the inmate to negotiate. Significantly enough, these survival sayings were not heard on the Death March. Here, despair muted speech. Now I was standing on the roll call grounds looking across at Irena, gathered in the group with other women awaiting transportation, with the Polish phrase *"Trzymaj się"* ringing in my ears.

## The Messiah is Nigh

It was on a hot August day when we, a selected work force of inmates, arrived in Sulejŏw, a neighbouring village of Chęstochowa. We were greeted by confusion. Unlike the regimented arrival at Majdanek and even the less rigorous Skarżysko Kamienna, Sulejŏw seemed to be run by a rudderless contingent of Ukrainian and Bialo-Russian guards. After rambling orders were given in pidgin German, we found ourselves in a huge barn that held piled-up stacks of straw. A rush of hope ran through my ached psyche in the face of this chaotic reception. Were these signs of approaching liberation?

The haphazard supervision of our assignments went on. The Ukrainian auxiliary soldiers paid scant attention to our work — their interests lay elsewhere. From the little Ukrainian I had picked up in Majdanek, I could make out snippets of the guards' conversations with Ukrainian-speaking inmates. Fearing that other guards might rat them out, they made sure that no one was within earshot. They wanted to know the whereabouts of partisan fighters in the forests. Rumour had it that many guards fled to the forests with their weapons to join the partisans. The regime seemed to have turned volatile. This precarious situation prevented the emergence of an inmate hierarchical structure. The daily routine began with an early rise and the staples: a piece of bread and coffee. Some strong-willed inmates portioned out their bread; I could not do it no matter how hard I tried. I devoured my bread portion with ferocity as soon as I got it, only to become prey to the clawing monster raving inside me later in the day. I still had fat resources gathered at the Mansion in *Werk C* that fed the monster, but these swiftly dwindled with each passing hour. As I was digging antitank trenches in the hot August sun, my entire being was focussed on the evening soup. With the exception of the lax supervision, I was going through ordeals similar to those that I had endured during the first few months in *Werk C* before meeting Irena. Hunger, loneliness, and efforts to resist the pull to go under were interspersed with nostalgic daydreams. But I also felt a glimmer of hope. Watching the guards wearily overseeing our digging and escorting us back to the barns at an ambling pace strengthened the "holding on" impulse.

Lying next to me in my straw bed was a Rabbi who shared with me his faith in our imminent redemption. In his mellifluous Lithuanian Yiddish, he predicted that the *"guleh* is coming any day now." *"Geula"* resonated deeply with the inmates. Its theme of redemption from oppression, which ran through the liturgy, had a singular meaning in the Sulejŏw reality in which the first cracks in the ironclad Nazi regime appeared.

While taken with the Rabbi's stories of redemption, which entailed Divine miracles, I could not relate to them. I was brought up in what can be best described as a traditional family, which did not observe the religious strictures. My strictly observant maternal grandfather made numerous attempts to persuade me to accompany him to the synagogue on the Sabbath. Mother, though not insistent on my attending synagogue, encouraged me to go for "grandfather's sake." But the services bored me, and at every opportunity I and the other boys slipped out of the synagogue to engage in more attractive ventures. Cognizant of my growing reluctance to keep him weekly company, grandfather proposed a monetary incentive by which he would give me one Zloty each Monday. It was a generous reward, which I immediately accepted. On the first Monday, I rushed after school to my grandfather's store to collect my pocket money. But in the hands of my grandfather the silver Zloty coin turned into small copper change, accompanied by a promise to fully pay me by the end of the week. When this pay deferral recurred the following week, I began turning down the Sabbath synagogue visits where I might have become familiar with the messianic mission. Thus the Rabbi's evocation of the Messiah, entailing redemption, hardly registered with me. The messiahs I awaited were Red Army tanks, rumbling into the camp in a cloud of dust and smoke.

Even as the Red Army was slugging its way west, the Ukrainian mercenaries transported us from Sulejŏw farther west, to the outskirts of Chęstochowa, which comprised three *Hasag* plants. We arrived in a Chęstochowa camp on a rainy October day and were taken to our barracks. The camp organization was loose, as was the working regime. I was assigned to the hall that was repairing damaged tanks. My job was to haul parts from the supply warehouse to the hall. In comparison with the Skarżysko Kamienna plant, the work pace here was relaxed. My two supervisors, one a *Wehrmacht Stabsunteroffizier* and the other a German civilian engineer, did not bother me as long as I provided the parts they required.

## The Predator Matrons

I only have a partial picture of the Chęstochowa plant, for I stayed in it only a few months. The plant bordered on the camp and the kitchen was located on the camp's edge. Upon my return to the camp from the plant, I had about half an hour until Soup Time. This thirty-minute window allowed me to scour the kitchen surroundings. In character with the camp's relaxed regime, the kitchen environs were accessible. Surprisingly, there were no inmates foraging through the garbage bins. I would position myself at the back door of the kitchen, patiently waiting for the door to open, and sneak a peek into the kitchen. From what I could tell, three matronly ladies were bustling around the kitchen space and what I assumed was one elderly man was waddling around the huge vats in a supervisory posture. Chęstochowa was my fourth camp, and I had never seen such a composition of cooks. The camp's loosely structured organization, which had the semblance of a ghetto, intrigued me. It was not intellectual curiosity that piqued my interest. Rather, it was the survival instinct that triggered it.

Information obtained and wisely used was part of any survival strategy. What I found out was that the elite, or *prominante*, that ran the camp had been part of the Chęstochowa Jewish community, which had been deported directly to the camp, in many cases in family groups. This explained the advanced age of the camp population and the strange make-up of the kitchen staff, the object of my pursuit.

Though Chęstochowa was not a starving camp on the Skarżysko Kamienna scale, a gnawing sensation persisted in the bottom of my stomach. The only way to get rid of this sensation would be to make contact with the kitchen staff. Back home about two years ago, I had ingratiated myself into the household of the *Kriminal Polizei* at Mother's insistence, but now grace itself would not do it. I would have to worm my way into the kitchen by other means. There was little art involved in this device, only persistence; unrelenting daily vigil might give me entrance into this Edenic place where many strove to be, but only few arrived at. And my stubbornness finally paid off: I became a junior member of the kitchen staff.

It was not a dramatic beginning. One afternoon I stood at the kitchen door hopping to keep my feet warm when the waddling "chef" came out, gave me a quick once-over and asked, "Are you from the Sulejów transport?"

He told me that he could use me in the kitchen and, to boot, he also filled my mess kit with thick soup, a charity that earned him my enduring gratitude. The following day I was ensconced in the kitchen. In my year-and-a-half internment, except for the short time at the Mansion, I had not had it so good: loaves of bread, marmalade, soups, chunks of margarine, and to top it all a bunk in the kitchen loft. I was content lying in wait for my tardy messiahs, in the form of Red Army tanks, to come liberate me. The tanks' rumbling echoed in my inner ear as I lay drowsing, wrapped up in two tattered blankets that I had bartered for with soup and bread. I ached from missing Irena, with whom I often held conversations in my mind. And while waiting for the rumbles to turn from mirage to reality, I was busy cleaning and doing an assortment of chores involved in kitchen routine work. Washing the walls of the soup vats gave me a lot of satisfaction. Back in Majdanek, and in the first few months during my internment in *Werk C* in Skarżisko Kamienna, when I'd been successful in getting hold of an empty vat I handled it as prey, furiously scraping morsels off the sides with spoon and nails; and even as I was thrusting them into my eager mouth, I was watching my back for intruders. But now I was blasé, treating the vat as a metal object.

Another of my responsibilities was to take out the garbage. There was nothing out of the ordinary in this chore, had it been done at the end of the day. But what was odd about it was that the garbage assignment had to be carried out about half an hour before the cooking of the soup was done. The "chef," usually casual about the performance of my duties, suddenly became a stickler for punctuality, and though I knew that it was none of my concern what went on behind the tightly closed kitchen doors, my ill-inclined urge prompted me to look into this conundrum. But I had to wait till a propitious moment when the kitchen door, left slightly ajar, allowed me a peek into the mystery. From my narrow vantage point, I could only see one vat attended to by one of the sumptuously rounded ladies. She was fishing out a half-melted chunk of margarine from the vat. The other two vats were outside my range of vision, but I surmised what the other women and "the chef" were about. This was a life-heist. Every bit of fat coming into the depleted inmate's body meant literally extending his or her lease on life. In this last stretch of the race against time, anything edible increased the chance of survival, as the Sulejów Rabbi would say. Each chunk of margarine netted equated to a life lost. What was worse, they did this not out of despair but out of greed. They bartered the loot for goods for themselves and their relatives.

Had I encountered these people in their respective neighbourhoods before the war, in their natural habitat, I am sure I would have found them to be morally upright and law-abiding members of their communities. So what had happened to them in the course of two to three years? The extreme conditions of the labour camp transformed them into predators. But the niggling question remains: had they survived, would they have been retransformed into their native humanness? It's hard to say. Survival modus operandi acquired under extreme conditions of deprivation may harden into habits even after the deprivation has ended. But extreme conditions might just as well make the sufferers noble and compassionate. I have encountered survivors of both kinds, both after Liberation and under siege in the forbidding environment of the concentration camps, and even in the ferocious environment of the Death March.

At these life-and-death crossroads, compassionate human faces made sporadic appearances. Out of this predatory God-forsaken land, a kind word was whispered; a helping hand was stretched out; a warning nod was made — and these seemingly small gestures literally made a life's worth of difference. If it were not for them, I would not be here to put down these words. Indeed, I was both the beneficiary of these acts of compassion and the target of punishing blows meted out to me by rapacious fellow inmates.

But what about me? Was I morally outraged when witnessing the matrons preying on the inmates' meagre subsistence? I was angry and resented them. But my resentment derived from being unfairly left out of the booty, rather than indignation at their outrageous behaviour. I too wanted my share of the margarine so that I could exchange it for clothes and shoes to meet the impending harsh winter. Do I feel guilty now for not speaking out then? No, I do not! There was no one to talk to, and confronting the perpetrators would have been suicidal. I am embarrassed by my own human degradation — but without being sorry.

Life in the *Lager* transfigured people from God's images, as the Judeo-Christian perception has it, into figures less Godly and more beastly. Even as the Red Army was thrusting its way west through the ravaged lands of Russia and Poland, the Hasag authorities evacuated the three Częstochowa plants and their forced labourers. In January of 1945, we were bundled into the now notorious sealed cattle cars going in a Westerly direction. It was my fourth cattle car ride, and not very much had changed in the behaviour of its occupants. The only distinct difference was that in the first shipping, from the ghetto to Majdanek, the sturdy and the deft had managed to pry the sliding door open and a few jumped out amidst bursting shots. Now, a languid passivity overcame the occupants of the car. They sat huddled together in resignation. What I remember of that journey was an embracing cold slowly making its way into my insides. I had tucked away bread and margarine in the kitchen loft in case of emergency. Now, crouched in a corner, encased in my bartered blankets, I surreptitiously nibbled from my hidden food supplies.

### *Jedem das Seine* — To Each his Own

This sign on the gate greeted us as we entered the Buchenwald concentration camp. The scene seemed turn the clock back to April 1943, when I had passed through the gates of Majdanek. Except for a selection and the SS guards' bearing, it was a replica of the Majdanek initiation. We went through delousing; changed back to the blue-and-white striped pyjamas and cap; marched in unison to the block — a second initiation into the concentration camp universe. But it was not for long. After a few weeks the entire Block was transported to the Rehmsdorf slave labour camp — a Buchenwald satellite. The place had a strange feeling; it was a kind of cross between a concentration camp and a slave labour camp, Majdanek and Skarżysko Kamienna rolled into one. The S.S. guards who escorted us to the bombed-out plant — which was about an hour's walk from the camp — had none of the vigour of the Majdanek S.S. Their backs, crooked with age, and the sagging shoulders from which rifles hung precariously, looked more like a gaggle of airport security officers before September 11 than representatives of the Thousand-Year Reich. Notwithstanding their weariness, they treated us with brutal rigour. Lined up in five rows and numerous columns, we dragged ourselves along on the back roads to the plant. The January cold bit through my tattered pyjamas and through the protective layers of paper I had managed to rustle up. They prodded us along with inquisitors' zeal to the bombed-out fuel plant. Notwithstanding their obvious fatigue, they showed not a scintilla of humanness. The Reich machinery was grinding to a halt, but the S.S. henchmen seemed to be oblivious to it.

Ironically, the freezing cold had an upside to it: the guards and the *kapos* hid from the cold in the burned-out skeleton buildings, only intermittently coming out of their shelters. This gave us an opportunity to establish contact with the French POWs on the site. While shovelling debris, the handiwork of the RAF and the US Air Force, into the craters, I was on the lookout for the POWs.

Staying behind the skeleton buildings, they would leave chunks of bread, cooked potatoes and other food tidbits. I would glide like a shadow to the appointed spot, pretend to relieve myself, and pick up my bounty. If lucky, I made direct contact with the prisoners, who hastily passed on news from the front. I shared the news with my fellow inmates, but the food I kept for myself. This was a venture not without risk, but worth taking risk for. Both the bread and the news were sweet.

Shoulders hunched, we slouched back and forth from the camp to the bombed-out plant in the dark every day except Sundays. It was a mechanical walk wound by a biological coil. Those regimented marches are blurred in my memory like grey grains on a T.V. screen. On recall I can see silhouettes of emerging images, but they never coalesce into a clear picture.

*Werk C* at Skarżysko Kamienna yields the image of the Tzarina clad in white, a cigarette dangling between her lips, accompanied by her whip-carrying enforcer, Heniek Eisenberg; Sulejŏw brings to mind the Rabbi spreading the word of Messianic redemption; Chęstochowa, greedy-eyed matrons bent over the cauldron, fishing out chunks of margarine — but here in Rehmsdorf memory lingers in an ethereal world intruded upon by snatches of awakenings. Recall needs a memory jolt. I see the water tap, wrapped up in a rag to keep it from freezing, located in the middle ground of the camp, I hear the cruel morning pounding on the bunk, I feel the grinding shuffle back and forth from camp to plant.

The instincts that shepherded me through critical moments in my survival saga seem to have been blunted. In the past, on arrival in a new camp, after having been assigned a block and a bunk, I immediately set out to sniff out the trail to the kitchen, scout out the food warehouse environs, and cajole information from veteran prisoners as to the behaviour patterns of the powers that be, but now in Rehmsdorf I lost the biological impulse that drives the organism's will to live. I somehow managed to stave off my hunger, but the exhaustion seeped into me. Mother seemed to have vanished too.

On returning from the plant, I would line up for the evening soup — without even trying to position myself in a spot conducive to getting a thicker ladle of the liquid — and would then throw myself on my shared bunk.

There was one very early morning when one of my grotesque nightmares must have startled me into wakefulness. The boy I shared the bunk with was just scrambling down to the floor. Had this happened a year earlier, when I was still hungering for life, I would have followed him in the hopes of finding something to eat. After all, what would an inmate give up sleep for but food? But now I stayed put. My aching body would not move. Some time later, my bunkmate happened to trudge alongside me on the way to the plant. I mentioned to him that I had seen him get up early one morning. "Yes," he answered, "We've a *minyan*, before the *Kapos* come." His relatively good physical condition indicated that he had been deported with the Hungarian Jews to the camps only a year earlier. There was not much more to talk about. My mind, though fuzzy, was occupied with devising a strategy on how to reach the French Prisoners of War. Apparently, I still had some life flickering inside me.

The ultimate test of my will to live came in April of 1945 during the Death March. Before recounting that, however, I must project into the future to discuss an episode that affords an insight into the survivors' remembrance mechanism.

## The Bond and the Rule

In the late '70s, I was doing research at Yad Vashem on children's writing during and in the aftermath of the Holocaust. I came across a microfiche of a prayer written by a boy named Moshe Flinker. Sixteen years of age, he and his family had lived disguised as Aryans in Brussels. Writing in a rather stilted Hebrew, Moshe looks into the future, where he intends to become a diplomat in a Jewish State in Palestine to help reconcile the two feuding communities there. The prayer, like his diary, demonstrated its author's emotional maturity and I was taken with it. But there was no microfiche printer in place. Only the Hebrew University had such a printer, and *Yad Vashem's* policy forbade taking materials out of its premises. The only person who had the authority to exempt one from this policy was Shmuel Krakowski, the chief archivist. On my way to see him in his small office, I was seeking an appropriate opening line. It was a hot summer day and he wore a short-sleeved shirt, his forearms resting on the chair's side supports. Still groping for an opening line, I glimpsed his inner arm: it bore a huge AK-tattooed number. "Shmuel," I asked, the words coming trippingly to my tongue, "what camps did you go through?" — a routine question one asked a tattoo-wearer. He listed a long list of camps, ending with Rehmsdorf — "the last of my odysseys," he said ironically, "not a widely known camp, followed by the Death March." When I asked, in a voice of feigned innocence, whether there was a water tap placed in the centre of the camp ground, he gave me an incredulous look and said in a tone of wonderment: "Yes... Yes... but how do you know that?" He paused for a fraction of a second, threw a searching glance at me and said, "You must have been in Rehmsdorf to know the tap; you had to be there," he repeated excitedly.

I have read somewhere that submarine sailors who survive hits from a destroyer's depth charges never lose their emotional bond with each other.

I felt the same way for Shmuel, and he for me. There was an instant surge of fractured pieces of memory, which dovetailed into reminiscing. Though we went through the same daily ordeal for about three months, and both experienced the infinitely long trudge to the Terezin ghetto, each one of us recalled different aspects of the camp and the endurance of the Death March.

It was an instructive lesson: despite the SS attempts to pound the concentration camp inmates into Pavlovian ciphers, they retained their native personalities. It was the first time that I had met a survivor with whom I shared experiences and yet found we had different narratives. While our memories emphasized different facets of our shared history, they were not at variance with each other. Though each one of us retained different aspects of the experience, they nevertheless bore similarities to each other. Though known as a stickler for rules, Krakowski did not turn me down. Our bond trumped the rule, a rule of his own making.

### "April is the Cruellest Month"

T.S. Eliot' opening lines of *The Waste Land* have elicited a wide range of tantalizing commentary. Heralding the roots breaking into the frozen land, the tulips popping up from the soil to meet the sun's rays, April evokes the rebirth of nature and, implicitly, faith. However, read within the context of the Death March, these lines bring back images of death and suffering.

In late April of 1945, the inmates of the Rehmsdorf camp were loaded into open cattle cars. The habitually cruel *kapos*, apparently scared by what might happen to them in the impending end, allowed us to take our blankets with us and fill cans with water. I remember very little of the train ride except that I held my blanket tight around me to keep the dawn chill away and slowly began unfolding it as the sun felt warmer. In the early hours of the next morning, as the train made its way through towns and villages, I heard a faint drone, which became increasingly loud. I got up from the floor and saw a plane with stars on its wings tearing down toward the train, leaving in its upswing the trail of an oval-shaped object cutting through the blue sky. That object landed on the locomotive, which screeched to a halt, followed by the cars of human cargo. What ensued was a cacophony of screams: "*Aussteigen, Aussteigen!*" Banging on the wooden planks with their rifle-butts, accompanying the pounding with shouts of "*Schnell, Schnell,*" the SS guards seemed to have lost their bearings. For a short while chaos reigned: the astounded inmates scurrying in confusion; the guards, still grappling with the disarray, were beating the unruly crowds into formation. This was the commencement of our Death March — the last leg of our ordeal.

The memories of the Death March that stay with me are blurry; when dragged from the recesses of memory, they appear like animated scenes moving through nightmare-motions of inertia. I remember the sun bearing down on me; tongues of heat sporadically flaming out from the asphalt; intermittent shooting in the back of the column; the parching thirst; the few drops of water left in the canister. Occasionally, I glimpsed peering eyes behind curtains.

There are two incidents I remember more clearly than the rest. One of them is the night when, at dusk, our ghost-like column reached the Marienbad train station. There was no shelter for us there. We were ordered to lie down in the field for the night. The field became a mother lode of sustenance. I dug my spoon into the earth, pulling out roots of various sorts, some of which were edible. I was lying on the edge of the field next to a boy my age, who was destined to become my traveling companion for a long while thereafter. A bright light coming from the moonlit sky fell on the blacked-out railway station. No guards were to be seen. Sounds of muffled cannon shots were heard. Were these muffled shots what sparked the little life still left in me? Or was it the pounding heartbeat of the sprinter in his last stretch of the race? I slid toward the boy lying next to me and whispered into his ear, suggesting we make a run for it to the nearby forest. We crawled out of the marked enclosure till we reached a row of bushes.

Our white-and-blue striped pyjamas stood out even from a distance. We kept on walking for perhaps half an hour, and when we hit a dirt road a *Hitlerjugend* sentinel, probably no more than a couple of years older than us, was leaning on his bicycle waiting for us, as if by a scheduled appointment. He didn't yell, he just told us in a nonchalant voice to turn back. I was the first to speak: "We're hungry and are looking for food. We're not running away." He turned the bike around and ordered us to follow, heading back to the train station.

Even now, sixty-three years after this event, I find it difficult to sort out what my feelings were as we walked towards the station where the SS guards billeted. No, I did not want to die so close to the last stretch of the race, but I did not dread death either. Unlike the rabbit incident, when the SS officer Kurt Schumann was poised to pull the trigger at me and in preparation of meeting the imminent bullet I voided my entire inner being, now, as we were nearing the station, the void had already been lodged inside me. Someone, not dressed in an SS uniform, stood outside the station, smoking a cigarette cupped in his palm. After listening to the *Hitlerjugend* sentinel's report, he hastily waved us to return to the field where the others were lying. The following day the Death March resumed.

The other incident I remember happened at one point along the road, toward the end of our walk: fruits of all sorts, loaves of bread, and cans filled with cool water were scattered on the side road. It looked like a mirage steaming out of the hot asphalt under my feet. The first to snatch the food were the *kapos*, followed by the strongest inmates in their rapacious hunger. Like packs of hungry wolves preying on a carcass, the strong inmates swept aside the weak and swooped on the food. Nothing in the world could have held them back, not even lethal bullets. It was all over in a second, like lightning. Even the guards ignored the stampede to the side road. As we dragged along, the side roads kept on yielding food and water in abundance. After the strongest inmates filled their stomachs and grabbed as much as they could carry, the weak and the apathetic stretched out their hands to scoop up food and pick up water canisters. This time, the manna did not fall from heaven. It came instead from Czech villagers, who at considerable risk lived up to their humane convictions by demonstrating that they were their brothers' keepers.

Earlier in that same day, the column had passed a huge mansion. A group of young German pilots stood at the gate watching us with neither pity nor hate registering on their blank faces. In sight of the demonstrable evil engendered by their regime, a regime on its last legs — in fact three weeks away from surrender — these young men chose to uphold fealty to the *Führer*. In retrospect, one cannot help thinking that these same people joined the political and economic reconstruction of post-war Germany and, after a couple of beers with friends, might have recalled the poor striped white-and-blue pyjama people shuffling along on the road. But right then, as the column was painfully dragging forward, blind obedience retained the upper hand.

Finally, one night, we reached our destination. Somehow the rumour spread that we were outside the Terezin ghetto. I held on to some chunks of bread that I'd picked up on the road. Surprisingly, a couple of bonfires were lit. When dawn broke, the *kapos* and the guards had gone. A puffing locomotive was pulling two cargo cars out of the station. I looked around; there were a few hundred of us left. Soon women dressed in civilian clothes came and led us through the gates into the ghetto. I was taken, with a few other teenagers, to be disinfected and showered. For the first time in two years, I did not dread what would flow out of the showerheads.

What I remember of my two-week stay in Terezin is being in a kind of sleep-immersion, mind and body free from sudden intrusion. I got woken up to take my meals, ate, hastily went to the washroom, and slipped back into sweet oblivion.

### Latter-Day Messiahs Have Come

Still drowsy with sleep, I woke up to the noise of clattering wheels. I could instantly tell that these sounds did not come from train wheels. Leaning out of the window, I watched with the other boys as Red Army vehicles rolled into the centre of the ghetto. There were only a few of them, but they were enough to mark our liberation. I thought of the Lithuanian Rabbi in Sulejŏw who had seen redemption in his mind's eye about eight months earlier, and wondered whether he survived to see it. I was free to go. The boy who had joined me in my attempted escape from the Death March joined me, and we quickly dressed and walked out of the ghetto compound, this time without having to look over our shoulders.

The spectacle on the road was fascinating. In the shimmering May sunlight, a long column of military vehicles was moving west; and on both sides of the road, in single-file lines, German POWs were slowly making their way in the opposite direction, toward Prague. Deeply impressed by the Czech people's benevolence during the Death March, we headed to Prague ourselves. Our shaven heads, pale faces, emaciated bodies and ill-fitting clothes unmistakably gave away our identity. As we walked, the Russian drivers showered us with loaves of bread. *"Khleb, Khleb,"* they shouted jovially. We also picked up tinned food of all sorts, which was fated to make us ill.

However, for the time being, we had an abundance of food, enough to have fed many a "Death Marcher," when only four weeks earlier, I would have bartered my life, or what was left of it, for a tiny bit of bread. As we walked, I saw out of the corner of my eye two German soldiers under a tree in the field, one of them bent over, apparently digging. "Let's see what these two are doing," I said to my buddy. There was a sergeant, squatting next to a high-ranking *Wehrmacht* officer. When he noticed us, he stopped digging. Both looked at us. On impulse, I took one of two loaves of bread I had, broke it into two halves, and tossed one half to each of them. I made sure to observe the protocol of rank, honouring the officer first. The astounded expressions on their faces are etched in my memory. "A few weeks ago," I said in a tone of contempt, "I was also digging in the soil for food, but *you* wouldn't have given me bread, you might have shot me…" I was agitated and could not account for my behaviour to myself or to my mate. Three days later, while lying in a Russian military hospital with food poisoning occasioned by those tins from well-meaning donors, I had time to reflect on this strange episode.

The young Russian lorry driver who picked us up on our way to Prague took us directly to a makeshift military hospital when he saw the state we were in after consuming the tinned foods. An officer met us, looked us over quickly and asked us: "*Amcha?*" — a code word for "Jews," used by my co-religionists for identification purposes. At last my Jewishness got me preferential treatment.

He had two cots set up for us at the end of a long line of beds filled with wounded soldiers. The following afternoon the same officer, accompanied by a rather tall man wearing a white coat over a *Wehrmacht* uniform, paid us a visit. They sat down on our cots and, after routine questions related to our health, the German doctor delicately negotiated a series of questions. He wanted to know whether we had any knowledge about our families and whether we knew what we were going to do next. Among a series of questions put with great sensitivity, one caught me with utter surprise. I do not remember the exact phrasing, but the gist of it was whether we might have done something illegal that landed us in the concentration camps. He sounded incredulous that boys of our age would be incarcerated in concentration camps. "Is this German doctor feigning ignorance or is he genuine?" I mused. "Is it possible that a high *Wehrmacht* officer is ignorant of the crimes perpetrated by his countrymen?"

While I was lying in bed, my encounter with the two *Wehrmacht* soldiers kept coming up in my mind. Why did I offer them bread? It was not pity, so what made me do it? My traveling mate quite understandably thought that I'd lost my mind. So it must have been revenge. Two Jewish boys, racial victims of the Nazi State, giving bread to two German soldiers, unwitting instruments of persecution, symbolized a triumph of humanness over savagery. At the time I probably did not formulate my feelings in these terms, but it was, I've since realized, what I felt.

## Death Stalking Life

The Feldafing Displaced Person Camp was a gathering place for survivors of the Nazi occupation, and for the flight refugees who had escaped to the Soviet Union and found shelter during the war. I arrived there in the summer after my short and unsuccessful visit to my hometown in search of family members. Seeking surviving family was a compulsion, like a muscle tic over which you had no control.

Viewed from the perspective of the Jewish tradition, Feldafing symbolized Ezekiel's resurrection prophecy, the raising of the dead. A tremendous effort was made to breathe life into the moribund Yiddish culture after its new, painfully acquired experience, to bring the eighteen-hundred-year-old culture into the new post-Holocaust realities. Driven by a biological need to make up for the unprecedented population loss suffered in the Holocaust, younger and older people went under the marital canopy at an unusually accelerated rate. Amid the jingling of the wine glasses celebrating weddings, mourners prayed for the dead. Out of this wasteland new life sprouted, heralding a new beginning. It was a triumph of life over death. Into this incongruous environment where death stalked life, I arrived.

Now that my single-minded focus on physical survival was gone, Mother and Irena made their presences felt more often in my reveries and dreams. Menachem too appeared in my reveries. I relived his bolt from the marching column, my ear capturing the shrieking bullets chasing him. I noticed that my feelings toward Irena had changed. In my reveries the sisterly warm hugs that she had given me took on a different quality. They still oozed warmth, but it was not the sisterly kind; it had an erotic thrill to it. I came to Feldafing wanting to believe that she had survived. Unexpectedly, I came across some girls who had been in *Werk C* in Skarżysko Kamienna, who told me that indeed she had, and that she was on her way to Feldafing to visit her ailing husband in hospital. I was longing for Irena as a regular sixteen-year-old would long for his girlfriend. We met in her friends' residence. I had not wept in years; even at memorial ceremonies for Holocaust victims, where Mother appeared to me as a virtually physical presence, only a few salty drops trickled down my cheeks.

After all of the buffeting about by life's circumstances, my well of tears seemed to have dried up. But when I saw Irena alive, they began to flow again, and freely poured down my face. I had last seen her on the roll call grounds in Skarżysko Kamienna just before the liquidation of the camp, about eleven months earlier. Her radiant eyes had not changed; nor had their sadness. With her graceful, light steps, she rushed to hug me. It was a prayer come true.

As became customary among survivors, we did not dwell on the past. She confided in me that she was going to divorce her husband, but would wait till he got out of the hospital. They had married in the ghetto when she had lost her parents to the *aktion*; ten years her senior, he had been like a father to her.

Of course she loved him, but in a daughterly way. I asked her whether she had met someone else. The tone of my question must have betrayed my state of mind for she gave me what can best be described as a knowing look. Women, as I later learned, know these things. "No, Edek," she said in a measured pace, "I need time, lots of time, time to heal." She had earlier visited her husband, and the doctor had promised quick recovery. "He would like to meet you," she said. I was eager to meet him as well.

He was sharing a hospital room with another patient, who happened to be a Marxist. My entrance interrupted a heated discussion about the merits and demerits of Communism. He looked older than his age, wasted away by the tuberculosis that he had contracted in the camps. The irony of the situation did not escape me. He was a father figure to Irena and I was a brother figure. We shared a passionate love for the woman that he was about to lose and that I would never have. In the concentration camp, my young age had turned out to be an advantage, but now it became an impediment. We had a casual conversation in which Irena was mentioned a few times. I told him about my chances of emigrating. I felt pity for both of them, casualties of tragic circumstances.

Irena and I saw each other daily over the short period I stayed in Feldafing. We met one final time a day before I left for Foerenwald in preparation for my flight to Britain. Irena had found relatives in Australia and she hoped to receive immigration papers soon. Inadvertently, we referred to our last meeting in *Werk C* camp, before the evacuation. At that time we'd had no control over our destinations; they were determined by our Lords and Masters of the Aryan race. Now we had plans, though we could not predict how they would evolve. Nevertheless, the sadness of parting was no less painful. The losses I'd sustained in the previous three years had left scars in my psyche. I longed for a place away from the anxieties, the marks of suffering, the agitation involved in meeting survivors, and yes, the joys of rebirth. I needed tranquility as an antidote to my inner turmoil. This I hoped to find in England.

## At the Birth of a Dream

Gathered from the Europeans ruins, a few hundred boys and girls were navigated back to civilization by a group of dedicated people with considerable success. However, my own anxieties manifested themselves in an obsessive wanderlust that did not abate. I was gripped by restlessness, in search of something I could not identify. I aimlessly roamed the streets of East London, whose people fascinated me. In their simple conduct and colourful speech, they struck an intriguing contrast to the properly comported North West Londoners, my fellow residents.

My unabated restiveness was exacerbated by my discontent with the maritime school I attended. It was largely my restlessness that took me to Palestine in 1948, on the eve of the Israeli War of Independence. I wish I could boast of burning patriotism that made me volunteer to join the fledgling Israeli Defense Force, and say that I felt holding a lethal instrument in my hand would give me the confidence to meet my enemy on equal terms, as a reaction to my long years of submissiveness. Alas, the truth was that I simply needed to get away to somewhere, an elusive somewhere.

At our first meeting with the *Yishuv* emissary, when he wooed us, the three naval cadets, into joining the imminent war effort against the attack of the Arab armies, he conveyed to us the urgent need for naval personnel. He put forward a persuasive case. On our arrival we were told that the newly formed Israeli Defense Force had no fleet. "We have rowing boats, would you like to get on one of them?" our new superiors asked somewhat whimsically. As soon as our boat anchored in the harbour, the volunteer group was taken to a makeshift military base for basic training. My unit was assigned to the south of the country to hold back the Egyptian columns moving north to Tel-Aviv.

Notwithstanding the post-Zionist historians' claim that the Jewish community had the upper hand over the six invading armies in terms of arms and logistics, my combat experience proves the opposite. The armoured Egyptian vehicles came swarming over our positions at daybreak. We encountered them with machine gun fire and mortars. In a confrontation, we were no match for them. What saved the day were the "Fiats," anti-armour grenades made in Italy, coupled with the raw courage of the fighters. Groups of two soldiers would burrow themselves into the sandy hill and fling the grenades and Molotov cocktails onto the passing armoured vehicles and tanks. In fact it was not a classical war between two armies; rather — at least in the first stages of the war — it resembled a guerrilla war in which the weaker party took advantage of darkness, ambushes and other tactics to counter the overwhelming advantages of the Egyptian Army. Between the battles, we would get occasional pep talks to lift our morale, and we'd listen to them in between snatching drowses. But there was one talk that pulled me out of my exhaustion.

Weary-eyed and craving sleep, we were crouching on a sandy mound on the Southern front on a hot June night, waiting to be driven to the front line to take Hill 69, which controlled the road to Tel-Aviv. I thought that we were in for another morale booster. But it turned out to be different. The words delivered in a rich baritone sounded cruel in their directness: "The Jewish people are once more besieged by an enemy intent on its annihilation," a voice piercing through the darkness told us. The slightly foreign-accented speech brought home to us, a motley company of newly recruited fighters which included a good number of survivors, the precariousness of the Jewish enterprise. The speaker was Abba Kovner, second in command of the Jewish underground in the Vilna ghetto and later a partisan fighting the Nazi occupiers in the forest. Subsequently, he bodied forth his war experiences in a series of memorable poems. What was significant about this short speech was an implied reference to the Holocaust, a word that I had not heard before in any of the speeches.

Lying in ambush during the long hours of the night, my thoughts wandered back to those dark days living under siege; now I was the besieger lying in wait for an Egyptian detail trying to slip into the surrounded town of Feluja. Inadvertently, I compared my state of mind as besieged and now as besieger. In the concentration and labour camps, particularly in the last stages of the war, death came as naturally as hunger and humiliation. When someone you knew failed to appear on the roll call or to the labour detail, you glossed over it or remarked nonchalantly: "Well, he didn't make it." On the battlefield, in contrast, no one expected to get killed or injured. And when people got killed, their deaths were noticed and mourned. I also learned that I was able to obey orders when they made sense and were not made simply at the whim of the superior in command. However, in one particular case I, and some of my volunteer buddies, refused an order. This manifestation of disobedience landed us in prison.

### My Initiation into Scooping Humus

They came out of nowhere. Three husky men wearing stubble on their faces and light machine guns over their shoulders drove into the military base where we were quartered. Our brigade took a lot of casualties in the summer of 1948 fighting in the south; consequently we were pulled out of the front line for rest and reorganization. My company was called to the mess. "*Haverim*," one of the three addressed us in the then-conventional salutation of comrades, "we need volunteers to help us in taking care of a radical group who have done a lot of damage to the State." He identified himself as a member of the *Palmach*, an elite command unit of the Israeli Defense Force. The radicals he was referring to were LECHI, an underground organization popularly known as the "Stern Gang," named after its founder Yair Stern. The speaker told us that they had shot Count Folke Bernadotte, the United Nation mediator to Palestine. "We're rounding up these people and need reliable '*Chevre*' to guard the dissidents."

While he was speaking, his eyes surveyed the listeners' expressions, at times resting on one face or another. This entire proposition seemed to me unacceptable. First of all it was a demotion in status, going from fighter to prison guard duty, and secondly, I did not understand the ideological rift between the leadership of Israel and the armed dissidents. In addition, the war was drawing to an end; it was time to go back to school. Even as I was contemplating these points, the speaker pointed at me. I chose the argument that would make most sense from his point of view. "I don't know what this is all about," I responded in halting Hebrew, "and anyway, I'm MAHAL." In contrast to his rough demeanour, his voice was gentle as he tried to persuade me that I would be performing a noble deed for the State. And in a somewhat determined voice, he added that we were in the military and disobeying an order, "volunteer or not," incurred punishment. There were about six of us who refused the order to become prison guards, each one for different reasons, and we were ordered to pack our kitbags and unceremoniously escorted to a van. Two young soldiers, our age, were leaning on its hood.

I was naturally curious to know where we were being taken, and I was about to use roundabout questions aimed at finding out our destination when our escorts freely offered us information. We were heading towards Jalami, a former British police station. It was a great place to be in, they asserted cheerfully. From what they told us, it did not sound like a penal colony. There was not a hint of irony in their tone. And yet, the sceptic in me doubted their account of the place. I wondered aloud whether there was something confining in this place; after all, it was a prison, not a resort. "Yes," they said casually, "the guys who don't do guard duty or fulfill other assignments are not allowed to leave the compound."

Jalami sat on the top of the Carmel Mountain; it controlled a strategic junction between the north and the south of the country. Its spacious compound comprised offices, a small prison and other facilities typical of a police station. When I arrived, it immediately struck me as prisoner-friendly, and the following days bore out my first impression. Our two informants were quite accurate in their description. We enjoyed such amenities as comfortable sleeping accommodations, meals in the mess and cultural activities. In the course of time I found out that Jalami was a detention for dissidents who were brought to the police station for informal re-education. The group I belonged to turned out to be slow learners.

This was my first sustained encounter with Israeli society. Of course, in the army I met Israelis, but our social contacts were limited and under the stress of combat conditions. In these relaxed and friendly surroundings, I was introduced to the Middle East culinary style and the attendant eating etiquette. Thus, for eating humus, you used a pita with which you cleaned the plate of its contents, and there was a curving movement to the wipe; and the boys working in the kitchen would prepare black sweet coffee in tiny cups.

Sitting on the lawn in the gentle autumnal sun, I learned about the mores of the Israeli mentality. It was still in its embryonic stages, but already showing the characteristics of a people different from the Diaspora Jew. What mostly intrigued me was their unshaken self-confidence. They had never doubted the final outcome of the war and were equally convinced of their moral claim to the land.

While feasting on homemade cakes ranging from Viennese *Strudel* to Polish *pierogi* to Arab *baklawa*, each one representing the Diaspora provenance of the family of my fellow prisoners, I realized what attracted me to them. This first generation born in Palestine, whose parents immigrated there from Europe and other continents before the war, linked their Jewish roots to Biblical and Talmudic myths and identified with the heroic stand of their ancestors against the Canaanites and the ancient Greek and Roman conquerors. At school as well as in youth movement groups, they had been taken on hikes crisscrossing the country under the guidance of field instructors who showed them villages, hamlets and hills that still bore Biblical and Second Temple-era names. It was an evocation of the historical past brought into the political discourse, with a view to achieving moral vindication of the Jewish claim to the land of Israel. This educational process only marginally touched on the Holocaust, for reasons that I came to learn about later, during my permanent residence in Israel. For a dislocated young Jew like me who felt alienated from his surroundings, the nascent breed of the rooted Israeli Jew was admirable.

Yitzhak, the nurse who was responsible for the infirmary, was getting ready to enter medical school. Part of his studies involved operating on frogs. He found choirs of croaking frogs near the compound, brought them back, cut them open and studied their entrails with the reflective devoutness of a Buddhist in prayer. But Yitzhak also had other interests that he generously shared with me. He introduced me to classical music and to Freud's psychoanalytical theories. When I finally got out of my detention, Yitzhak took me to concerts in the old auditorium of Ohel Shem in Tel-Aviv, but more often than not we couldn't afford the tickets and would stay outside listening to the melodies streaming out of the concert hall. He was like an older brother to me, and I tried to reciprocate his kindness.

Otherwise outgoing and sometimes garrulous, he was shy with girls. I first noticed this in the compound when we were in the company of female soldiers. Later in Tel-Aviv, when I learned to pepper my Hebrew with current slang and managed to borrow *Sabra* mannerisms, my traffic with the Israeli girls on the beach became as natural as the lapping waves on the shore. I tried to bring him into this casual beach chitchat, not always with great success.

Getting out of detention required some manoeuvring. The war was drawing to an end and partial demobilization was enacted. What I could infer from my casual exchanges with a junior officer was that we, "the six rebels with a cause," as we were referred to, might be sent back to our unit to either await discharge or to engage in the skirmishes still going on along the Northern front. This latter option boded ill. Going back to lying in ambush at night or staying indefinitely in the compound were dim propositions. For a while it was fun indulging in Middle Eastern cuisine, reading Freud and watching Yitzhak exploring frog entrails; notwithstanding these indulgences, my patience was wearing thin. Time was running out and the fact that we were confined to the compound exacerbated our irritation. As for myself, my latent restlessness resurfaced. It was time to have a chat with the boys to plan our next move.

We were in agreement that we ought to immediately apply for discharge on the grounds of our special MAHAL status. This request was to be put verbally to the station commander. Upon request, we were given an audience to present our case to the commander. And then a funny thing happened. We came loaded for bear, only to find an amiable officer who invited us to sit down. We spoke in English, and to show off our passion for Israel I threw in some Hebrew phrases, to the officer's delight. There was no problem in letting us go, he said. Of course, he would have liked us to pursue our studies or our careers in Israel, but he wished us well whatever we decided. Within two weeks we received our discharge papers and made our way to the MAHAL offices on Benyamin Street in Tel-Aviv to collect our tickets and travelling papers.

I stayed behind for a month or two to get a better flavour of the new Israel. Yitzhak introduced me to his serious-minded friends and to Israeli high culture. The Israelis I befriended in the army had gotten me used to the lighter aspects of Israeli society, but high culture was something new to me. I also signed up for a Hebrew crash course with a teacher whose quilted shirt, known as a *Roebuck*, tightened by a colourful girdle, looked like a museum artefact. But when animated, he assumed the characteristics of a revolutionary Bolshevik — an outtake from a Soviet propaganda film. His fluffy shock of flowing grey hair on his small, tilting head, accompanied by broad theatrical gesticulations using the Stanislawski method, transformed the class into a stage. He became especially enlivened when reciting stanzas from Pushkin's poetry in the original and in the Hebrew translation, neither of which we could follow. Another favourite of his was Andrei Gromyko's speech, given at the United Nation General Assembly in 1947, in support of establishing a Jewish State. He considered this speech a turning point in relations between the Zionist enterprise and the Socialist State. I thoroughly enjoyed his thespian temperament and kept attending the course in the remaining days before I decided to return to England. But before returning, I had to fulfill a commitment to two friends who fell in the War of Independence.

Though I was only in my late teens, the line-up of those I had lost was as long as my eyes could see. The number of family and friends I had lost to the Holocaust could fill a midsize cemetery, and an even greater number of people were simply lost to oblivion. With the passage of time, old age had taken its toll among my seniors. In sum: I had been in consort with loss most of my life. Some of the dead make frequent appearances in my life to this very day: Menachem, who negotiated me into the art of survival in the ghetto; Hochman, my former classmate who helped me survive Majdanek; and of course my mother, who appeared at the most critical moments in my life to strengthen my flailing spirit. Now the time had come to visit two fresh graves: that of my British foster-brother Jonathan, buried in the military cemetery in Rosh Pina, located in the northern part of Israel, and another, belonging to a soldier I had befriended during the fighting, buried in a civilian cemetery in Tiberias.

Eulogizing the dead takes on a variety of forms. Deliveries in third person singular range from praising the good deeds performed by the deceased to extolling the pristine character of his personality. Another form is speaking directly to the dead in first person singular. Usually a long-time friend positions himself by the grave in front of the mourners and in a solemn voice, fitting the occasion, draws on shared memories recalling the times

> when we were kids playing basketball in the butcher's backyard…
> and in the blink of an eye you've grown up,
> become a prosperous businessman

and a pillar of our community, raised a family,
the pride and joy of the community.
Most of all, you will be remembered for being a *Mench,* you've spoken
from the heart and made good on your words.

And to round it all up, he would add, "You put your money where your mouth was. You'll be sorely missed," ending the eulogy in a flourish.

Listening to this type of gushy outpouring, I could never help but wonder why all these redeeming qualities could not have been celebrated when the subject of the eulogy was still alive. Thus, strands of conventional hypocrisy are woven into a verbal tapestry and usually taken by the mourners for what they are. A cynical mourner might wonder: if so many virtuous people tread this good earth of ours, why is it that so much evil has been plaguing the lands since time immemorial? From fratricide to genocide to the Holocaust, humanity has been gripped by a killing frenzy, as if Cain handed to us a legacy of killing.

These thoughts were running through my mind as I stood in the military cemetery in Rosh Pina on a spring day. Amidst the hundreds of freshly-covered graves, emblems of the young lives given to gain Jewish sovereignty, I looked at Jonathan's headstone. Headstones are mute, like the dead themselves, and I wanted to bring out Jonathan's person from the stone's muteness. In his short life he embodied the very opposite of hypocrisy. He tried to dissuade the survivor boys from going to Israel to take part in the war. "You have already done your share," he said one afternoon as we walked on the Heath. But he himself, he volunteered to join the fledgling Israeli Defense Force, leaving medical school and home behind. He was the epitome of idealism, free of self-interest and committed to the cause he believed in. In the course of my life, I have met people of many different backgrounds and life experiences, but I have never met a person whose words and acts dovetailed with such grace.

To conjure him from the dead, I felt I had to project the past we shared into an imaginary future; to reattach the severed life just as surgeons reattach severed limbs nowadays. The walks we took on Hampstead Heath, the unforgettable high tea at his parent's home, and other memorable moments became a seamless whole with the future. In my mind's eye, I see Jonathan suntanned, driving on a dirt road, heading to a kibbutz to attend to the sick. I see him bustling in the infirmary, speaking to his patients in an English-accented Hebrew, compassionate and yet professional. I visit him in his small room on the kibbutz; he has turned it into a visible mixture of

Hampstead Heath and kibbutz cultures. He serves me English tea and Israeli biscuits.

But eventually I snap out of the reverie. I still have another obligation to the dead.

Company 3 of battalion 53 comprised young men in their late teens and early twenties. There was one soldier, I believe a corporal, somewhat older, who stood out among the youngsters because of his age and religious inclinations. Originally from Tiberias, a city by the Sea of Galilee, he had different behaviour patterns from the freewheeling Tel-Aviv boys. We called him the Tiberian. I liked him a lot precisely because he was different from the other native Israelis. When he was wounded during a night raid on an Egyptian position, we carried him on a stretcher about three kilometres to an ambulance waiting on a dirt road. The commanding officer asked me to board the ambulance, which drove us to the nearest hospital. It was dawn when they wheeled him into the operating room.

Exhausted, I plopped down on a bench in the hospital corridor, my World War Two Canadian-made rifle next to me. When I woke up, I noticed through my squinting eyes a grey-bearded elderly man, garbed in a black garment with a huge skullcap on his head, rhythmically swaying back and forth while reciting a prayer. I surmised that the man was the Tiberian's father. I left my rifle lying on the bench and approached him in cautiously measured steps. He raised his eyes from the holy book. Even as I was telling him who I was, a surgeon came through the door. I knew instantly that the Tiberian was dead, just as his father must have known. And as soon as the surgeon finished expressing his regrets the father, shading his eyes, let out a cry, a cry oscillating between resigned acceptance and mild protest: "The Lord gave, the Lord took away. Blessed be Lord's name." I had heard this before but could not at the time identify its source. The anguished cry, as I learned later, echoed Job's when told that his seven daughters and sons had been killed. It has become a classic lament in the painful history of the Jewish people. It was, indeed, theodicy at its most profound.

I never made it to that last cemetary. I could not bring myself to confront yet another grave. It was time to put my life together and return to London.

## The Schnitzel Riddle

The intimate affinity I had felt for London during my stay there from 1945 to 1948 weakened somewhat after Jonathan's death and the Balters' divorce.

This family was my emotional anchor. On my return to England, I met members of the family only separately, on different occasions. Their foster care guidance vanished — and I still needed it. The Finchley Hostel boys I knew had left the residence and new arrivals had taken their places. My friends came into their own; a few attended universities and art schools, others went into business, and quite a number emigrated to families across the Atlantic. I could not go back to the regimented life of the naval school in King's Lynn. The restlessness that overwhelmed me in the wake of Liberation seemed to be seeping back into me, in search of an indeterminate purpose. It felt like I was groping my way in the dark along a road splitting off in multiple directions. It was this same restiveness that had driven me to join the War of Israeli Independence. Occasionally I tell people about my combat experience in Israel, and from their expressions I infer that they expect me to recite a tale of burning patriotism that made me volunteer. I was interviewed for a Jewish weekly recently that profiled volunteers for the Israeli War of Independence. My interviewer piloted me toward cutting a heroic pose. He wanted me to tell the story of a boy survivor who had left school to fight for the newly emerging Jewish state, the longing of a wounded nation. I almost submitted to this tempting indulgence.

When I returned to London, in the absence of the Balter family, I tried to contact my former speech therapist — apparently, her magic was still working on me. But she had already moved to another place.

Whitechapel still fascinated me. The Cockneys' simple mannerisms and colourful speech struck an intriguing contrast to the properly comported Northwest Londoners.

I located a boarding house owned by a Viennese lady, a flight refugee whose other residents were also Austrian flight refugees who had escaped the Nazi invasion in the nick of time. Single, sophisticated and in their late forties, they had a hard time shedding their cultural inheritance. At the dinner table they still conversed in Viennese German and ate Viennese dishes, prominent among them the legendary Viennese schnitzel.

Obsessively attentive to everything concerning food, I noticed that the sizes of the schnitzels served varied. While the side dishes were approximately the same, the schnitzel came in large, medium and small sizes. I received the smallest portion. The first time I observed this discriminatory schnitzel distribution, I thought it might have been a fluke, but when the same occurred the following week, it was time to launch a snooping inquiry. I had to be circumspect in my investigations, since my weekly payments were rather irregular and the owner, bless her memory, though both large in size and generous of heart, was ill-tempered. It did not take much effort to find out that the size of the schnitzel was proportional to the room size, which in turn was proportional to the amount of the weekly payment. My weekly check paid for the smallest room, and hence the smallest schnitzel. I felt no resentment toward the Viennese lady. After all, her enterprise was founded on capitalistic principles, sprinkled with compassion for the "less fortunate," such as myself. Once I was in the neighbourhood of the Highgate cemetery and stopped to visit Karl Marx's grave. I recalled there what my schnitzel informant had told me: "Capitalism is guided by a profit principle, and this poor woman does what's necessary to keep her business afloat." Marx did not answer.

I landed a job in an import citrus warehouse thanks to a web of connections. I started as a clerk registering the orders placed by retailers from all over Britain. As long as the telephone callers originated in the Greater London area and its vicinity to the south, I got the orders all right, but once they started coming in from the northern regions of Manchester and Leeds, things got mixed up. Despite having been exposed for a while to northern accents at the naval school, on the phone the phonemes and the intonation seemed to have different sounds, consequently causing me to mess up the orders. And the Scottish accent was way out of my linguistic hearing range.

As a result of my slip-ups, I was given the registration job, counting the incoming crates and making sure that they were intact. It was a satisfying job, even exciting at times — particularly when the Jaffa orange crates arrived busted, giving out a pungent aroma that brought back memories from the times I had fought in the south. Back then, the orchard would provide shelter for our Company; we morbidly dubbed it "the warrior's resting place." After long days of fighting, we would lie down under the trees and fill our lungs with the intoxicating orange fragrance.

Now in the shed, my coworkers and I would sit on the crates at lunchtime and bite into the juicy flesh of the oranges — a feast to the palate. I could have gone like this for some more years. The wages I made, supplemented by assistance from a Jewish foundation, saw me through the month, though I could not afford a bigger-sized schnitzel. What really bothered me was that I could not rekindle the glow I'd felt for London during my first stay there. The overcast skies, the drizzle, even the foggy days still gave me a sense of security, odd as it may sound, but I still missed the warmth and cohesiveness of the Balter family and had a painful longing for Mrs. Rubin's hugs.

Jonathan's father, Dr. Balter, seemed to have been affected the most by his son's death and the divorce that followed. The stooped back, the wrinkles on the face, and the bulging veins on his hands belied the keen look of his eyes, from which emanated a kind of knowing wisdom usually associated with tragedy on a Jobian scale. Over tea and sandwiches in a spot at Regents Park overlooking a pond, he told me about his experiences in Israel, where he volunteered to serve as a physician in the newly-developing settlements in the south of the country. "I went from a Rolls Royce to a horse buggy," he quipped, an ironic glint flickering in his eyes, "driven by a local who also stood in for a translator." Though the switch was quite remarkable, it did not bother him as much as the climate. I knew exactly what he meant. He administered medicine in the same area where I had fought the Egyptian invaders a couple of years earlier. "And the living accommodations... well, they were not quite suitable for the needs of an elderly doctor," he said in a typical British understatement.

Surely, moving from a Hampstead Heath mansion to a hut in Nizanim baked by a scorching sun must have caused him significant discomfort. I could not quite figure out why he volunteered to go to Israel at all, and particularly to go to Israel in its infancy, when the living conditions in the outposts, so to speak, verged on the primitive. It was a tantalizing question. After all, he was not a banner-waving Zionist, unless he kept his Zionist sentiments to himself, nor was he a romantic. Then what made him take such a radical step at his age?

Though spurred by curiosity, I knew that I should not submit to my impulse to ask. Was his venture a tribute to his son, an offering to his memory on the altar of Jewish sovereignty? Perhaps it was his way to pay his dues for his good fortune for skipping that free ride east from Vienna which so many of his fellow citizens experienced. It would take a Freudian therapist and numerous hours of analysis to answer these tangled questions, and I will never know the answers. As we parted, I knew that our last words to each other would not be an *auf Wiedersehen*, but rather a goodbye. I saw him to the street, where he hailed a cab; he too knew that we would not see each other again.

It took me two years, but eventually I understood that nothing kept me in England, and I returned to Israel, more permanently this time. Unlike Dr. Balter, who internalized his grief, his former wife, Jessica Balter, channelled hers into bustling activities both in England and in Israel. She would come to Israel on Remembrance Day, when we drove up to the Rosh Pina cemetery to pay our respects to Jonathan. The difference between her restrained mourning and the demonstrative expressions of the other bereaved, who were mostly natives of North Africa, was striking. She stood over the grave in quiet solemnity punctuated by the wailing of the neighbouring mourners, who threw themselves on the graves, giving voice to their sorrows in lamentation. When the military ceremony was over, they picnicked with great gusto — a reaffirmation of life over death. It was obvious that Mrs. Balter did not appreciate these unreserved outbursts of emotions. Her English upbringing was offended. I explained to her once the Eastern mourning traditions, which were generally emotionally effusive. Later, we would visit the kibbutz with which she was involved and spend the following day sightseeing.

Mrs. Balter fluttered through life's offers with a vivacity that would pique the envy of women half her age. She was well connected both in Israel and abroad, and thanks to her I met some influential people in Israel. Apart from our annual meetings there, we used to meet when she came to visit on charity missions and she always welcomed me to her London flat on my rare visits to London.

## Israel and I — An Uneasy Co-Existence

Israel in the fifties was an odd combination of democracy and monocracy. It had a functional democracy with the conventional democratic institutions and, at that same time, was ruled by a monocratic party. MAPAI, the predecessor of the current Labour Party, held the majority seats in Parliament and wielded power in the National Workers Union as well as in the Health Care system. The powerful Workers Union owned heavy industry, a bank and major real estate properties. MAPAI's economic and political tentacles reached into each nook and cranny of everyday life.

Applying for a job within or outside the government required the prior approval of some mysterious entity. Though presumably unwittingly, the structure was modeled on the Bolshevik apparatus, adapted to the Israeli realities. This wasn't surprising, for the MAPAI leaders were the disillusioned children of the Russian Revolutions, who had jilted Marxism-Leninism for Socialist Zionism. Architects of the State, they identified the interests of the party with that of the State: what was good for the party was good for the State, to paraphrase Henry Ford's infelicitous epigram.

This monolithic socio-political situation greeted me as I disembarked in the Haifa port on my return to Israel. Finding a job turned out to be a difficult task. Without *protekcia* — a sobriquet for connections to the apparatus — the chances of landing gainful work were as promising as sowing seeds on the barren Judean hills. To weave myself into this pervasive *protekcia* network — the equivalent to the "ol' boys club" — I would have to join the youth wing of the MAPAI party, the old-timers counselled me. Apparently joining was a necessary condition to getting a job; but the prerequisite was to personally endear myself to the job's custodians. It was string-pulling time in Israel.

Though still in my mid-twenties, I was a veteran in juggling fate, so this sleight of hand should have been a bagatelle. My credentials were impeccable: I had volunteered to fight in the War of Independence; I had returned from England to join the Zionist Socialist enterprise; I swore fealty to the Party in power. Seen from a Zionist Socialist point of view I had enough points to qualify for a job — even to the secret service. And the time was just right, but not for a secret agent job. I was a certified radio operator, and right then the government, in collaboration with the Fishery Union, was opening a radio station in the Jaffa port. But I was still missing one crucial ingredient. This ingredient I found in a party functionary. A friend referred me to a cognoscente of Israeli local politics, who coached me on how to approach this person of significance.

Sitting in a relatively spacious office, the person of significance addressed me as *Chaver*. "*Chaver Eliahu*," he said to me, very significantly, "with your experience you must know new young immigrants; we could help them to integrate into the new life."

The subtext of this pregnant line was that he expected me to haul in young people to follow in my footsteps into the party. In other words, he designated me to become a party hack. I thought that fulfilling this mission would not require much creative imagination, and fortunately was not too far mistaken. I kept in touch with a few former Jalami detainees. What a shame that Yitzhak, my doctor friend, was at the time studying medicine in France. His serious demeanour would have impressed my benefactor.

When I approached my three fellow ex-detainees from Jalami with the proposition to accompany me to a couple of meetings at the MAPAI youth movement, they hesitated. They had already been spoken for by other parties. After my repeated explanations that they did not need to change allegiances, "just show up with me at the appropriate time to parade your presence," they agreed, though coyly, to present themselves. The ploy worked like magic. My three-month incarceration in Jalami was not in vain after all. At long last, I got the job as a radio operator, and a new era opened for me.

The Radio Station 4XT took me into the mainstream of Israeli life. The nature of the work connected me with the government and labour union bureaucracies, various suppliers, fishermen who came ashore, and of course shore men, who made up a colourful collection of specimens all by themselves. They would drop in at the station in inclement weather, smelling strongly of sea spray, for a chat and a cup of coffee. The discussions centred mostly on current political topics. Their party affiliation was with the MAPAI ruling party, which kept veering to the right. In the discussions, I took the leftist position, sometimes acting the contrarian, at times in order to keep the discussions flaring up and on rare occasions on principle. What offended me most was the ironclad grip that MAPAI had on society. Having been an object of arbitrary orders in those lands of the grotesque ingrained in me objections to absolute domination.

The MAPAI's party machinery was invasive and irritating. Curiously enough, the more I integrated into the broader Israeli society and the more my shares of the land increased, so to speak, the more I resented the latent MAPAI policy of assimilation. I had already experienced the prodding to merge into the Israeli mainstream on my first stay in Israel in 1948. On my return to Israel three years later the pressure to "be like us" increased.

## The *Sabra* Model

The rage of the fifties, into the late sixties, was to become a *Sabra* (the name was borrowed from the desert fruit that is prickly on the outside and sweet on the inside), a native-born Israeli who, like his fruit namesake, wore a rough exterior hiding a kind core. New immigrants received a warm welcome from the Jewish Agency and government officials in charge of absorption on their arrival. Flying banners accompanied by patriotic music greeted them as they disembarked from boats and planes. This was a time of the Ingathering of the Exiles, Isaiah's prophecy come true. But this miraculous multicultural gathering needed to coalesce into a social-cultural conformity. With Israel's enemies in wait to launch a second-round attack — as the Arab propaganda liked to call it — on the nascent state, accelerating the melting-pot process became a priority, and the young immigrants were expected to cast themselves into the model of the muscular, tanned, somewhat socially awkward *Sabra,* disposed to action rather than words, preferring the plough to the text, never flinching in the face of the enemy. In short, the *Sabra* and the *Sabarit* were the antithesis of the Diaspora Jew.

Exalted in the contemporary literature and adored by society at large, the *Sabra*, put up on a pedestal, became the national paradigm to be emulated. A newcomer to the country in search of an identity, I too aspired to emulate the paragon, or at least to dwell in its shadow. And as things sometimes happen, help came unexpectedly. My meeting with Rivka was providential.

Rivka was born into Zionism. She was just about finished with nursing school when, in the wake of the U.N. Security Council Resolution of 1947 to partition Palestine, riots broke out in the region. The Palestinian Arabs, with the logistic support of the Arab countries, launched a bloody attack against the Jewish community. Soon after the declaration of the State, Rivka joined the Israeli Defence Force and was assigned to the Shiba military hospital. It was there that I had met her on my first stay in Israel in 1948. I was visiting a wounded soldier, a fellow volunteer from Canada, who had lied about his age to enable him to "join the fight," as he put it.

A dyed-in-the-wool Israeli patriot, Lieutenant Rivka embraced us for volunteering for the Israeli army. Vivacious, smart and unique in many ways, she was surprisingly unoriginal in hawking the Zionist slogans with a fruit market vendor's enthusiasm: "Your place is here," and, pushing an old Zionist saw, she punctuated it in syllables: "Grow with the country's growth." I believe that she saw in me the potential to become "one of ours," a current phrase in those days. It was my Hebrew, which I made sound vernacular, and my simulated *Sabra* mannerisms that seem to have found favour in her eyes. When I called to tell her that I was returning to England to finish school, Rivka must have seen my departure as her own failure. To her credit, she did not load me with a guilt trip, but made me promise to look her up when I came back. She did not entertain the possibility that I might stay in England.

On my return to Israel two years later, I called Rivka. At first I was of two minds on whether to make the call. By now, she might have been married with children and I would be barging into her life. I waited until I had secured the job at the radio station. I rented a room in a less prosperous part of the city, in closer proximity to the workplace to which I bicycled for the day shifts. Finally, I felt confident enough to make the call. To my relief, Rivka's marital status had not changed and her Zionist passion had not been damped. She was now a civilian working in the same hospital, now as head nurse.

When we met again I soon found out indirectly that she harboured a partial curriculum outline for me, which in the course of time developed into a full-fledged educational programme. Notwithstanding her openness, she was not without guile, as I initially thought her to be, though that guile was in service of a good cause.

She had that rare knack for easily bridging time-gaps by bringing the past into the present. Still vivacious and still spicing her quick speech with an Israeli style of humour, Rivka told me rather sketchily about her life in the intervening two years: the break-up with her boyfriend Shlomo, her promotion, and what social activities she was engaged in. Of course, she was eager to know, or, as she put it, "dying to know" what made me come back. Falteringly, I tried to share my mental confusion with her. There was no rational motive for my decision to return to Israel. Rather, I had drifted to Israel in search of a motive. But how could I articulate this emotional turmoil with my limited vocabulary? I answered somewhat frivolously, "a change of climate; this might do me good." At the time I was unaware that my motives for returning were much more complicated. She smiled, intimating that she knew there was more to it than a change of climate.

Her immediate objective, as I found out, was to launch a makeover programme to convert me from a Diaspora Jew to a *Sabra*-like creature. One late afternoon, while leaning against the railings separating the beach from the street, she gently led me to the first makeover step. "'Eliahu' is a ghost figure that appears at the door at the Pesach Seder," she said. Prefacing her next line with a gesture, she held out her two hands wide apart to indicate distance: "It's too long." She suggested, "We cut it and just leave 'Eli,' short and crisp." The use of the first person plural "we" sounded odd, but I attributed it to her profession; the "we" was part of the lingo, like the morning-shift nurse greeting the quintuple-bypass heart surgery patient with a chirpy "How're we doing this morning?" I liked Rivka, I liked her a lot, but I was not sure about her feelings toward me. "Does she fancy me?" I ruminated in the common English phrase. Was this a deeply felt friendship or an infatuation, was it a kind of Zionist Salvation act or an act of aesthetics attempting to reshape an object *d'Golus*?

Cajoling replaced the sloganeering she had engaged in when we had first met in the hospital in 1949, which made conversation more pleasant. On reviewing the suggested name change, it occurred to me that "Rivka" was a common Diaspora name. Why then did her parents not give her a name drawn from nature, geography, or the like, native to the country, as was the custom in those times? Or more pertinently, why not apply the scalpel to "Rivka" the way she did it to "Eliahu?" I suggested that she change from Rivka to "Riva" when we met the following evening. "No, that won't do, it sounds like a quarrel." What about Rivee: an endearing name — it has a nice ring to it? Her usual expression of good humour suddenly clouded over. "All my siblings wear the names of family members killed in the *Shoah*," she said. "Rivka is my maternal grandmother's name. These are our only links to the past." I did not mention that "Eliahu" was my paternal grandfather's name.

At the beginning of our relationship, I misled Rivka into believing that I spent the war years in England. I did not actually outright state that I was a flight refugee. Rather, by a series of interlacing anecdotes and vague references to places, I wove together a narrative tapestry that told a story of escape from Europe with the *Kinder Transport* arranged by various Jewish agencies. This story became part of the identity I carried into my late thirties — in fact until I finished my doctoral dissertation. I kept my past ordeals from my friends and even from my wife and daughter. And not all my reasons for doing so were groundless, as I will discuss later.

My coworkers readily accepted my name change, but my distant cousins thought that I should retain the name "Eliahu" in memory of the family. Rivka praised the progress I was making in Hebrew, in which she justifiably took much pride. Her next move was sartorially-related. Looking over my wardrobe with a critical eye, she instantly dismissed half of it. "Your winter stuff is all right," she said, giving it a qualified approval, "but you've got to get new summer clothes."

We set out shopping. The word "shopping" should be taken as hyperbole. Israel in the late fifties was quite austere and the clothing choices were limited. Khaki trousers together with strapped sandals made up the fashionable wear, with a limited variety of shirts. I could afford these inexpensive items. Soon my appearance took on an Israeli caste. When putting my mind to it, I could take on the *Sabra* body language, facial expressions and general mannerisms. One day as Rivka watched, I looked in the mirror and a full-fledged *Sabra* looked back at me: suntanned, with a short-sleeved shirt hanging loose outside my khaki pants and strapped sandals on my feet. To complete my newly-reshaped appearance I mimicked an Israeli buying falafel from a stand: "Give me half with everything," I made a sweeping wave of the hand, getting an imaginary falafel from a street vendor. After receiving my order, I peeked inside the pita and said: "You've given me only three, Yoseff always gives four." "So why don't you go to Yoseff?" asked the vendor, bristling with contempt. "I give four only to soldiers." For the vendor I used a *Sephardic* accent, easily imitable. It was a thespian demonstration for Rivka. She stood behind me and burst out laughing. I had passed the test.

When the spirit took me, I could affect a host of accents and intonations reflecting the different layers of Israeli society. The immigrants from Poland in the thirties or the immigrants from Germany in the wake of the Nazi advent to power, for example; each one had its own verbal mannerism. The immigrants from North Africa had their own vocabulary, spicing up the language.

I realized eventually that if I wanted to become the real thing, I had to go beyond virtual reality. To make a genuine Israeli out of me, who had taken root in its cultural soil, the desire had to come from the inside. Rivka must have known that it was up to me to continue the process of assimilation. This was the hardest part. My mimetic skills could only lend me the appearance of a *Sabra,* so I decided to invest the appearance with reality, the affectation with substance. This would first and foremost require Hebrew immersion.

I had already been reading the tabloid *Yediot Acharonot,* but I realized that it would have to be supplemented by more serious readings, like Hebrew novels and a respectable weekend magazine. Going to see plays was also a boost to language immersion, as well as an entertainment that stimulated my thespian inclinations. The challenge facing me was to inject into my vernacular the multi-layered cultures embedded in the multi-layered Hebrew language. Any Israeli worth his salt was familiar with the Bible and the Talmud. You could easily tell a virtual Hebrew speaker, who had taken a crash course or picked up the language on the job, from a real one who was raised on Hebrew. The former was what could best be described as a one-dimensional speaker of functional Hebrew; the latter spoke it in a way that resonated through the annals of cultural history. There was another brand of Hebrew speakers derisively called *Maskilim,* derived from "Enlighteners," a reference to the Hebrew Enlightenment of the nineteenth century. They acquired the language at Hebrew schools and teachers' colleges in Eastern Europe before the war. Their Hebrew sounded like a recital of the Bible, and was derisively called "Shabbat Hebrew."

I went from borrower to leaser to what I had hoped to become: a Hebrew language owner, though the words would never evoke Mother's lullabies or childhood memories. Morphing into the proverbial *Sabra,* I gained recognition as an Israeli: perhaps not "one of ours" but neither "one of them." By the end of the process, I could pass as a genuine Israeli, but it took a while, a long while, to achieve this designation.

I found myself in the company of people with leftist leanings. Urbane and sophisticated, their Hebrew homegrown and further enriched by post-secondary education, these young intellectuals in their late twenties advocated a Zionist vision endowed with a progressive perspective. I was attracted to these people my age, who displayed a fine blend of idealism and humour, a humour not marred by millenial graveness. I was taken with their aversion to power, particularly the wielding of arbitrary power. Had they lived in Russia in the late nineteenth century, they would have joined the anarchist movement. It was comforting to be in the company of my spiritual kin. Their sympathy toward the Soviet Union earned my appreciation, as my feelings of indebtedness to the Soviet liberators had not faded with time. The image of the young soldier who had given my friend and me a ride to Prague and drove us to the hospital when we were sick was inextricably lodged inside me.

In the ill-lit spacious room which was the headquarters of the "Young Chapter" of the MAPAM party — a hard left Socialist Zionist party with a strong Kibbutz base and city factory worker membership — heated discussions raged till the wee hours, devoted to making Marxism compatible with Zionism. Inspired by its founding father Karl Marx, Communist ideology in its various metamorphoses perceived the Zionist movement as nationalistic and hence reactionary. I was fascinated by the casuistry exercised in trying to synthesize Socialism with Zionism. It seemed as futile an exercise as fitting a square peg into a round hole. Still the believers did not relent in their efforts, arguing that a truly socialist Israeli government would bring about a change in the Kremlin position toward Zionism and the State of Israel.

This encounter with the world of ideas generated in me an intellectual curiosity about Zionism and Socialism. The ideologues made sure that I had the proper books on the subject; ploughing through them required a lot of self-discipline. Assisted by the dedicated help of the girls, who took turns educating me in the ideological schism between Zion and the Kremlin, I was able to marginally take part in discussions on the subject. It was an intellectually exhilarating experience.

The girls' mums frequently invited me for dinners and when I'd be sick would bring me chicken soup. What was odd about it was that the mums rarely asked me about my parents and where I spent the war years. This was also true about the army, where I served a month in the reserve every year. By contrast, when I had first arrived in England, questions of this kind were part of the introductory conversation. Refugees bereft of family were such a common phenomenon in Israel in the fifties that questions of this kind became mundane. In Israel, you either made it and became part of the whole, or you would always be "the other."

In her book *1948 — Between Calendars*, Netiva Ben-Yehuda captures the general attitude toward immigrants in the staccato lingo of her generation: "We didn't ask the newcomers about their past. There was some kind of anathema about their experiences. The Diaspora is bad so you don't talk about it. They were blemished." And how does one remove the blemish? By shedding "his [the newcomer's] Diaspora mannerism and taking on the authentic image of the *Sabra*," Ben-Yehuda counsels, with tongue in cheek. Thanks to Rivka I peeled off the "blemished layers" of "the other," though, as I later realized, only the surface ones. And thanks to Sarah, my girlfriend, I put down cultural roots in the Hebraic ethos.

Unlike Rivka, Sarah was not inclined to inculcate me with Zionism for Zionism's sake. She looked at me as a person whose growth into Israeli-hood required time and care. Though utterly patriotic — and, like other teenagers, she had carried messages for the *Hagana* underground during the British Mandate — she did not spin out template Zionist slogans. She had been a very successful message carrier, incidentally: her braided, blond, shoulder-long hair perfectly complemented her blue eyes, and the two together projected a calmness that fooled the Tommies guarding the check posts. They just waved her through, assuming she was on her way to buy milk.

I first met Sarah at the leftist group meetings, where we would engage in small talk, lightening up the grave issues of the debates. During a demonstration in support of the sailors' strike in the late fifties, Sarah and I walked side by side holding hands in a show of unity, as instructed. When the tumultuous applause died following a rather long speech at the end of the march, I asked Sarah whether she would like to come for a walk along the *Yarkon* street beach. As we dragged our bare feet through the warm beach sand, Sarah told me about her underground errands without a hint of bravado. Her high school classmates also took part in different assignments in the struggle for independence. I got a detailed description of the *Yishuv*, or the Jewish community in Palestine, during the critical 1945-48 years as it made its way to statehood.

When my turn came, I shared my fictional Kindertransport story with her, claiming I'd come to England just before the war. It sounded credible. When we next met at the group meeting, Sarah kept an empty seat next to hers ready for me, and I walked her home after the meeting. She attended the "Levin Teachers College" and had an early class. In the course of the next few months we engaged in a song-and-dance wooing game. We went to the theatre, and though the plays were straightforwardly realistic, reflecting the realities of the fifties and early sixties, I missed quite a bit of the dialogue, which Sarah filled me in on during the intermission. She also advanced my musical education. As I've mentioned, Yitzhak, the frog-dissecting nurse at the Jalami prison, had initiated me into classical music, mainly the loud and dramatic symphonies by Beethoven, Tchaikovsky and other Romantics. In Jalami, we would sit in his crowded room sipping tea and listen to the melodies being emitted from his gramophone till late at night.

Sarah, however, thought that chamber music, which she considered the jewel of the crown, would further refine my taste for classical music in general. The director of the Chamber Music programme was a family friend and gave her free entrance to the concerts. In the nascent Israeli Museum on Rothschild Boulevard in Tel-Aviv, flight refugees from Germany and Austria filled the small auditorium to capacity. Apart from their attire, nothing about them hinted that they had ever left the Rhine River for the Jordan River. They held on to German culture with the passion of neophyte lovers. They conversed in German, took their respective seats with deliberate German courteousness — even their spoken Hebrew had a German sound to it. Chamber music was not just a cultural event; it was, indeed, an affirmation of the *Kultur* they had left behind in the wake of the Nazis' rise to power.

Once I became part of Sarah's life, the free entrance privileges had to be renegotiated. After I was introduced to the Programme Director, he looked me over and apparently liked something about me, and I was cleared to continue attending the concerts. We would usually sit on the stony steps. Whereas Sarah was totally immersed in the performance of the quartets, trios and duets, my head alternated between swivelling around to the various paintings on the walls and stilling itself to observe the ladies fanning their perspiring faces in the muggy Tel-Aviv evenings. My auditory system seems to have had a hard time making the transition from symphonies to chamber music, but the bane of my musical experience was Schubert's *Lieder*, which met with fervent enthusiasm from the audience.

In one of the Lieder concerts, after having explored the paintings innumerable times, observed the fanning ladies and the wincing facial expressions of the soprano, I ran out of distractions. But lo and behold, a fly buzzed forth from nowhere and landed on a patron's glistening pate. The patron swiftly waved the irritant away and it took off and settled on another shining head. My eyes suddenly caught a forest of domes in a variety of shapes in the auditorium. By the time the fly finished its rounds, the concert came to an end. Amidst the thunderous clapping of hands, the fly either met its death or merely hid to lie in wait for the next concert. Despite occasional bumps in the road, eventually I did become a devotee of chamber music — to Sarah's delight.

By now I was considered, by myself and by my peers, an Israeli in the making. My literary Hebrew improved immensely under Sarah's tutelage, as did my music skills. I was moderately active in the political life of the country. To further complement my integration, I felt it necessary to get to know intimately the lay of the land, which meant following in the footsteps of the Biblical and Second Temple heroes and vicariously reliving their triumphs and defeats. I was not the only one who thought in these terms: in some miraculous way that signified national memory, these places still bore their original Hebrew names in Arabic forms. Thus, exploring the country marked initiation into Israeli adulthood, assuming the ritualistic character of a Bar Mitzva.

Since I missed these rituals, the cross-country walks that were part of the youth movement's focus, I suggested to Sarah that we tour the country. Ritualism was far from Sarah's mind; her sensibilities were shaped by cultural values. Crisscrossing the country on foot with the view to seeing historical landmarks would enrich me culturally and would give me an understanding of the Hebrew idiom and its linguistic ramifications. Rivka would have framed the tour in strict patriotic terms. For Sarah, however, it was a hike into the country. At that time the Judean hills were under the Jordanian rule, so we had to settle for a trip to the Galilee, once a flourishing community in the aftermath of the Bar-Kochba Revolt.

Equipped with food, water, a map and a sten gun, we set out to the Galilee. It was spring, a fitting season for tracking its ravines, hills and mountains, and we met other young couples and small groups hiking the country. From the brief encounters we had with them, I could tell that they were not out on a reconnect expedition with history; rather, they took advantage of the clement weather and the Passover vacation for a pleasant hike. I came back a more integrated Israeli.

The Jewish community in Palestine had been passionate about archaeological excavation long before the establishment of the State, but its archaeologists were geographically limited under the British Mandatory rule. Now it developed into a national pastime, at times verging on the obsessive. The children of Zion were digging up the past so as to reinforce their historical link to the land in their own eyes and in the eyes of the world. On our tour, I was deeply impressed with the digs we chanced by. They provided tangible proof of the historical research that described the volatile fortunes of the Jewish Galileans over hundreds of years. At the time, it did not occur to me that these archaeological passions that gripped the Israelis were, in addition to methods of reconnecting with the Jewish heroic past, reactions to the Diaspora martyrdom tradition. I was swept away into the assimilation frenzy to the point of self-obliteration. I avoided meeting fellow-survivors of my age and similarly did not openly observe Shoah Remembrance Days. Auschwitz was not in fashion in Israel in the fifties.

## The Other

In 1952, David Ben-Gurion, the first Israeli Prime Minister and the founder of the State, and Konrad Adenauer, the first post-war Chancellor of Germany, signed the *Wiedergutmachen* Agreement, under which, among other clauses, the Jewish State would be compensated for the destruction of European Jewry.

This agreement sparked a fervent national debate between the right-wing and left-wing political parties, each basing its position on moral grounds. While the right argued that any payment from Germany was "blood money" and called for a boycott of Germany, its rivals on the left evoked the Biblical injunction, "thou murdered and inherited?" In this bitterly fractious controversy, which went so far as to be accompanied by violence, Holocaust survivors, who then comprised approximately a third of the population, were not asked on what side of the divide they came down. Their mute voices were a telling sign of how Israeli society and its political and cultural institutions treated the eyewitnesses to the events that were the cause and reason for the agreement. Marginalized, they were mentioned in *sotto voce*, as if the speaker was referring to a deformed relative.

The Israeli ethos evolved in a fiery struggle of existence, battling the swampy and arid land and implacable foes, and found it hard to accept the survivors, who had not demonstrated similar mettle in confronting their enemy. The only survivors upon whom honour was bestowed were the armed resisters. All the rest remained "the others." And when the billions of dollars came pouring into the country following the agreement, the monies were invested in the development of infrastructure and industry; the survivors' well-being was not factored into the budget allocation.

The shadow of neglect that fell on the survivors manifested itself in many walks of life. One of the egregious areas of neglect was in the field of psychiatry. Shamai Davidson, a Scottish psychiatrist, immigrated to Israel at about the time the German reparation agreement came into effect. He was astounded at the lack of awareness in the medical profession concerning survivors' needs, and by the corollary that there were no appropriate psychiatric facilities to meet the specific needs of the survivors. Frustrated, Dr. Davidson went to the United States to fundraise and to start basic research on the subject. While the survivors were languishing in transit camps, the Israeli custodians of the German restitution money did not find it necessary to allocate a budget for building housing accommodation for them; nor did they allow money for training young survivors to meet job market demands, or grant scholarships to those who aspired to get post-secondary education or even secondary education. We were left to fend for ourselves, and many of us succumbed to gnawing loneliness and feelings of abandonment.

My disguise as a flight refugee rather than a survivor saved me from being branded with an, "Oh he comes from there," and made assimilation easier. It is mainly for this reason that I did not apply for *Wiedergutmachen*, which would have given me a monthly pension. I craved assimilation to the point of oblivion. I also wholeheartedly believed in the psychologically redemptive character of the Jewish State, which, transformed the image of the passive Jew, waiting in line to walk up to the sacrificial altar, into the new Jew with rifle at the ready and plough at hand.

The Israeli Parliament passed a law of Remembrance in 1953, but as before, so after the legislation, sacral-ritual ceremonies propped up by canned speeches marked the Days of Remembrance, and the newspapers ran their routine editorials and repetitive radio programmes. Since I exiled myself from the survivors' community, I was not privy to the commemorations taking place behind closed doors. Survivors, comrades-in-suffering from the ghettos, the concentration camps and the Displaced Person Camps, met in small circles in their homes to give expression to their anguished memories. On this day, in my room, I would light a memorial candle for my mother, its flickering flame rhythmically reviving the image of her unclasping my hand from hers and ordering me to run for my life. When the flame died, the image receded into a nightly whirlpool of images. The following day I would again wrap myself in my Israeli disguise.

For five years or so, my intellectual and spiritual home was the youth chapter of the left Zionist MAPAM party. As I improved my knowledge of Marxist dialectics and Zionist history, I increasingly took part in the ideological discussions. My scattered knowledge of Freud's writings, acquired during my short stint in Jalami prison, helped me negotiate these stormy discussions. I was the beneficiary of two rabbinical minds: one analyzing trends in human history, the other dissecting the human psyche — both demonstrating shifts in human behaviour.

Despite the feeling of closeness with my co-believers and their radical social and political ideas, I was reluctant to formally join the party, and remained a fellow traveller. My reluctance derived from the personality cult of Stalin, which caught up with all the international peace crusaders inspired by Moscow. Mordechai Oren, a leftist Zionist with impeccable Marxist credentials, was invited to the International Peace Conference in Berlin in 1952. On his way back to Israel he stopped in Prague with the purpose of securing the release of a few of his fellow party members who were accused of collaborating with Rudolph Slansky's anti-Communist spying ring. An easy prey, Oren got netted in that fabricated plot as well and was charged with espionage.

I had read Oren's articles and attended some of his lectures, in which he steadfastly endorsed Moscow's position vis-a-vis the West's. I ascribed his arrest to an unfortunate bureaucratic mistake. Surely, soon the truth would come out and he would be released, I argued when the topic came up with my political adversaries. When Oren was eventually freed and returned to Israel, he wrote a book describing his ordeals. Hard on the heels of Oren's episode followed the 1953 accusation of the Jewish doctors who allegedly tried to poison Soviet leaders. These incidents caused the first fissures in my belief in the redemptive value of Communism. The fissure widened into a clean break from Marxism when I read Khrushchev's speech at the Twentieth Congress of the Communist Party in 1956, at which he exposed the criminal nature of the Soviet regime.

Even after the passage of over fifty years, right now, as I am putting this down in writing, I still feel the pain caused by the precipitous let-down I felt upon seeing Khrushchev's speech. This is what the idol worshipper must have felt upon realizing that his gods were made of clay. Khrushchev came closest to the patriarch Abraham and to Paul of Tarsus, the two iconoclasts who ushered in monotheism — though the latter with significant concessions to the reigning paganism of the times.

During those emotionally rocking days when realization hit me — that the Communist redemption was a sham; that my expectations that Socialist forces would free humanity from Capitalist indenture turned out to be hollow; that Peace sloganeering only served to rally masses around Soviet aggressiveness — it plunged me into despondency. I had invested much hope in Marx's redemptive ideology and it had come to nought. Sarah and I talked about these events. She was still hesitant to make the break. Ironically, these let-downs brought us closer.

With wooing taking its course and the gentle prodding of Sarah's brother-in-law making itself felt, we began contemplating marriage. The logistics involved were simple: Sarah and I had incomes from our respective jobs that would enable us to save money for purchasing a small apartment. In the interim, we would move in with her parents, a prospect I obviously did not look forward to. There was, however, one foreboding hitch. According to state law, Jewish marriages have to be registered with the Orthodox Rabbinical Courts, which acted in compliance with the Talmudic rules. One of these rules was the mandatory immersion of the bride in a *Mikvah* administered by a female, who would supervise the immersion. Sarah regarded this ritual as demeaning. "I'm taking daily showers. And for the wedding, I'll immerse myself in a hot tub," she quipped. She adamantly refused to take the *Mikvah* plunge.

When we were sitting in the waiting room at the rabbinical offices to be called in for an interview, I casually mentioned to Sarah that I would like to have a few words with the interviewing Rabbi concerning the water immersion issue. She did not mind but doubted its outcome. When our turn came, I asked to see the Rabbi separately. Relatively young, sporting a short beard and possessing a pleasant demeanour, he asked me what my concerns were. His Hebrew was a normative Israeli vernacular that indicated that he was the product of the new generation, Rabbis more attuned to the secular Israeli mores. The Rabbi's tutored eye immediately identified my spiritual provenance. The way the black *Kippa* was sitting on my head and my rather loose-hanging attire signified that I was not an adherent of the faith. "Rabbi," I exerted my most reverent voice, "it's about my bride. She won't go to the *Mikvah*; please help me." To my utter surprise, the Rabbi smiled; it was an understanding smile. "Why? It only takes a few minutes, and the *Mikvah* lady is considerate," he said. I summarized Sarah's upbringing in *"Shomer Hatzair,"* a youth movement that mixed Marx with a heavy dose of Freud, underpinned with Borchov's Socialist Zionism — all these more akin to paganism than monotheism of any creed. Similarly, her high school *Tichon Chadash* was steeped in anti-clericalism. The Rabbi asked the secretary to usher in "Ms. Ribowski." The interview was short and perfunctory. I thanked the Rabbi for his sympathy and walked out bouncing in joy. Sarah too was relieved. "How much have you paid him?" she asked. And in the same jocular spirit I said, "They'll garnish my salary for the next six months."

## The New Day's Rhythm

Man cannot live on bread alone, say the Scriptures, and I felt a need to fill the spiritual vacuum left by the fall of Stalin. Sarah thought that I should enroll in a university part-time; there I might find answers to my relentless questions, or at least get a better sense of my Judaism. I agreed. After all, I had suffered for the sole reason of being Jewish, so it would make sense to find out the sources of that hate that had been visited upon my forbears and had subsequently robbed me of my adolescence. Bar-Ilan University, with its Orthodox character, was conducive to my search for answers.

Entering into the environment of the religious Bar-Ilan University was akin to being introduced into a new culture. Though everyone was amiable, an invisible line of demarcation separated the male and female students, and a kind of first-date shyness hung between conversing parties who might have known each other for many years. While sitting on the campus lawn in a mixed-gender semi-circle cramming for exams, the male students sat in a group, facing their female counterparts, and the two groups kept a respectful distance from each other. Only glances, like Cupid's erotic arrows, were exchanged between them. I am left to assume that after arrows, there must have been more intimate traffic between the genders. The day was portioned out by rituals: the morning prayer,[12] *Shaharit*, and the early afternoon prayer, *Mincha* — both in remembrance of the sacrifices performed in the Second Temple. The third prayer, a late addition and not Temple-related, was *Maariv*, Vespers. Of course there were blessings before and after meals, along with less formal rituals. I had maintained my life thus far thanks to my ability to adjust to abruptly changing circumstances, and so blending into this new environment did not entail too much of an effort.

At the beginning I found the prayers intriguing and at times meaningful, but after I had been attending them for a while, my mind started wandering from the text. The prayer became routine, and the phrases repetitiously monotonous. I looked around and wondered what percentage of the people present prayed with their mind focussed on the meanings of the words and what percentage was mumbling perfunctorily. To put the prayers in a historical context, I signed up for a course on "The Development of the Prayers," given by Professor Joseph Heinemann, a renowned scholar of liturgy. His work in placing them in context, as well as providing a rationale or them, proved immensely helpful.

The two subjects that interested me diverged from each other, but since I did not intend to follow an academic career and planned to hold on to my radio operator job, I felt free to indulge in my whims. I was attracted to the era of the Second Temple and the aftermath of its destruction in 73 A.D, the traumatic turning point in the destiny of the Jewish people, and I was equally drawn to the malignance manifested in Elizabethan and Jacobean drama.

What interested me about the Second Temple era was the dissenting group of Jews — later labelled Judeo-Christians — who drew their inspiration from Jesus' teachings and gave him the title of Messiah. But it was Jesus' personality that I was taken with. His deep compassion for the poor combined with his rebellious nature rekindled the ideals which had been lost in the wake of Khrushchev's speech. Asked by Caiphus, the High Priest, whether he was the Messiah, Jesus stared him down, saying: "You've said it." He gave an identical answer to a different question, this time from Pontus Pilate, the Roman procurator of Judea. Pilate's concern was political rather than religious. "Are you the king of the Jews?" asked Pilate, to which Jesus answered again: "You've said it." A foe of the hypocritical priests and the

---

[12]    The Jewish Orthodox practice is to hold prayers three times a day.

Roman tyrannical occupiers — one he dared in court, the other in a fortress — he castigated the rich and provided for the poor; he healed the sick and resurrected the dead. These characteristics aroused my admiration. Was there a historical Jesus or was he a composite of many young radical Galileans who roamed the countryside? These issues did not bother me. It was the ideals embodied in his personality that fascinated me.

Equipped with the knowledge acquired by poring over the New Testament and the other related works that were accessible to the intellectual capacity of an undergraduate, I set my mind to getting as close as possible to this young Nazarene. Riding on my motorcycle, I crisscrossed the country in search of monasteries, which the Holy Land was plentifully blessed with. What struck me was the number of Jewish converts to Catholicism who eventually had taken the vow. A substantial number of the converts were involved in some manner with the Holocaust. Those who agreed to talk to me about their experiences told me that they had found peace in Jesus and his teachings. By then I knew enough about the Hebrew prophecies to wonder what Jesus' teaching offered that the prophets missed. While I shared with my former fellow Jews the emotional immediacy in encountering Jesus, we parted ways on one crucial point. To them, Jesus was the Son of God and Man, the expiator of our sins and the eventual harbinger of redemption; to me, however, he was a historical figure inadvertently instrumental in a spiritual paradigm shift in human history. In his attempt to transform conventional perceptions, he was a forerunner of Galileo. Had he been alive nowadays, Jesus would have been nominated for the Nobel Peace Prize. Of course, I did not divulge my heretical views about Jesus to his believers.

## The Temptation of the Cross

The question of religion brings up an earlier recollection. After Liberation, when my trip to my hometown in search of surviving family had ended in failure, I had kept on looking for family in Displaced Person camps in Germany and Austria. I'd also kept on inquiring about Menachem, whose memory stayed with me. The same rails on which sealed cattle cars had run, loaded with human cargo destined for destruction, barely three months earlier, now held passenger carriages carrying human beings in search of salvaged lives. In both cases, we got free rides.

The designation "Displaced Person Camps," is woefully lacking in descriptive accuracy. The people residing in them were not refugees of earthquakes and floods or of other disasters brought about by nature. They were victims of man-made destruction. Uprooted from their homes, they had drifted to these camps hoping to put together their shattered lives, using the places as a kind of pontoon bridge over which they could scurry over to sanity. Resilience, imprinted on their genes through centuries of persecution of their ancestors, stood them in good stead. As determined not to submit to spiritual extinction as they had been resolved to resist physical destruction, the survivors of the Manquake resuscitated their lives by drawing on the rich Jewish tradition and culture. It was truly a moment of spiritual resurrection in the mode of Ezekiel's prophecy.

While the majority of the survivors held on to their ethnicity and religion in defiance of the Nazis' dark designs, a considerable number of survivors distanced themselves from the Jewish communities and from Judaism. These were mostly parents with young children who had been hidden by the Righteous Among the Nations during the war. They did not want their children to keep on bearing the yellow-starred triangle that had become the mark of Cain. Unlike the convert-monks, however, they did not accept Jesus as their Saviour; their alienation from Judaism was a reaction to the failings of the Emancipation that had swept Western Europe in the nineteenth century: the triumph of religious bias and the failure of human progress. The Second Coming Church Dogma predicated on the Jews' acceptance of Jesus turned out to be fallacious. In the aftermath of the Holocaust, many of those Jews who abandoned Judaism did not do so to fall into the embrace of Christianity; they did so to excise the Deicide stigma branded on them by the Church, which undeniably contributed to the virtual destruction of European Jewry. I had actually met such a family in Munich while randomly travelling across Germany, soon after liberation. At that time I was too bewildered to form an opinion on this issue of assimilation.

My travelling buddy and I had stumbled into Munich and needed a place to stay overnight. By chance we met a refugee who directed us to a house of refugees who might be able to help us. A man, and a propped-up cross on a mantelpiece, greeted us. The room was cluttered with Christian icons and children's toys. The room had the unmistakable appearance of a household in transit. The man was visibly Jewish and carried a sprawling Auschwitz number tattooed on his forearm. His ready hospitality indicated that he recognized our shared concentration camp history. He must have seen the bewilderment on our face as we took in the room's decor. Pointing to the cross he said, "It's for my grandson." In a weary voice he continued to tell us its background.

Just before the deportation of their town, he and his daughter had found a shelter for the three-year-old boy with Christian friends. They knew that if the boy's mother did not survive, he would be baptized into Christianity. Both the grandfather and the mother had survived, however, and had returned for the boy. As expected, they had found him totally estranged from his family and immersed in the Christian faith. He had not wanted to part from the people whom he considered to be his parents. Even as we listened to the story, mother and son came back from a walk in the nearby garden. The mother joined in the conversation. They were still of two minds as to what to do. We looked to them K.Z. (concentration camp) poster persons, and they must have felt that we'd understand. "Should we impose on him our suffering or just bring him up as a normal person?" the mother inquired of us.

Decades later, when researching a history seminar paper at Bar-Ilan University, I had an opportunity to revisit this situation when I met with Carmelite monks who had been born Jewish. They brought back fleeting memories of my own doubts about my relation to my religious and ethnic origins. The thought of melting into the vastness of humanity had crossed my mind more than once. A Freudian might have interpreted my decision to go to the maritime school in King's Lynn as motivated by a desire to leave my Jewish heritage behind me. But what I was certain about was that my choice to attend an Orthodox Jewish University was prompted by a deeply felt need to invest my Jewish identity with substance. Similarly, my dogged pursuit of the truth about the Jewish Nazarenes and my fascination with Jesus were driven by a passion to understand the Jewish-Christian schism that had bred into a culture of animosity, an animosity that had destroyed innumerable lives.

My extended and detailed seminar paper did not provide the answers I was seeking. Nevertheless, I got a better understanding of the divide between the mother religion and its Christian progeny along with its tragic ramifications. My professor, Moshe Bauer, a newly minted doctor of Hebrew University, was proud of me; my dedication to the project impressed him. Upon my mentioning that I was looking forward to presenting it to our seminar, the professor demurred. "Not yet," he said. Looking me straight in the eye, he added, "I'm up for tenure and there're some covert black hats" (a derogatory name for Jewish religious extremists) on the committee who might take exception to your paper's subject-matter." Though disappointed that I could not take on some of my fellow students, for whom Jesus and Judeo-Christians were anathema, I fully sympathised with my tenure-anxious professor. My pugilist impulse would have to wait for other occasions. This was also my first lesson about the politics of academia.

# Harold Fisch — My Patron Saint

Parallel to pursing the emergence of the Jewish Christian movement, inspired by Jesus' charismatic personality, I signed up for a class on English literature with an emphasis on Elizabethan and Jacobean drama, taught by Professor Harold Fisch. A Cambridge graduate and a scion of an Orthodox Jewish rabbinical family, Fisch seemed to elegantly straddle both worlds. He espoused the Creation as described in Genesis without rejecting the Big Bang theory, holding that both appealed to different human facets. Though not engaging in missionary pep talks either in class or on campus, he would nevertheless have liked his students to see their way to Heaven.

Sporting a goatee that sprouted from a face covered with stubble, he strode the campus grounds projecting a contemplative aura. When in a thespian mood, he turned the class floor into a stage upon which he acted out the dramatis personae at hand. With the open text serving as a stage prop, Fisch would simulate the scene in which the stooped Lear lugs Cordelia's corpse offstage amidst a dying whimper. As if with a magic wand, he could transform a text into a dramatic moment: voice modulated, body language shaped, facial expression delineated–all working in tandem to take on the role play of the moment. Macbeth, shuffling his feet across the floor, mumbling, "Out, out brief candle," brought home the futility of ambition and the unalterable fate of man. He was apt at doing comedy as well as tragedy; Fisch's Malvolio, strutting the floor while reading the letters supposedly from his mistress, sent the class into bursts of hilarity. Sometimes I came to his classes exhausted after working a nightshift at the radio station, but his analyses, burnished by histrionics, kept me awake. I made up for my sleep deprivation in other classes, where I vacillated between a nod and a wink. Indeed, theatre's loss was academe's gain.

Fundamentally, the evil that hunted me down and hustled me into cattle cars that hauled me into a penned land absent of cause and effect — that same evil, in different permutations, drives the characters of the Jacobean plays. They are mostly fuelled by irrational impulses. Ferdinand of "The Duchess of Malfi," for instance, is stirred by jealousy and fear of tainting the family's blue blood, and has his sister, the Duchess, killed. But on seeing her dead body, he utters the famous line in a strange mixture of remorse and regret: "Cover her face; my eyes dazzle."

Archival documents report that after a day's slaughter of men, women and children, the Nazi killers were plied with alcohol to calm their shattered nerves. I am not comparing the conduct of the Jacobean dramatis persona with those of my tormentors, either the SS men or their collaborators. Rather, what I'm suggesting is that the evil that stalked me sprang from the same muddy source as the one that motivated the characters of the Jacobean plays, namely the dark side of the human condition. The analogy that comes to mind is attending a funeral procession, which naturally evokes intimations of mortality; by the same token, viewing a Jacobean play brought back to me intimations of a concentration camp. My everyday life encounters and the events happening globally reinforced my views that this malediction ingrained in the human species afflicts society when contributing socio-political conditions occur. The following story, told to me by Rabbi Brumur of Toronto, is a case in point.

The year is 1961 or thereabouts. Adolf Eichmann is on trial in Jerusalem, his state of mind a subject of psychiatric inquiries: is this man in the booth, watching the newsreels showing piles of emaciated corpses shoved into collective pits, clinically normal? Has he regrets, and does he admit to being part of the death machinery? Or is he a psychopath incapable of human sympathy? Rabbi Cyperstein, a known Talmudic scholar, who is teaching a course in Talmud at the same time at Yeshiva University in New York, naturally takes an interest in these questions. One day he comes to class in a despondent mood. "The psychiatrists have established that Eichmann is normal," he says, "and this frightens me, because I consider myself normal and therefore capable of committing atrocities as Eichmann has done," he muses aloud to the astonishment of his listeners. "What shields my humanity from degeneration," Rabbi Cyperstein continued, "is my faith in the Torah."

Rabbi Cyperstein's deductive reasoning was validated by the so-called Frankfurt Denazification trials, at which scientists, physicians, and defrocked clergymen stood in the docks accused of genocide. The killings raging on the European and African continents in the last two decades of the twentieth century and at the dawn of the twenty-first century put to mockery the slogan "Never Again." It's a delusion to believe that people learn from history, and the delusion is easily dissipated by watching the evening news on television. The optimistic futurists may predict that bio-scientists may be able to implant a new gene in humans that will thwart their aggressive impulses and perhaps convert evil into the milk of human kindness. Professor Harold Fisch, like Rabbi Cyperstein, saw the skull beneath the skin, to quote T.S. Eliot, and I saw the skull insignia attached to my SS tormentors' hats.

Whether it was the emotional immediacy of my responses to his presentation of the dramatis personae in action or other aspects of my personality, Fisch must have intuited that I'd had an intimate rendezvous with evil. As Fisch and I drew closer, thanks also to our shared love of the sea, I was tempted to tell him about my encounter with Man's malediction, but inhibitions held me back. I wanted to be judged on my own merits and not on the basis of my experiences. If the experience factored into the sum of my merits and subsequently afforded me insights into the human psyche, I considered it a by-product. Fisch undoubtedly influenced many of his students, but on me he left a lasting impression. He would present an issue, generating questions that invited answers which in turn stimulated new questions. This made for a discourse of intellectual inquiry that led to new levels of discovery. He had a gift that combined inspiration and challenge.

For all his seriousness and depth, he had a mischievous side to him, a trait often manifested in class and outside of it. In class, he often played to the gallery, so to speak, and at parties entertained his listeners. But a gift he passed on to me which has proved invaluable was the knowledge of how to formulate questions. When the spirit took him he could spice his analysis of a text with subtle ironies, sardonic comments and a colourful range of humour. I still remember one of his gibes aimed at curbing my flight of the imagination in interpreting a certain text. "Mr. Pfefferkorn is often original," he enunciated, sprinting a couple of steps onto a low pedestal, "but equally often wrong." The chuckles of my fellow students indicated approval. The gibe was like music to my ears, an acknowledgement of my presence; others, however, smarted under them. And then came my opportunity to have my own little jest at Fisch's expense.

The Jewish tradition observes two Dionysian festivals: One is Simchat Torah, which celebrates the giving of the Torah to the Israelites at Mt. Sinai; the other one is Purim, which celebrates the saving of the Jews from persecution in ancient Persia. Consuming liquor in abundance, dancing to the point of dizziness and singing with full-throated enthusiasm mark both festivals. These are times of merriment. Purim is also a mask festival that allows the celebrants to masquerade and do parodies. Its counterpart would be Halloween.

Purim also provided an occasion to take on the professors who, in the course of the year, enjoyed immunity from parody due to the hierarchal structure of universities. The girls in the English department took it upon themselves to organize the Purim party and asked me whether I would do Fisch. "His outstanding physical characteristics and eccentricities," they pointed out, "make for good parody." This was true, and I felt that Fisch deserved a gentle dig, but prudence weighed in against the opportunity to show off my thespian skills. "But there are other students whose body build and height are more similar to Fisch's than mine," I argued halfheartedly, "and some of them even grow stubble and goatees that resemble his." "No, no," they insisted, inserting a flirtatious tone into their persuasive efforts, "you're a natural for this." Few mortals would remain indifferent to such flattery coming from pretty maidens, their playful eyes squinting in the early spring sun. I finally succumbed, but not without apprehension.

I knew that my thespian reputation was on the line and was not sure how Fisch might take it. I went into character, as the fashionable cant had it, and moulded myself into Fisch's persona, body, psyche, mannerism and intonation. And on that angst-inducing evening, I walked into the small auditorium mimicking Fisch's inflection and stride, carrying a pile of papers and all wrapped up in musings, lifted my eyes and uttered one line: "I'm awfully sorry, this must be the wrong class," to which a rehearsed group of students shouted in unison: "No! No! This is the right class."

I turned on my heels and walked out. Lights off! When the lights came back, I was standing at the podium, text lying open on my palm, reciting from Macbeth's banquet scene the moment that Macbeth notices Banquo's ghost making his second entry:

> Avaunt! And quit my sight! let the earth hide thee!
> Thy bones are marrowless, thy blood is cold;
> Thou hast no speculation in those eyes
> Which thou dost glare with!

I chose this charged scene because Fisch excelled in its performance when teaching the play. And it was a felicitous choice. The sketch received an ovation and I left the podium in Fisch's long strides amidst peals of laughter. Even as I, surrounded by a ring of congratulating fans, wondered how the subject of my parody took it, Fisch threaded his way through the crowd and, patting me lightly on the shoulder, murmured, "Good show, Eli, good show," words delighting my ears. I had finally earned my thespian feathers.

We lived in the same suburban neighbourhood and would sometimes run into each other. One late Sunday afternoon, I met him not far from the synagogue that he belonged to. After a short exchange of customary pleasantries, he remarked casually, "I don't think I saw you in the Shul yesterday," a shade of a sardonic smile forming on his lips. Without admitting my transgression, I replied, "I usually go to the other Shul." Fisch often indulged in tongue-in-cheek pastimes, and I was delighted to respond in kind.

Fisch's strict Orthodoxy matched his radical politics. A founding member of the movement "The Greater Israel," which claimed the Land of Israel from the Mediterranean Sea to the Jordan River, he pursued his political goals with the same passion that he held for his faith. In both politics and religion, I diverged from him. But whereas his politics were intolerable to me, his Orthodoxy intrigued me. The repetitious glorification of God in His multiple attributes of ubiquity, omnipotence, omniscience, compassion — among other endowments — immediately conjured images of being trucked in cattle cars. It was then, at the time when thirst had blunted hunger, when the biological instinct to go on had given in to despair — it was then that I had cried out for His redemptive powers to make their presence. The emerging images rendered the prayers meaningless. When we prayed in the same place, I would give Fisch a sideways look. Wrapped in the traditional prayer shawl and attended by a rhythmic sway, he wholly submerged himself in prayer. I envied him. I too wanted to gain peace of mind through acceptance of the Divine and submission to His decrees, but the past weighed too heavily on me. God's attributes did not help me in my time of need.

I encountered a similar reaction to redemption many decades later in Toronto, where we lived in an ethnically mixed neighbourhood. My family was in Italy, taking in the Renaissance marvels, leaving me to my own culinary devices. On a hot Friday afternoon, I went to the supermarket to get some food items to tide me over for the weekend so I would have time to finish the play I was writing. As I came out from the supermarket carrying one meagre bag, I noticed a young woman, unseasonably dressed for the weather, holding a bunch of pamphlets and greeting shoppers with a question: "Are you Jewish? Are you Jewish?" After having identified the religion of the person in question, she thrust a pamphlet into his or her hand, accompanied by a commanding voice: "Read about the Messiah, He is coming." When my turn came she gave me a quick glance and didn't ask, declaring in the affirmative with stress on the "you," "You're Jewish." She stuffed a pamphlet into my hands and without much ado immediately turned to the next shopper. She seemed to be in a hurry, presumably heralding the Messiah's coming not far ahead of his intended arrival.

Something in me abhors millenial fervour of any creed, secular or religious, be this The Coming of the Messiah, The Second Coming, or Communism. (I should like to note that the Rabbis of the Second Temple took Messianic tidings with a grain of salt, to use an understatement.) This woman's demonstrable self-righteousness underlined by self-assuredness brought out the mischief in me. I obviously look Jewish. In the season of lights and goodwill, I am always greeted with "Happy Hanukah," never "joyful Christmas." Despite my visibly Jewish appearance, I asked her why she thought that I was Jewish, and making it more complicated, I added: "I may look Jewish but I could have converted to Christianity or Buddhism, God forbid." The "God forbid" trailer was a signal that I kept the faith. "I knew all the time that you were Jewish," she said. Quoting a Talmudic ruling in Hebrew which indicated that "a life-threatening situation supersedes the Sabbath" — meaning that one is allowed to breach the Sabbath Laws — I asked her whether "the coming of the Messiah also supersedes the Sabbath?" What followed my question was totally unpredictable. She darted a look at me full of fury and in colloquial Israeli Hebrew pronounced these memorable lines: "I know your kind," she intoned, her eyes fixed on me, "it's more like you, holding back the coming of the Messiah. Go home, wash up, and get ready for Shul." And to show that she had no bad feelings toward me, she wished me "Shabbat Shalom," the customary Israeli salutation on Sabbath eve. From the corner of my eye, I noticed a man standing in the shade observing the scene.

Even as I walked away from the place pondering this bizarre exchange, I noticed that same man catching up with me. He asked me in English whether I understood Yiddish and, turning his arm to the inside and saying "it's here," pointed to an unusually big Auschwitz number tattooed on his arm. "When I needed Him, waited for Him, prayed for Him, He didn't come. So what do I need Him for now?" In answer to my question of what had made him stand there, he told me that he was curious to hear how people would react to the coming of the Messiah. He shrugged his shoulders in resignation. "People, what do people know?" I would have wanted to continue the conversation, but I was emotionally overwhelmed by his reaction to the Messiah's messenger. It struck a deep chord in my memory.

Strangely enough, I was thinking of "*Waiting for Godot.*" First staged in the 1952-3 season, in Paris, the play had captivated audiences worldwide and swiftly became a subject of study at university drama departments. Attuned to the human psyche, Samuel Beckett drew on a religious yearning for Messianic redemption and transformed it into a dramatic metaphor. Estragon and Vladimir, the two characters of the play, are waiting for a Mr. Godot, who keeps on putting off the impending meeting through a boy messenger, but continually promises to come next time. Consequently, Estragon and Vladimir dangle between despair and hope. Here is an exchange between Vladimir and Estragon that encapsulates the tension between waiting and coming, promise and breach:

Estragon: Oh, yes, let's go far away from here.
Vladimir: We can't.
Estragon: Why not?
Vladimir: We have to come back tomorrow.
Estragon: What for?
Vladimir: To wait for Godot
……………………………….
Vladimir: We'll hang ourselves tomorrow. (Pause.) Unless
Godot comes.
Estragon: And if he comes?
Vladimir: We'll be saved.

Estragon and Vladimir sound like two dropouts from the Habbad-Hassidic movement masquerading as buffoons; the movement's founders made the coming of the Messiah an inconvertible article of faith. "Even if He tarries, He shall come," they sing in frenzy.

A friend of mine, who prodded me to commit my experiences to paper, has given the manuscript form of this book minutely critical reading. His major criticism was that I cut off the narrative flow by what he called intellectualizing. He conceded, however, that my occasional philosophical digressions allow me to gain a perspective that enables me to view the Holocaust within the wider context of the human condition. From this point of view, I could see the concentration camp and the behaviour of the SS as well as the inmates, notably the elite inmates, the *prominante*, as an extension, though twisted, of what was known as normal society. Ultimately, what we are depends on where we stand in the pecking order of society. Thus the homeless person bundled up sleeping on a steaming grill views life differently from his fellow creature who sleeps through the night in the comfort of his or her bed. Similarly, the ghetto resident looking over the fence had a perspective darker than that of the Pole freely roaming the streets, though both lived under occupation. And the concentration camp inmate reduced to a tattooed cipher felt differently from both.

I wish I had seen the implicit connection between *"Waiting for Godot,"* and the eschatological implication that informs this play, as well as other plays of the Theatre of the Absurd, while still studying under Fisch. He would have liked the idea of the Judeo-Hebrew influence on modern sensibilities. His seminal book, *Jerusalem and Albion: The Hebraic Factor in Seventeenth Century Literature*, as well as his other published scholarship, indicates his intellectual inclination. He identified the presence of the "Hebraic Factor" in literature, most notably, as indicated in the subtitle, in the literary seventeenth century sensibility.

### A Subject of Interest

My last year of studies was drawing to an end. Because of the academic pressure, I had to cut my working hours at the radio station, and I supplemented my income by moonlighting.

A neighbour of ours mentioned to me that he needed some private lessons in English. It was a God sent chance. Over the course of our tutoring sessions, we became friendly. He was an engineer and worked for the Israeli Armament Industry. He told me that the plant management was looking for a teacher of English to tutor a group of engineers bound for England, and asked me whether I would take the job, which I readily agreed to do. But since the course would take place on the plant grounds, I would have to have security clearance: "just a formality because of the sensitive nature of the plant." Those were the Cold War years, and the Eastern Block, siding with the Arab countries, had become their major supplier of arms. Israel, justifiably, was apprehensive about security breaches. But I was confident that I had nothing to fear. As far as security reliability went, I had a clean slate. I had veered away from my leftist leanings three years earlier, in the wake of the famous Khrushchev speech in 1956; had switched from *Al-Hamishmar*, a left wing daily, to *Haaretz*, a respectable moderate newspaper; had found myself a house in a middle-class neighbourhood; attended a religious University; and to top it all off, I was the proud owner of a Vespa, nothing to sneeze at in the Israel of the early sixties. In short, I was a budding bourgeois. So when I received the telephone call inviting me to "come to the *Quirya* for a conversation" regarding my job application, I took it at its face value, as a "conversation."

On a drizzly afternoon, at the appointed time, I rode on my Vespa to the *Quirya*, the location of the major government offices, for my appointment.I parked my vehicle under an awning to protect it from the rain and, raincoat dripping, entered the office, without first being vetted by a receptionist. Three men in their late forties and early fifties, drinking tea from glasses, greeted me. They made no bones about enjoying their measured sips. The man sitting on the right got up from his chair, took my wet raincoat, hung it up near a burning gasoline stove and brought me a hot glass of the beverage, generously sweetened. The atmosphere was cozy and the people amiable. The one sitting in the middle introduced himself as Alex, and the two others also introduced themselves by their first names. The sixties in Israel still had traits of a pioneering country, its life-style simple, its socializing informal, and its communication stripped of circumlocution, sometimes at the expense of civility.

Alex came right to the point, explaining the reason for inviting me. Addressing me as *Haver*, in keeping with the communitarian spirit of those days, Alex described the security situation of the State; that the Soviet Union had been trying to breach its security by planting spies in sensitive security positions. He then opened a file and spun out a litany of my political activities for left-wing causes, my association with subversive people and my professed sympathy for the Soviet Union. Most of the information they collected about me was general and needed no intensive snooping to attain it. Still it was flattering to be a person of interest to the *Sherut Habitachon*, Security Service. "How many of my classmates back at the university could boast of such attention?" I mused. My self-importance grew in my own eyes. One piece of information, though, that required close sleuthing, I resented.

"We've here a report that you went to *Rishon-Lezion* to meet Nissan," Alex read from the file — month, date and hour, all minutely recorded. Nissan was a hard-core Communist who envisioned a world revolution, inspired by Moscow, which would ultimately redeem humanity of its ills. Due to his extreme ideology, Nissan was expelled from his Kibbutz and lived with his parents. Penniless and out of work, he had once asked me for a loan. Apparently, Nissan's liberal interpretation of communal sharing did not jibe with mine, and when he was tardy in repaying the loan, I broached the subject with his father. It was for this purpose that I had gone to *Rishon-Lezion*.

Alex and his colleagues were waiting for me to explain the contradiction between my avowed severance of any links with Marxist ideology and its advocates and my connection with the subversive Nissan. Patiently, I explained to them that I had met Nissan at the Kibbutz of which my girlfriend was a member. At the time, we had shared similar political views. They seemed to accept my explanation.

I looked at these three men, their faces weatherworn, their hands covered with calluses. These people had tilled the arid land in the day and had guarded their outpost settlements at night; they had laid the cornerstone of the Jewish State and subsequently its foundation. They were dreamers with their feet planted in the soil of the newly redeemed land. Now, they had donned the mantle of the State's Guards. Their intuitions honed by experience, their intelligence endowed by nature, they were the salt of the earth, and also, undoubtedly, loyalists to the ruling party. I felt a lot of respect for them and I was getting to like them. They knew that I was no more a rebel with a cause than a church choirboy, and that I had gone through a social class metamorphosis. My newly acquired bourgeois status was documented in the file, and yet they persisted in probing me. But why would they do this? They were following a script: "Pfefferkorn may have moved on," they must have been thinking to themselves, "but one must make doubly sure; one must be so careful these days."

The earlier drizzle had changed into rain, and though I was ready to leave, I knew that if I did, I'd just have to stand under the awning until it cleared up. And the Nissan affair annoyed me. So I thought I would take them on, playing the game by their own rules. "Have you ever looked into the Prime Minister's endorsement of the Peel Plan of 1936?" I asked with a straight face. By their expressions, I could tell that my question had caught them off guard. "As you know," I continued, enjoying their bemusement, "the opposition on the right, the Revisionists, considered the Peel partition plan a sell out and they considered Ben-Gurion a traitor." They were catching on, and smiled. "But the same man, David Ben-Gurion, in the fullness of time, when the political constellation was favourable, declared an independent state."

By now I have seen enough of my professors' mannerisms to assume them. I fumbled in my breast pocket, groping for my glasses with the purpose of putting them on to give my lecture gravitas. Alas, they were in my coat. "Suppose, just suppose, that human beings did not change, that their consciousness had been frozen since coming of age. You would be out of a job. Alex, here, could be the custodian of the files, come in the morning and dust them off from time to time, have a cup of tea and then go to the beach — weather permitting." They recognized the ironic tone of my monologue and seemed to be amused. These people had a sense of humour that further endeared them to me. In keeping with this light mood, the taciturn one asked me whether I was taking Talmud at Bar-Ilan. I answered, "I'm right now missing an important Talmud class." We shook hands and I told them that I was withdrawing my application, because I did not want a shadow following me. "What if I get involved in some untoward act or commit adultery? There would be no chance of hiding my transgression," I said. And as an afterthought I threw another verbal punch: "With you guys shadowing me from the comfort of a car, I'd have to look over my shoulder while riding my Vespa, and that could be dangerous."

They were openly amused. Considering the weather, I was increasingly less so: I would have to ride back to my classes on the wet roads. On my way out, Alex politely asked me not to talk about this meeting, which was regrettable since I would have liked to share it with some of my friends back at the university during the long breaks. I could have retold the story with much gusto, perhaps written a little piece for the student newspaper, with the mysterious title: "Nothing is that is Not." But this was not the end of the episode.

About two years later, while riding on the top of a double-decker bus in London, I noticed a familiar face half turned toward the street. It triggered immediate recall. I slid across the aisle and sat next to the person. "Shalom, Alex!" I greeted him in Hebrew. *"Ma Nishma*, what's new?" His head jerked from the window toward me, eyes blinking with recognition. "Pfefferkorn! It's Pfefferkorn," he uttered, surprise written all over his face. "What you doing here?" he asked. Acting out a secret agent role that I had picked up from the movies, I glanced sideways at our surroundings, supposedly making sure that no one was eavesdropping, dropped my voice to a whisper and, ever so slowly, lingering on each vowel and stressing every consonant, I said: "I'm shadowing you." His face cracked into a broad smile. I would have liked to chat some more with Alex, perhaps ask him what status my file was now, but he got off at the next stop, wishing me *"Kol Tuv*," all the best. I hope his departure was not on my account.

## The Lure of the London Stage

After graduating from Bar-Ilan, I went to London in 1965 to study linguistics. This field was all the rage at the time in academia. At parties and in the university cafeterias, professors of literature and languages discussed the subject over coffee while puffing pipes, leaving trails of smoke in their wake. Academics have the skills to engage in earnest discussion on a topic with an appearance of expertise after having read an article or two on the subject. Modern linguistics took on a life of its own. I was intrigued by this new field, the excitement of its discovery, and its intricate methodology, which afforded insights into the way languages work. I broached the subject with Fisch. Unlike his colleagues, he did not pretend to know much about linguistics, yet he was quite receptive to the idea. By this point, my wife and I had a five-year-old, Vered, so relocating to London even for one year was complicated. We pulled together our resources and, with Bar-Ilan's support, we set out for England.

The course, entitled "Systematic-Functional Linguistics," and headed by professor Michael Halliday, drew students from the European and American continents. There were also some Englishmen returning from the British Commonwealth to their homeland in the wake of growing nationalism in the countries they had immigrated to decades earlier. It was an interesting group of people, and their mix of cultures and languages generated stimulating discussions that allowed for observation of the function of languages in a social context. The subject interested me, the group of students was engaging, and Professor Halliday was stimulating. I was, however, distracted by the allure of the London stage. While studying the Elizabethan and particularly the Jacobean plays under Fisch's tutelage, I would stage the plays in question in my imagination, construct the props, and arrange the entrances and exits of the characters. But the performances that I saw in London transcended the limits of my imagination. The gracious ease with which the actors moved on the stage, their melodious diction, enchanted me. Cutting-edge technology allowed the directors wider freedom in interpreting the play, as it was influenced by contemporary scholarship. Consequently, they transported the tempo of the Elizabethan and Jacobean periods onto the stage, giving them a modern perspective and yet being careful not to tamper with their authenticity.

While studying seventeenth-century plays with Fisch, I had intuited similarities between the plays' characteristics and the concentration camps' traits. Now watching the performances on stage, where the words were fleshed out and the characters became tangible, my intuition assumed a cerebral clarity. I saw with deeper lucidity the crossover of human behaviour from conventional society to the concentration camp environment. If the dynamics of the Jacobean drama intimated a siege environment, the Theatre of the Absurd evoked a semblance of the Holocaust.

The Theatre of the Absurd made its presence felt on the London stage in the fifties and sixties, with lasting effect on dramaturgy. One of its striking components was the severance between cause and effect — behaviour does not yield expected results. Precisely. This phenomenon plagued the ghetto resident and particularly the concentration camp inmate, and now I saw that it also appeared in the Theatre of the Absurd. Language was divorced from ambience. Thus, for example, Pinter's characters drink water and talk liquor lingo heard in pubs. Likewise, in Ionesco's plays, synchronization between word and action collapses amid farce in the shuffle of the chairs. These cognitive dissonances are fuelled by a crafted irrationality that moves in circles rather than leading to a resolution. The cumulative effect created by this dynamic was that of weariness and anxiety in anticipation of something happening that does not happen. It is as if the characters' faculties acted separately from and against each other.

Watching the performances from the security of my theatre seat, I experienced a sensation similar to that of having a nightmare. I was ejected into wakefulness, and memory started reeling out the nightmare images. The purposelessness, the ennui, the unpredictability, and the hovering threat — these haunting remembrances melded with the drama unfolding on stage. The malignance driving the Jacobean theatre, and its unshod absurdity, reinforced my dark vision of humanity. Strangely enough, I could watch the ferocity of the Jacobean theatre with some measure of dispassion, but I could not always distance myself when viewing the work of some of the Absurdist playwrights — Pinter, to mention one dramatist of many. The drama taking place on the stage was too close to home.

Doubts began nagging at me: did my observations, filtered through a dark prism, have validity, or were they subjective impressions derived from abnormal historical circumstances? Would an informed theatre audience see the resemblance between the Jacobean theatre and the Theatre of the Absurd? Furthermore, would they see that these two dramatic genres, drawn from a common humanity, were linked, though tangentially, to the human condition? Partial answers to these questions I found out later.

## Humouring the Jewish Agency

Meanwhile, I pursued Linguistics but invested my greatest energies into formulating my Master's thesis. I thought that establishing a sensibility link between the Jacobean and the Absurdist dramas was challenging enough without the intrusion of the Holocaust. I was short of time and money — two commodities whose absences had been the bane of my existence. Since making time *ex nihilo* is the purview of the Almighty, I felt that it was my obligation, as the family provider, to find additional income. I landed a part-time job at the Youth Department of the Jewish Agency. "Your responsibilities are to raise Zionist consciousness," pronounced my prospective employer from behind his large desk. His tone and mannerism were those of a public speaker. It did not take much time to identify the type, prevalent in Israel.

A political hack who failed to get elected to the Knesset, Moshe Gilboa had been given the position of Youth Director in the U.K. by the ruling party until a vacancy was made in the Knesset. What I understood by "raising Zionist consciousness" was "convincing Jewish youth of the correctness of the Zionist cause." This I tried to do two to three times a week, mostly in the East End London Jewish clubs. I would show films about Israel, play Israeli songs, and tell stories about the country. The teenagers preferred darts, billiards and ping-pong games to education about Israel.

It was in this spirit that I wrote my first monthly report. Here are some excerpts from it:

> The young people who come to the clubs have not been brought up in Zionism. This is their first encounter with the story of Israel. Nominally Jewish, their interest in the Jewish tradition is limited to the High Holidays. Despite the pedagogic difficulties ahead of us, it's a worthwhile project that should be further encouraged.

Sober and slightly embellished, but evidently not enough to meet Gilboa's expectations. An urgent message awaited me at home one day to immediately see Moshe Gilboa. On entering his office, I noticed my report lying on his desk. "Look, Eli," he said in his simulated authoritative tone, "with this report, Jerusalem will scrap the project." He held the three-page report in his hand, leafing through the pages and quoting from it. I was getting the drift of his intent. "Look, I don't want you to lie, but put together the report as we envision the situation in four or five years." The noun "vision" in multiple permutations was a staple of his vocabulary. As instructed, I wrote a visionary report predicting "the steady growth of the education programmes' population. One should see these young people as potential *Olim*." I also threw into this brew some Jewish Agency lingo: "They will grow with the growth of the country, the future generation making history," in an echo of Rivka's cant. Admittedly, it was written on the rosy side, a prognosis of a promising future. Moshe sighed. "It's not believable, it's too good." Noticing the frustration spreading on my face, he said soothingly, "Look here, don't worry, I've a practical solution. Find a middle course between the two reports," he said. This was precisely what I did, and concocted a report drawing from the first and the second, mixing vision with realism. It was the right concoction that found favour in the eyes of my employer and in the eyes of my employer's employer in Jerusalem. I came away from this farcical episode equipped with a greater knowledge of the inner workings of a bureaucratic structure.

### The Fateful Sukkah Meeting

Two months prior to our return to Israel, I sent Fisch the first draft of my thesis: "The Disfigured Image of Man in the Jacobean and Modern Drama." Himself an original interpreter of texts, Fisch encouraged his students to go out on a limb in their writing. Predicated on this assumption, I had reason to believe that he would like my thesis. He greeted me in his office and we chatted awhile. Yes, he had read my first draft, but "found it a bit farfetched," he said with a consoling smile. "Too much of a leap." The three hundred years separating the two eras seemed to bother him.

Naturally, Fisch's response to my thesis was disappointing, to say the least, and I wondered whether I should not follow my initial instinct and return to my radio-operator's job. After all, I came to the university to find my Jewish feet, so to speak, to get an understanding of why I was deprived of my youth; why my people were the world's pariahs. My fleeting musings were interrupted. "We have a chap here from Brown University on Sabbatical. I'd like you to meet him." He invited my spouse and me to his Tabernacle or *Sukkah*, a makeshift booth that commemorated the wandering of the Israelites in the desert. On our arrival at Fisch's home, we went straight to the *Sukkah*, where he introduced us to Rosalyn and David Hirsch of Providence, Rhode Island. Their complexions indicated that they were recent arrivals indeed and had not yet been exposed to the Israeli sun. He strategically seated me next to David. They were settling in with the help of their neighbours, and their rented house was in our neighbourhood, a fifteen-minute walk from our own home. Amidst the hum generated by the conversations across the table, Rosalyn asked me how long I had lived in Israel, following up with a second question on where I had spent the war years. To the latter I answered laconically, "In Europe," and Rosalyn shrewdly noticed that I was being evasive. Just before taking our leave, David mentioned in passing that Fisch had given him my thesis and that he was looking forward to reading it.

Normally, the rejection of a Master's thesis was no reason for redirecting one's career plans. These things happen all the time and M.A. candidates move on to new topics. My case, however, was different. I felt both an emotional and an intellectual commitment to the premise that the dark side of human nature occupied the Jacobean plays as well as those of the Theatre of the Absurd. To see the common source that fuelled these two historically divergent dramas required, perhaps, a leap of the imagination, but I felt the flow of human evil sprang from the same source. And at the back of my mind lingered a question as to whether one had to go through a traumatic experience — similar to the one I went through — to see the serpentine path intersecting these two drama phenomena. I was therefore waiting with trepidation for Hirsch's telephone call. It came on a muggy evening just before my bedtime. "I've just finished reading your draft," he told me on the phone, "I liked it on the whole, but it still needs some tinkering." We arranged a meeting for Saturday afternoon in the neighbouring national park.

As soon as I put down the telephone, I started counting the days and the hours remaining before the scheduled meeting. I expected to see David

Hirsch carrying my slim thesis under his arm generously sprinkled with comments and profusely underlined. But my expectations did not tally with his intentions. He came empty-handed. Swinging his arms sideways, as was his usual manner, he strolled through the gate to where I was waiting for him. After a brief accounting of how the family was settling in, David navigated the conversation toward my war years.

Apparently he and Rosalyn had been speculating about my whereabouts during the war, but instead of asking me directly, he only mentioned that his wife, her mother and her aunts were holed up in a hiding place at a peasant's house in Poland for about two years. Her father did not make it. This piece of information put a new complexion on our conversation. He went on to explain that when Rosalyn, then in her teens, and her mother had arrived in New York, they had found accommodations in Brooklyn not far from the Hirsch family's home. David had volunteered to teach her English, and after a short tutorship had married her.

A natural storyteller, Rosalyn's mother shared with David riveting stories about their experiences. His interest in the Holocaust grew exponentially as he met more survivors through Rosalyn's family. After receiving his doctorate in American literature, David obtained a position at Brown University, where he taught American literature. After a while, he fashioned a course on the Holocaust in literature, offered in the English department. This took me by surprise. Teaching a course on Holocaust literature at an Ivy League University in the sixties was a pioneering act. The subject was at that time hardly recognized in academia, nor was it popular in the mass media in the United States. David inadvertently anticipated a trend that evolved a couple of years later. Obviously, he related these anecdotes with the purpose of making it easier for me to talk about myself. I had to overcome a series of emotional hurdles to throw open a past that I always held at bay. So I opened up a crack just wide enough to indicate that I had trust in him. "You see, Israeli society is ambivalent about the *Shoa*. They like heroes, not martyrs." I gave him a thumbnail review of the Israeli attitude toward the Holocaust, an attitude that at times verged on alienation toward the survivors. David listened to my short lecture with incredulity. "But the Holocaust vindicates the Zionist ideology," he rightly observed. "The events prove that the Jews have to take destiny into their own hands. When Rosalyn asked you in the *Sukkah* where you spent your war years, you dodged the question. Why?"

"I've many reasons for masquerading my past. One day, I'll share my thinking with you. It's rational," I assured him.

Imagine, two people sitting on a park bench on a Saturday afternoon assuming reversed roles: the one with a life experience veiling it in silence; the other, with knowledge derived from books and stories garnished from survivors, further transmitting them through an educational tool. The irony of this situation did not escape me. Indeed, it was curious: a closeted survivor in dialogue with a vicarious survivor. To make himself a credible narrator, David had to shorten the perspective of the events; I, on the other hand, to make my ordeals bearable, had to distance myself from them. Consequently, we viewed the Holocaust from two different points of observation. On the way back from the park, I briefly recounted to David my experience in Fisch's seminar on the Jacobean drama and my discovery of the Theatre of the Absurd on the London stage.

At the time, the Holocaust was hardly a social topic discussed in the living rooms on Friday nights, when Israelis customarily got together and reviewed (and griped about) the week's events. The passage of time created mental space for the survivors to talk about their experiences among themselves, making sure that their children were out of earshot. My milieu, however, was made up of my fellow students at Bar-Ilan and fellow workers at the radio station. I did not seek the company of survivors. I even avoided meeting the London hostel boys and girls who had immigrated to Israel. It was almost a decade after graduation when I finally managed to find my way through this psychological labyrinth. Until that point, I believed that if I wanted to make it in academia I needed to unshackle myself from the past, or at least view it dispassionately as much as possible. At a certain point I must have decided to pursue my academic goals assiduously. I say "I must have" for it was not a conscious decision of the "go, get it" kind. Rather, it was of the meandering kind you don't notice until many years later.

Fridays were the appointed days when David and I met officially to work on my thesis. At the same time, we indulged in creature comforts, for Friday happened to be the preferred day to satisfy David's cravings for freshly baked pastries and an assortment of breads. He was a cake and *Challa* connoisseur. He picked the pastry with a surgeon's precision and an epicurean's passion. His choices would elicit conspiratorial winks from the sales person at Kapulski, one of the pre-eminent bakeries of Tel-Aviv. The aroma of the Kapulski Bakery, we were told, had once filled Nalewski Street in Warsaw. This was not unusual; Tel-Aviv boasted cafés and bakeries whose provenances were European countries ranging from Vienna to Warsaw to Kraków. It was an aficionado's delight, a cosmopolitan display of bakeries, shapes, tastes and colours — a paradise for the senses. It took me back to my incarceration in

Jalami prison eighteen years earlier, when our guards, returning from weekend furloughs, brought with them homemade cakes representing the various countries their mothers hailed from.

Loaded with assorted cakes and *Challa* for the Sabbath, we sauntered down to the beach where we sat down under a café awning to shade us from the sun and had our first pieces of cake, washed down with au lait coffee. This mini-ritual was followed by a review of my thesis. David was considering one or two chapters for publication in an academic magazine. The review provided a natural point of departure for a wide range of topics for discussion, which usually veered toward my wartime experiences. David's quest to learn about my survival reminded me of my walk with Jonathan on Hampstead Heath twenty-one years earlier. But unlike Jonathan, for whom the concentration camp universe was suffused in the apocalyptic images seen in Brueghel paintings, David knew its granite facts. He had a panoramic view of the Holocaust thanks to his voracious reading of its history and the literature of memory written by survivors.

It was a painfully slow recall of my ordeals that I shared with him, though I related only those that pertained to the specific subject under discussion. Since our families met socially, I asked David not to mention to my spouse where I had spent my war years. This request struck him dumb, and it took a while for him to regain his speech. "It's that I want to be judged on my own merits, without crediting success or imputing failure to my experience," I explained. Nor did I want people to attribute my often volatile behaviour to my tortuous past, but this I did not mention. I dreaded the moment when people might be nodding their heads, saying: "Oh well, you know, he went through hell, we must be forgiving." Ironically, many years later I found out that Sarah had known about my wartime history for years, and wisely chose not to bring it up or tell our daughter until I did. My Friday conversations with David were an enriching experience not only intellectually but also psychologically. Inadvertently, they loosened up some of my tangled memories, making my nightmares easier to bear.

### My Brother — Yusuf

In May of 1967, President Abdel Nasser marched a division of Egyptian troops into Sinai, blocked the Tiran Straits and unleashed a barrage of radio propaganda predicting "the end of the Zionist entity." This had a particularly traumatic effect on survivors and their children, who comprised about a third of the population at the time. A siege mentality gripped the country. Between

May 16 and June 5, known as "the three-week waiting period," the country braced itself for the imminent onslaught by Egypt, Syria and Jordan.

The habitually bustling Dizengoff Street in Tel-Aviv, dotted with sidewalk cafés and boutiques, was shut; long lines stretched out in the supermarkets. An eerie stillness descended upon the cities and villages, a kind of taut-nerved stillness waiting to break open at any moment. The shadows of doom crept back into my traumatic nightmares. I bore the shadows in silence.

Every historical event generates folklore and anecdotes. One of my own experiences gives an inkling of the country's mood at the time.

Amid the increasing tension, rumours spread that Arabs perched on roofs of the hilltop village houses were eyeing Jewish property below on the coastline. The Israeli press carried statements by the P.L.O. Chairman, Achmad Shuqayri, declaring open season on Israel. He made no bones what he was planning to do. Against this ominous background, Yusuf, our gardener, knocked on our back door one early morning. As usual, he spoke in Hebrew but saluted me in Arabic. "Hawadia Eli," he said, somewhat timidly, "I've come to collect my tools and the pay from last time."

Yusuf and his extended family came to our Ramat-Gan suburban neighbourhood to tend the gardens. On hot days, I would invite him in for a drink of cold water and Turkish coffee. At twenty-one, he wanted to marry and have his own family, as was the village custom. Our conversations were short, for he had work to do to, as he put it, save money for a dowry and "God willing build a wing attached to my father's house."

We walked down the steps toward the shed where he had left his tools. And then he stopped abruptly, his lazy eye fixed on me, his other darting about, and said: "Eli, you're my brother, and nothing will happen to you." I did not ask for further elaborations, nor did I need them to understand or follow Yusuf's promise of protection. That was the first time in our acquaintance that he'd called me 'Eli,' omitting the deferential 'Hawadia,' and said 'you're my brother,' not 'like my brother.'"

I was deeply disturbed by his statement. His words stirred murky memories of promises broken even by well-meaning Christians to give shelter to their Jewish fellow-citizens. Still, I felt Yusuf meant what he said, without, of course, realizing its effect on me. I did not share this episode with my wife, and luckily, I did not have to put Yusuf's brotherly loyalty to the test.

A couple of weeks later, after the dogs of war were reined in, Yusuf came and asked whether the garden needed work. This time he greeted me with the customary "Hawadia Eli." The recent intimate moment in the garden was replaced by the distance between victor and vanquished. His demeanour projected a subdued mood. His parting words of concern at our last meeting nibbled at my mind and I broached the topic. "Tell me, Yusuf," I said gently, "What happened to the Egyptian army?" He looked at me in disbelief, "You don't know…you don't know," his voice betraying agitation. "Mr. Dulles gave Hakim Amer, right in his hand, 5 million, perhaps 10 million." And to drive home this shocking news, he grabbed the palm of my hand and simulated the act of the money transfer.

I was amazed at the fast working of rumours — the grain of myth. That Field Marshal Abdul Hakim Amer, a son of the Egyptian revolution, would betray his country for money was beyond belief. What made sense was that Amer, the architect of the 1967 war, committed suicide in the aftermath of the defeat, and that the myth mill quickly went to work to shift the blame for the rout from the army to its Commander-in-Chief. But it would have been useless to try to disabuse Yusuf of this notion.

I felt the tide of my puckish disposition swiftly rising. "This is true, I've heard it on the BBC," I confirmed, "but how do you know it?" I wondered aloud.

"Our elders know everything," he replied with a hint of pride. We were standing in the garden in the scorching sun. I needed a cool head to be able to come up with something more shocking than the bribing of Marshal Amer. I invited Yusuf to the house for a cold drink of water. We both needed it. Mustering a naïvely affected expression, I asked Yusuf whether the village elders knew about Abdel Nasser. "What about Nasser?" he asked his voice strained with anxiety. Drawing out the "Well…" as long as vocally sustainable, I said, "Nasser has sent his family to Switzerland but himself is still in Egypt." And to make this news credible, I referred him to his reliable source of information: "Ask your elders, they know." At the time I had no clue that just then, in the heat of the day, in our tiny kitchen in the presence of my adversary and well-wisher, I was stitching one more thread into the Six-Day War myth tapestry.

A few of days later, I was called up for reserve duty for fourteen days. When I returned home, my wife told me that Yusuf was looking for me. I ran into him the following day in the street. He was on his way to work. "Hawadia Eli," he greeted me with exaggerated respect, "you're right, the President sent his family to Switzerland, but only for the summer, and they will soon return."

I did not dare to question the factuality of this news item, spun in the coffee shop where the elders congregated to sift truth from fiction while sipping small cups of bitter black coffee. How did this canard find its way into the deliberation of the elders in the coffee shop? I could only speculate, using deductive reasoning, how it had gotten a foothold in the village.

On the way back to the village, while riding in the truck, Yusuf must have related my information to the others. On their arrival home, they walked to their houses and on the way met their neighbours, to whom they imparted Yusuf's story as heard from "the professor," as they sometimes called me. By the time Yusuf showered, ate supper and went to the coffee shop to check out the latest news, the tale had already transmigrated there. Thus Yusuf became the loom of a myth spun by me, though modified to save President Nasser's face.

### In the Aftermath of the Six-Day War

A tremendous sense of relief swept across the country in the wake of the unprecedented victory over three Arab armies that closed in on Israel from the South, North and East. Only the Mediterranean Sea on the West remained open. Together with the victory celebrations, manifestations of jingoism seized the country. Confronting this chauvinistic intoxication, sobering voices were heard in the progressive media, revealing cool-minded Israelis who had not lost their historical perspective. One of these voices found its expression in a collection of interviews titled *The Seventh Day*,[13] and in its translation into English: *Soldiers Speak*.

The interviewees were combat soldiers who had come back from the war. One, named Menachem, tells of his uneasy feelings being part of an invading army, a victorious army, a powerful army:

> If I had any clear awareness of the [Second] World War years and the fate of European Jewry it was once when I was going up the Jericho road [Arab] and the refugees were going down it. I identified directly with them. When I saw parents dragging their children along by the hand, I actually almost saw myself being dragged along by my own father.

Menachem's sentiment resonates throughout the interviews, which covered a spectrum of emotions. Two events had a lasting emotional impact on another soldier, Yariv, and both provided an insight into his Jewishness, rather than his "Israeliness." When they heard of the conquest of Jerusalem,

---

[13] Avraham Shapira, ed., *The Seventh Day: Soldiers' Talk About the Six-Day War*. England: Penguin, 1971, pp. 216-217.

"There wasn't a single one who didn't weep, including me. Then, for the first time, I felt not the 'Israelness' but the Jewishness of the nation."[14] The other event was the time when his unit had to evacuate the inhabitants of a village. He could not do it. "When you come to carry out an order like that, you have a very uncomfortable feeling. The Arabs said to me not once, but two or three times, or more: 'Leave us to die here.' And it's very hard, simply on the human level.

I could not stay in the field, I took my jeep and drove off, there and back."[15]

These two events reveal Jewish consciousness on a high level. Yariv became preoccupied with this new-found Jewish identity, which clashed with his Israeli one, but hoped that "perhaps, they'll eventually come to some sort of resolution."

Unlike Yariv and the other interviewees, I did not experience dual identities in opposition to each other. My Israeli identity, though proudly worn, was after all an implant. Shadows of barbed wire, not the Galilee mountains or Sinai desert, hovered over my mental landscape. No matter how much I made an effort to blend into the Israeli background — and by appearance and language I could almost pass as an authentic Israeli — there was this invisible separation line between "them" and "me." Ironically enough, it was the images of barbed wire and watchtowers, a reminder of what might happen to a defenceless people, that narrowed the space between "them" and "me."

These nightmarish ideas brought back memories of helplessness, that third plague, next to hunger and cold. The sight of the Israeli flag fluttering on the Golan Heights, from which destruction had rained down on Israeli residences in the valley for decades, reassured me and vindicated the Zionist ideology that advocated a militarily strong Jewish state. Similarly, I took pride in the self-assured strides of the combat soldiers on return from the battlefields. True, there was bravado in their bearing and even a hint of bluster as they related their stories. But I took these to be the inevitable manifestations of the tasks of fighters who literally carried the fate of a people and a country on the brink of extermination. As Yariv put it succinctly: "Extermination: We got this idea — or inherited it — from the concentration camps." Surely, at the time Yariv's was still a minority voice, but it eventually became that of the majority.

---

[14] Ibid, p. 220

[15] Ibid, p. 220.

My views in the wake of the Six-Day War victory assumed a somewhat modified perspective during a guided bus tour of the captured territories. (I advisedly use the word "captured," for they were originally meant to be bargaining chips to be swapped for peace — a policy known as "Land for Peace.") The people on the bus, from what I could tell, were representative of the liberal part of the population, mainly academics and their families or academics in progress like myself. What I observed among the Arab population was despair. My attempts to engage people in political conversation were met with silence or evasion. No, it was not fear; rather it was resignation, the acceptance of fate.

In Jericho, we stopped at a restaurant for a meal. Obsequiousness is an integral part of people waiting on tables, but the Arab waiters displayed a kind of deference that exceeded the usual waiterly compliance. Behind the winning smiles, anger lay in waiting, ready to turn into a snarl. After all, we represented the occupier of their land and deserved their resentment. On the way back from Jericho to Jerusalem, Menachem's image of being pulled along by his father haunted me for a long time. I came back from the trip deeply troubled.

## A Critic at Large

Whatever misgivings I felt, daily humdrum demands overshadowed them. Professor Fisch employed me as coordinator of Second Language English Studies. This seemingly innocuous position wielded lots of power. It partially controlled the students' schedules. The coordinator would determine the students' competence level, required credits and decide on a whole series of other issues. I must admit that the position gave me satisfaction partly because of the way the students tried to endear themselves to me. The female students showing their best profile, and the male students making up for their gender shortcomings by trying to establish comradely relations, made me smile. Though mindful of their needs, I felt that I often made decisions on a whim, particularly on my bad days. I also discovered that this seat of authority planted inside me seeds of aloofness that in due course would make me a full-fledged bureaucrat. In Israel bureaucrats were ranked below politicians in terms of civility. In my work at the university, I went out of my way to avoid being branded a bureaucrat. It was not uncommon to walk into a government office to find the clerk reading the evening tabloid, acknowledging your presence only after having finished the paragraph. One clerk vividly stands out in my memory.

For some reason, I had neglected to renew my passport, and urgent action was needed to expedite the renewal of the passport. This clerk, who was handling my case, was in the habit of sneaking peanuts into his mouth. Any day I came to inquire whether my passport was ready, he would be cracking peanuts, apologizing for his unbecoming behaviour: "It's a matter of health," he would say. I would not dare to question the veracity of his remark for fear that I would jeopardize my effort to get the desired passport.

The university position was intended to tide me over until I received word from Brown University, to which I had applied for graduate school. In the interim, I read up about the United States with an emphasis on American university culture. Browsing through books became my pastime. I would leisurely flip through pages, read amusing blurbs, and when financially possible treat myself to buying a book.

I was at the time in a poetry phase, and I came across a book of criticism on Modern Hebrew poetry. Azriel Ochmani, the author, a known Marxist, had moderated his political ideology over the years, but only slightly his views of literature. Still an adherent of socialist realism, he harnessed the aesthetic values of the poems to the "Proletarian Culture," which advocated, in Stalin's formula, the engineering of man's soul. Ten years earlier, I would have relished Ochmani's approach. But now, a follower of the New Criticism School inspired by the Keatsian philosophy that "beauty is truth and truth is beauty," I found Ochmani's analytical method glaring with absurdities. Skimming the pages of his book, I felt both embarrassed and challenged. And the challenge I translated into writing a critical review of it. By the time I finished reading the book, its pages were covered with coloured remarks pointing out the fallacies of the author's arguments. I titled my review "The Peacock and the Coloured Feathers," an image borrowed from the author's own vocabulary. I retained the derisive phrase and turned the derision towards the author.

Since my political conversion, I had subscribed to the prestigious newspaper *Haaretz*, and occasionally sent letters to the editor. Because of the paper's liberal leanings, I thought that the review would receive a sympathetic reading by the editor of the Literary Supplement. About two weeks later, I received a telephone call. The caller identified himself as Tammuz, apparently assuming that I should know his name and position. He would like to talk to me regarding my review. Naturally, I wanted to know what he thought of it, but he demurred and only said, "We'll discuss it when you come."

The Literary Supplement office was spacious and, as might be expected, cluttered with books. On my entry through the open door I saw a middle-aged man wearing a bushy moustache and a tanned complexion reading galleys. From the corner of my eye, I noticed a young woman, to whom I was not introduced, sitting at the other end of the office. Without rising from his chair, Tammuz greeted me with a hearty smile and said: "You must be Pfefferkorn." He seated me opposite him, lit a Turkish cigarette, pulled out my review from a desk drawer and launched into a monologue. "There're cases when materials merit publication and don't get published, and there're cases when materials don't merit publication and get published. Your piece belongs to the former category." He looked at me making sure that I was internalizing his words.

Taking advantage of his momentary pause while wiping his moustache, I managed to squeeze in a single utterance: "Mr. Tammuz, why…?"

He interrupted me in mid-sentence: "Everybody calls me Tammuz, there is no appendage to it." Then he continued his homily in a measured pace. "You see, Ochmani is a sick man, publishing this piece might do him irreparable damage." Punctuating the sentence with what must have been meant as a rhetorical flourish, he asked, "Do you want him to die?"

I looked him straight in the eye and said: "I don't mind." A kind of picaresque gleam appeared in his eyes. Looking back on it, I think that must have been in appreciation of my cavalier answer. He got up from his chair, pulled a stack of books from the shelf and put it on his desk. It was then that, for the first time, I saw him in his full length. He was a well-built stocky man whose presence filled the space of wherever he happened to be. Sitting down, he treated me to a question and answer exchange that was more engaging than the homily:

Tammuz: Tell me, Pfefferkorn, is the creation perfect?

Pfefferkorn: Of course not.

Tammuz: Are you perfect ?

Pfefferkorn: Like the creation.

Tammuz: Am I perfect?

Pfefferkorn: Just like me.

Tammuz: So what makes you think that these (pointing to the pile of books on his desk) are perfect?

I enjoyed this repartee as much as he did. He kept it fresh as if he had made it up right then and there. And without much ado, he switched back from dialogue to homily form. "If you want to be taken seriously by the literati, Pfefferkorn," he emphasized, "you must expose their fallacies, flaws, foibles. Remember, deconstructive criticism gets noticed. Take 'em apart. Let the others put 'em together." Since I had never entertained the idea that any mortal's work was perfect, I took Tammuz's instructions to be an initiation sermon into his circle of critics for the Literary Supplement. Eventually, I departed with a pile of books under my arm. Truth to tell, I felt a rising glow of pride. I wished that David Hirsch had been with me and that I could have shared the news of my new status with him, but he had already finished his Sabbatical and could not immediately share in my literary elevation. I hesitated to tell Fisch, for he might have had qualms about my writing for a literary supplement before having established my academic credentials. Paying tribute to David, I went to his favourite Kapulski café and had a latte, reinforced by a big chunk of cake.

The day after my visit to Tammuz's office, in the late morning on Friday, the phone rang. The voice sounded familiar, but I could not quite place it. The caller identified herself as Ruth Almog, the person who had sat in Tammuz's office typing. It all came back in a flash. I had first met Ruth when she was still a college student. She would come to the coastal radio station where I worked to communicate with her boyfriend, Yair, who was the skipper of a trawler. At the time she wore shorts and looked like a high school kid. Now she was married, a published author of fiction, and the literary editor for the Supplement. She had recognized me on my entrance to the office yesterday but had not wanted to let on. It transpired that what Tammuz had told me about Ochmani's illness was not the whole truth. "Eli," she said, "Ochmani is ill but not as ill as dramatized by Tammuz. The truth is that Tammuz is planning to go on a Sabbatical and applied for a grant to the Writers' Union that Ochmani chairs." So this was a matter of calculated compassion, worthy of a master manipulator. She made this call because my piece deserved publication and because she did not like her boss's manipulative modus operandi.

The review was published in the Literary Supplement of *Yediot Acharonot* and elicited a slew of letters to the editor that made me both famous and infamous. I cherished both reactions, for they put me on the map of Israeli literary critics. But it was not before my critical pieces began to appear in *Haaretz* and I was inducted into Tammuz's coterie that I was taken seriously. For a neophyte literary critic, this was quite a feather in my cap.

The reviews appeared Friday in the weekend edition of *Haaretz*. On Friday afternoon, I would take a walk along Dizengoff Street, where the Tel-Aviv literary figures congregated for their weekly ritual rant. Sitting on the café sidewalks around tables piled up with the weeklies, they would call over a passing reviewer either to vent their displeasure or to express their appreciation of his reviews. I could tell ahead of time whether I was in for praise or condemnation. If the call was, "Pfefferkorn, come over here," and was accompanied by jerky beckoning, that boded ill; if they said: "Eli, come over," and accompanied it with a wide wave of the arm, that signalled their pleasure. Whether called out on the carpet or seated at the table, I had lots of fun, and either sort of conversation was a balm to my ego.

One of those Friday encounters I recall in fondness, though not in detail. That week, I had reviewed a book, written by a novelist, which was influenced by the French existentialists. I pointed out this aspect of the work in a tone that must have had a sarcastic edge to it. By Israeli critical standards it was a mild comment. He saw me pass by and I saluted him in a gesture of peace that was met with an ominous voice: "Pfefferkorn! Come over." Eagerly, I threaded my way through the tables and sat down without being invited to do so. "Pfefferkorn, you know how to criticize, but do you know how to create? You know how to destroy, but do you know how to build?" He pointed his finger at the review in front of him. The verbal match was on, and the fellows at the table were watching like spectators in an arena.

I immediately confessed that I did not know, humbly adding, "I equally don't know how to lay eggs, but I can still tell a good egg from a bad one." The retort, though not original, was propitious. This sort of needling could go on for a long or short while, all depending on the number of barbs left in the arsenal. I would be remiss if I did not mention that at times intellectual dialogues also took place.

My working relationship with Tammuz slowly evolved into friendship. My spouse and I became regulars at his soirees, where discussions ranged from literature to the arts to politics, underscored by a healthy dose of gossip. The more I got to know Tammuz the more curious I became about his personality. Studying him was akin to digging into an archaeological mount made up of many layers. In his youth, he had belonged to a movement that was derisively dubbed "Canaanites" after Canaan, the ancient name of the Promised Land conquered by the Israelites in 1200 BCE. The movement, comprising writers and poets, developed an ideology culled from the ancient cultures of Mesopotamia. The main plank of this ideology was the importance of creating a "Hebrew nation" as opposed to "a Jewish nation." "Tammuz" was the name of the Phoenician and Greek Adonis god, as well as the Samaritan and the Babylonian fertility gods. The other members of his group also carried names of ancient deities. Obviously, the movement embraced an atavistic ideology that took a backward leap of approximately 3000 years. By the time I met Tammuz, he was already a defrocked pagan priest.

Though pathetically out of touch with the pulse of history, this group left a legacy of poetry and work in other literary genres that enriched the Hebrew language and influenced its literature. As I became closer with Tammuz,

● I was enchanted by his stories about people he had met and places he had visited. Occasionally he allowed me to peek into his personal garden, the dwellings of his muses, and that allowed me a deeper understanding of his literary work. In the course of our growing friendship, he entrusted me with reading a manuscript of his and even gave me unlimited license to make critical comments. I took this opportunity to demonstrate that I was an attentive pupil by searching for imperfections, and dutifully scrawled my critical comments on the margins. But I also scribbled an appreciative note at the end: "Your fiction sounds true."

He jealously guarded his editorial prerogatives and whenever he found my criticism favouring an author for personal reasons, my review did not get published, despite our friendship. Unsurprisingly, I don't recall a single case when he rejected a review that was flagrantly adversarial. Adverse criticism often generated polemics and Tammuz thrilled to it; it also made for good copy.

Over the years, we have occasionally been at odds, particularly in the later phase of our relationship, once I felt that I'd come of intellectual age.

One tiff involved Elie Wiesel. To my chagrin, he had been a virtual pariah amongst the Israeli literati. They considered him a poseur who tailored the Holocaust to suit American sentiments. One of his critics put it picturesquely: "He conjures up the victims going to the gas chambers as if with a magic wand amidst the gasps of his audience." On one of his visits to Israel, Wiesel interviewed the Israeli Defence Minister at the time, Shimon Peres; the event had the literati in stitches. Training his eyes on the interviewee, Wiesel addressed him in Biblical Hebrew: "My Lord, Minister of the Israeli Armies," a salutation that sounded to Israeli ears like a parody of the Bible. The down-to-earth Israelis scoffed at such maudlin language, which provided fodder for the weekly funnies. I felt embarrassed for my friend.

Wiesel sent me a book titled *A Jew Today*, comprising a collection of excellent essays and short stories, and asked me whether I would review it for *Haaretz*. One of the short stories caught my attention. Cast in a Kabbalistic mode that resembled Chagall's surrealistic style, it dealt with anguished memory. My review met with Tammuz's dismissive chortle. "Eli, you're too intelligent to be taken in by this bathos. Kabbala, Surrealism, Chagall... I won't run it." In response, I made it clear that "I'll go to any length to have the piece published in *Haaretz*." He didn't believe that I would dare to go behind his back. But Ruth, his assistant, warned him that I would. The review appeared in the paper the following week; it earned me the sobriquet "Wiesel's champion."

Tammuz was, as I've already observed, a master manipulator who would exercise his skill on his friends whenever the fancy took him. Aharon Appelfeld, a widely published writer whose novels limn in evocative vignettes the ordeals of the pre- and post-Holocaust eras, wrote a memoir in Hebrew entitled *"In First Person Singular"* describing his painful assimilation into Israeli society. Tammuz handed me the memoir for review, attended by a typical wince, skewing his moustached upper lip, and said, "Another philosopher has come to town."

Appelfeld was a friend whom I used to meet occasionally in a Jerusalem café where he made notes for his next novel. Notwithstanding Tammuz's disparaging comment, I was favourably disposed to the memoirist. Laced with abstract thinking, the memoir was, nonetheless, wanting in cogent thinking. This time I agreed with Tammuz' observation. But I was reluctant to review the memoir lest I offend its author. By a combination of flattering — "you're the best man for it" — and questioning my professional ethics, Tammuz persuaded me. I gave in. While I tried my best to point out the positive aspects of the memoir, my critique nevertheless retained a rather harsh tone. I ended the review by saying that "philosophy's loss is literature's gain," intending to blunt my critical thrust, but the readers took it to be a back-handed compliment. I felt bad about the entire episode and feel a sting of repentance to this very day. Viewing it in retrospect, I should have withstood Tammuz's seductive manipulation.

My status was elevated thanks to my reviews in *Haaretz*, endearing me to my colleagues and earning me prestige among my neighbours. But most of all, Fisch was proud of me. Not so my spouse, who deemed the haggling with the authors a waste of time.

The letter from Brown University arrived on an unusually rainy day. I had been expecting it for the past few months. On my return home, I would nervously shuffle through my mail in anticipation of its arrival. I was forty years old with a wife and eight-year-old daughter, about to travel to a far-away foreign country, unfamiliar with its culture. I had moments of dread. To ease my anxieties, I became a regular visitor at the American Library in the US Consulate in Tel-Aviv, poring over the New York Times and a variety of American magazines. Their pages carried Richard Nixon's and Hubert Humphrey's faces, always wreathed in smiles. It was the year of the 1968 presidential elections, and each candidate tried to gain advantage over the other by the width of his smile. I also noticed that both boasted symmetrically lined-up sets of teeth. Nixon's Cheshire grin contrasted with Humphrey's expansive one, but both exuded joy. They must have made excellent fodder for cartoonists.

I had seen a few prime ministers in Israel, and they had all run for elected office without smiling. David Ben-Gurion, a seemingly tenured Prime Minister, wore a permanent gloom made audible by foreboding statements reminiscent of Isaiah's dark prophecies. Prime Minister Golda Meir wore on her face the alarmed look of a person hearing about an imminent pogrom. Swaddled in the Jewish tragic chronicles, she openly carried her presentiment in her pocketbook to the world's capitals with the alertness of a watchtower guard heralding the enemy at the gate.

I was therefore perplexed by these smiles jutting out from the pages of the American newspapers. An Israeli-American acquaintance unlocked the puzzle for me by taking me behind the smiles. "The average American is by nature optimistic," he explained to me. "The gold mines are just around the corner; you just have to take the right turn to find them." In Yiddish folklore America was referred to as The Goldene Medine, The Golden Country. "You never stop dreaming of becoming rich," he said, chuckling, "and that's why the presidential aspirants and other elected politicians keep smiling into the camera." This was an instructive lesson for me, which became a reality on our arrival in New York in the summer of 1968.

## Kosher Style

A family of thrice-removed cousins met us at the airport. My first encounter with Americana was in the form of a sandwich. Packed between two slices of rye bread was a slab of pastrami that would make at least two sandwiches back home. Our daughter, Vered, got a child's sandwich that could easily be taken for a regular one in any European restaurant. Since we came from the Holy Land, they expected us to keep Kosher and took us to a "Kosher Style deli." I could easily understand "Deli" but "Kosher Style" was an original that had never made it across the Atlantic. I was used to Kosher or non-Kosher. My business-minded cousins believed "that all that stuff is a marketing ploy."

I marvelled at the marketing ingenuity of my people. I felt, however, that the Kosher Style concept enfolded more than just clever marketing. I made a mental note to broach the subject with David Hirsch, who is good at making the complex simple without simplifying it.

David and his chum, George Montero, who also taught American literature, gave me a preliminary introduction to the human and academic make-up of Brown University's English department. Like zoologists, they divided the faculty into categories. Themselves of a sparring disposition, they put the categories in pugilistic terms that ran from light flyweight to lightweight to heavyweight. Only a very few defied pigeonholing; one of those was Professor Damon, an eminent Blake scholar. "You'll like him," they assured me.

When I first met him at the mail-box, Professor Damon was in his early eighties, wearing a bulky hearing aid attached to an earpiece by a cord. I waited until he finished sorting out his mail and then addressed him. He beckoned me into his office, shut the door and turned on the switch of the receiver. "When I go into the corridor, I switch this off," he said, pointing to his hearing aid. "There's too much drivel going on out there."

I instantly liked old Damon, as he was referred to in the department. He seated his tall frame with a heavy sigh and engaged me in a lively conversation that belied the frailty of his body. It was as if his head was planted on an alien body — nature's mischievous mismatch. In the course of time a close relationship developed between us, one of teacher and disciple. Damon scoffed at the vanity of his colleagues and I adored him for his cynicism.

The crash course that I received from David and George allowed me to tiptoe my way through the various competing cliques, asserting my presence without offending anyone. It was an achievement not to be sneezed at, and one duly recognized by my two coaches. After having settled in, becoming familiar with the library and being introduced to the rabbis of the three denominations, it was time to explore open vistas in the Rhode Island scenery before the beginning of the semester. Usually on weekends, David and Rosalyn would take us for a day's ride into the country and into the small mill towns, once vibrant but by that time depopulated.

As time went by, I became aware of the multi-layered American ethos. I was struck by its unique characteristics: its theatrical nature; its stylized substance; its hasty change of style; its inventive genius — all these, and many other aspects, never stopped amazing me. These socio-cultural dynamics confronted the East European Jews who landed on Ellis Island and adapted to the new culture with reservations. The Kosher style idea made it easier for the immigrants, and particularly for their children, to acculturate into the American life-style and yet retain their Jewish identity. "Style" connoted American, "Kosher" Jewish.

A ritually slaughtered chicken prepared according to the *Kashrut* laws but cooked in a dairy utensil became Kosher Style. As David put it: "What drives this entire undertaking is a passion to be '*an Amerikaner*,' the marketing enhances it." In an effort to acculturate, the Jewish culinary menu offered kosher bacon, which was actually beef flavoured with bacon taste. Thus a semi-observant Jew could have his bacon and his gefilte fish, a traditional Sabbath meal.

The imitation of the authentic extended to other aspects of Jewish life. The phrase "belonging," for example, I first heard from our landlord. Bow-legged and waddling up the creaky stairs, he would make his way to our apartment to collect his bi-weekly rent. He was born, bred and had prospered in Providence, and yet he still spoke a kind of English in which Yiddish influences manifested themselves in intonation, diction and syntax. When he came the first time to collect his rent, he asked me whether "you belong already?" The question caught me unaware; bewilderment must have shown on my face. Up to this moment I thought that I belonged to my family and by extension to the State of Israel, where I paid taxes, fought its wars and usually obeyed its laws. "What I mean is that you belong to a *shul*," he added for clarification. I discovered later that there were three categories of belonging: 1) dues-paying member of a synagogue or temple; 2) former members who for a variety of reasons stopped their affiliation with the religious institution; 3) non-affiliated but planning to belong. I decided to join the third category. In one of his collection visits, we talked about the advantages of higher education in life. Chuckling between slurps of tea, he asked me a rhetorical question. "Tell me, Eli, who has more *smartkeit* (sic), you or me?" And without pausing, he added another rhetorical question: "Who gives money to who, every two weeks?" I thrill to disputation but do not dispute obvious facts. My landlord's conclusion deriving from the fact that I shelled out a bi-weekly rent to him was irrefutable: "Obviously, you've got the *smartkeit*," I humbly conceded. Glowing in victory, he wobbled down the stairs to knock on the door of his next tenant.

### Black Cats versus White Cats

It was a gloriously crisp New England autumnal morning as I strode across the Brown campus to my assigned class, carrying under my arm a copious bunch of syllabi for "Poetry 101." It was one of those days when the Creator smiles upon the earth and the Psalmist praises His creation, a day that makes life worth living. The freshmen were hurrying to their classes, the juniors and seniors sauntering to theirs. My state of mind must have been closer to that of the juniors, though my walking pace was not. I was looking forward to meeting my class and at the same time felt apprehensive about the meeting. What I had learned from my teaching experience was that the first encounter with a class shaped — to a large extent — its contours and subsequently determined its character. I breathed deeply, taking in the fresh morning air.

As I walked into the dusky classroom from the bright, sunny outdoors, I noticed through my squinting eyes about fifteen students of various complexions, some sitting upright, others slightly slumped in a more leisurely position. A rather lean and small black-skinned student sat erect up between two white-skinned counterparts, in the front row. The seats in the deeper rows were mostly taken by white students and a few blacks.

I liked that chequered class composition and tacitly welcomed the presence of black students. I felt an emotional closeness to black people because of our similar experiences. The active participation of the Jewish community in the Civil Rights movement made me proud of my people. I therefore expected a rapport between the class and me.

Actors can tell the mood of an audience as soon as they come on stage. Back in Israel, I got a sense of a class on the first day of teaching. But here, my senses were not yet acute enough to guide me. After making some introductory remarks, I handed out the syllabus and waited for questions. The lean black student in the front row was the first to raise his hand. Waving the syllabus, he announced in a defiant voice: "There're no black cats here, only white cats." This announcement was followed by an orchestrated choral demand to know, "Why are there only white cats here, no black cats?" I had been in the country for about six weeks, watched television as time permitted, read the New York Times daily, occasionally saw both white and black cats lurking in alleys, but missed what their colours signified beyond their blackness and whiteness. Surely, my coaches, David and George, would have told me that black folks do not take kindly to white cats, or did they miss this one? I was flabbergasted at the way events were turning out.

I needed to gain time; I needed time… I needed time to sort out my wildly racing thoughts. My distress increased by the second. I was seeking signs of help among the blue-eyed blond students who sat erect in their chairs, looking straight ahead in silence. Suddenly a thought crossed my mind. "The entire uproar is due to medical reasons… perhaps an allergy to cats, cats that have found shelter in the building from the morning chill." But I could not brace myself to open the door to the hallway to verify my notion. So I fell back on the last delaying tactic. Stuffing my pipe with tobacco allowed me time to stall and finally come up with a combative ploy. I got up from my chair, looked the syllabus-waving kid straight in the eye and stressing each word with a sculptor's chiselling precision asked: "What do you mean?" In response, they unleashed a harangue. While the thrust of the harangue was aimed at the white establishment, they targeted me as its representative. Each of the four students briefly told a story of his ancestors' suffering. The stories were moving. White society had not owned up to its wrongdoing; the absence of black poets from the syllabus was indicative. Throughout the indictment of the white establishment, I wavered between sympathy and resentment towards the black students. Their stories deeply touched me, but the misplaced venue and the ill-timing of telling them distressed me. What most disturbed me, however, was the way they told them. The telling was orchestrated and synchronized, akin to a well-rehearsed recitation, consequently dulling the pain encased in the slavery experience. It showed that even an authentic story, when lacking in spontaneity, might turn into bathos.

Now that the white and black cats were put in a racial context, I slowly came to grasp what offended the protesters. Stripped of their felinity, the felines assumed anthropomorphic characteristics. This I could handle. During a short lull, I took the opportunity to offer my rebels a compromise. First I explained to them that I had nothing to do with writing up the syllabus outline and then I told them that I would agree to teaching black poetry, though it might not exactly fit in with John Donne, Keats and Yeats. They rejected my offer and renewed the class warfare, but at a lower level of intensity. In the course of my teaching, I knew that maintaining one's composure in such circumstances was critical. I tried hard not to lose my cool. But when my attempt to reason with them failed, my anger burst out in a confrontational rebuke. I was offended and I gave voice to my feelings. Raising my voice above the din I went into a monologue: "Your pain you take out on me without knowing who I am... I belong to a people that trod the bloody paths of history for two thousand years. My ancestors endured expulsions, persecution, pogroms; they were quartered, burned on the stake. I belong to a historically victimized people... I'm Jewish."

Emotionally drained, I plunked down onto the chair. Silence fell in the room. Even the blue-eyed students' chairs squeaked, registering vital signs. My accusers sat in silence, their postures somewhat shrunk. I only now became aware that I had used my unlit pipe as a pointer to underscore my litany of agonies. Though there were still about fifteen teaching minutes left, I called it a day. Even as I gathered my things, the four black challengers approached my desk. "We're dropping the course," the small, lean kid spoke.

Putting on a face of mild disappointment — lest they change their minds — I asked, "Why?"

"It won't work," he said in a hushed voice. He was the most vociferous among them. They showed signs of discomfort. Surprisingly, they asked me what other section of the course I'd recommend they take. I was flattered by the trust they put in me. The name that immediately sprang to mind was Mr. Harold, who, hailing from California, seemed to have the right mix of sensibilities to deal with these racial issues. They thanked me and left.

I needed a long walk to sort out my feelings and thinking. Why did the white students keep silent? Were they intimidated or was their silence a tacit admission of guilt? I knew why the black kids dropped my course; they wanted to avoid a victim rivalry. What they really wanted was a full-blooded WASP professor, preferably with slave ownership ancestry. But why choose a class as a place to raise your resentments? And then I had a question for myself: why did I not mention the Holocaust and my ordeals? By the time I got to David's office, I had calmed down, but my face must have shown turbulence, for David immediately noticed. I gave him a step-by-step account of the episode, anticipating an enormously stunned response, but instead he smiled. Apparently, protests in classes against the Vietnam War and against discrimination against blacks had been happening quite a bit of late. Politically energized by inflammatory speeches on campus, and without time to cool off, the students would simply carry the heat of the speeches into the classroom. So there was nothing sensational about it, except that it happened in the morning and the haranguing was done by freshmen. David actually praised me for standing up to the black students.

While the term "political correctness" had not been coined yet, the climate in which it originated already reigned at Brown as well as at other universities. The faculty as a whole at Brown, as I learned later, tried to avoid confrontation with students. There was a wide range of reasons for faculty reluctance to react to the protesters' abrasive behaviour. Some professors agreed with the substance of the protests; others just did not want to turn the classroom into an arena for verbal warfare. Still others believed that sanity would return and the life of the mind resume, so why get upset about it? Had I known then the faculty's conciliatory disposition — for want of a more fitting term — I might have absorbed the offences in mournful silence. But the assertive position that I had taken in the class paid off. To begin with, David spread the word among his peers over coffee and croissant, and I shared my adventure with my own peers over beer. In the department corridors, I was acknowledged with a knowing nod and smile: "This fellow from Israel really dished it out." In recognition of my assertiveness, I was invited to join a makeshift literary club. I myself did not consider my response to the class' disruption as anything extraordinary. Intimidation should be met with determination, harassment with deterrence. The nearly sweeping approval of my reaction to the provocation that I was subjected to exposed the Achilles' heels of human nature: the reluctance to take a stand when risk is involved.

One early morning as I was collecting my mail from the mail-box, a significant tap on the shoulder made me turn around. There stood Handsome Mr. Harold, to whose class I had directed my provocative students. His posture did not bode well. Eyes shooting flaming arrows at me, he hissed through his perfectly aligned teeth one pointed question: "Why do you hate me?"

For the record, I would like to state that I do not usually hate people, nor do I necessarily love them. I judge people by what they say and whether they act on their words. In this particular case, I neither hated nor loved Harold; I was emotionally impartial to him. He was a fellow graduate student who embraced humankind with a Mormon's missionary passion. He loved humanity at large and the underdogs up close. In short, he was an underdog lover. These sentiments Harold had expressed in our short conversation over coffee earlier in the month. It seemed then that he had the right sensibility to channel the black kids' anger into creative activity. Evidently, I was wrong. Now I was facing a fuming Harold.

"Why should I hate you? I hardly know you," I said with a shade of affectation.

Even as I was about to elaborate on the subject of our relationship, he cut me short and spat out, "They're destroying my class," and with this he turned on his heels and left in a huff. Handsome Harold was out of my life for many months.

The Brown campus was not an oasis of calm in 1968. Planted all across the green lawns, loudspeakers emanated inflammatory speeches amid cheering and jeering from the crowds of students sprawled on the grass, the words stitched into each other like threads in an exotic tapestry. Capitalism, Fascism, Socialism, Plutocracy, Democracy, Hypocrisy and a string of other "isms" and "cys" liberally bounced around. It was like a Hyde Park Corner event without the self-deprecating irony of the speakers and the humorous taunts of the audience.

I would amble from speaker to speaker in search of some idea variations, but all the speeches sounded the same and the speakers bore a strong resemblance to each other. They wanted a revolution and they wanted it now; and the way to get it was to destroy the Military-Industrial Complex, as Republican President Dwight D. Eisenhower put it in 1961. Occasionally, I engaged the proponents of the revolution in discussions. Having been trained in the thinking of Marx, Engels and Lenin in my own messianic days, I was well equipped to probe the intellectual plausibility of their radical endeavours. My point of departure was that a revolution could not be made without the active participation of the working class and the acquiescence of the middle class. As I expected, my discussants were better versed in the art of love-making than in the art of class warfare, greater celebrants of Dionysus than followers of Marx. As soon as they finished their exams they screeched out from the parking lots in their Jaguars and BMWs, leaving the revolution and the Vietnam War in a trail of gas emissions. To be fair, some took the train to Washington, DC, to join the antiwar demonstrations on the Mall. In all, it was a spectacular retreat from the campus rhetoric.

The veteran faculty took all the upheaval rather badly. The University, situated on the hill that perched over Providence, registered a tremor; the daily rhythm of academia got disrupted and mitres ruffled. I took the campus uproar as a farce, a youthful joyride masquerading as a generational rebellion. I had been witness to and victim of the calamities that ravaged the European Continent, an experience that equipped me with an intuitive warning system. The sight of the students hanging out on the lawns, singing folk songs accompanied by strumming guitars and punctuated by speeches, did not trigger my alarm system. Indeed, when they returned for the 1969/1970 academic year, their revolutionary passion was considerably deflated. Bowing to the *Zeitgeist,* the University adapted its curriculum and the undergraduates returned to their studies in earnest.

The years of my residence in Providence, Rhode Island, were the best years of my academic career. The tranquility that wrapped my surroundings allowed me thinking space, and the intellectual vibrancy that pulsated in the university further challenged my inquisitiveness. It was not as if I had been deprived of stimulation at Bar-Ilan University — Harold Fisch provided me with plenty of intellectual challenges — but the daily tension of life in Israel sapped my emotional energies. What struck me were the different questions asked by Brown and Israeli students concerning papers that they'd handed in for grading. The Brown student, relaxed and congenial, asked, "Did you like my paper, Sir?" In contrast, the anxiety-ridden Israeli student asked, "What did I get?" No wonder. The Israeli student comes to University in his early twenties, after a three-year stint in the army, and is therefore in a hurry to finish his studies. Unlike his Brown counterpart, he is goal-oriented to a fault. Indeed, they live in two contrasting worlds.

Whether it is my personality or fate (and I tend to believe that one's personality is one's fate), I am often led to commit follies that I subsequently come to regret. I jeopardized my standing in the Providence Jewish community because of a critical article I published in *Haaretz* about Jewish education in the U.S., using Providence as an illustrative case. The article, entitled "The Silent Conspiracy of Jewish Education in the U.S.," was based on my observations of the local Hebrew schools, reading of the curricula, or the lack of them, and examination of the accompanying didactic books. My wife taught in the afternoon Hebrew school, and she related to me the educational flaws of the system. The pedagogy in the Hebrew Supplementary Schools was reminiscent of the Kosher Style food, symptomatic of the efforts of an ethnic minority to become part of the American ethos and still retain a Jewish identity. The Supplementary School was supposed to nurture the students' Jewish heritage, while the public or private school was to inculcate the Jewish child with Americanism. And because American culture has such a pervasive influence, Judaism, in due course, becomes diluted. The situation is not unlike the Kosher Style food construct, where the Style overwhelms the Kosher. It was a courageous attempt to maintain the hyphen between Americana and Judaism. At the time I had not realized the American Jewish resilience in a state of constant strife, its ability to retain religious and ethnic continuity in the face of assimilation pressures.

It was Rabbi William Braude of the Reform Temple who had me over for lunch to educate me about the American Diaspora. He had read my criticism in *Haaretz* — a paper he subscribed to — and found its author sadly wanting in understanding Jewish life in America. He began by asking me whether I was aware of the cultural pressures on Jewish tradition and consequently the drift away from Judaism. "Your article implies," he argued, "that the Supplementary Schools have little or no impact on their students' Jewish awareness and therefore should be done away with." I objected to his characterization, arguing that I meant to say that the Schools could be made didactically more effective. I came out of this dialogue with a deeper understanding of the religious and ethnically existential realities the Jewish community was facing. I realized that my observations were made from an Israeli perspective. I was humbled and conveyed my apologies to the Rabbi.

The Jewish identity is not questioned in Israel; there are other problems visited on its citizens, but not identity issues. Later I kept on asking myself why I would get involved in an issue that supposedly did not concern me — when, as the Texas argot has it, I had no dog in this fight.

I was into my second year of graduate studies and we intended to return to Israel as soon as I was done, so why would I want to malign the good people of Providence? They had greeted us with a welcome basket, saw to it that we got free dental work, invited us to their homes on holidays, and some of them became close friends — and despite their generosity I criticized their institutions of education.

As I was probing deeper into my motivation, it dawned on me that I was driven by an act of defiance, namely wishing not to hand Hitler a posthumous victory. Education was an antidote to assimilation and subsequently to the diminishing numbers of the Jewish population. I was neither religious nor nationalistic. Had I been given a choice of religion, I would not have chosen Judaism or Christianity. Monotheistic religions have a zealous disposition, consequently wreaking havoc. In Israel as well as in the Diaspora, I occasionally went to weddings, rarely to funerals, and when the spirit took me, to a synagogue. I also went to church to watch Mass; its stylized pageantry fascinated me. Had I lived before Paul's vision on his way to Damascus, I would have been a devoted pagan. But Jewish continuity gave purpose to my three-year suffering; my loss of youth and family constituted the core of my being.

In the course of my rather itinerant career, I often compromised my principles and bowed to opportunism with a view to advancing my interests, but not when it came to the Holocaust. Enshrined in a kind of closed garden, impenetrable from the outside material world or by my own evil inclinations, Memory was a driving force in my life. And I paid a high price for adhering to it. At the time, I was not conscious of the impact that my past ordeals had on my daily life and particularly on my life of the mind. Only in the clarifying process of writing my dissertation did I slowly come to understand the grooves they had worn on my consciousness.

I was overwhelmed by my daily responsibilities. Teaching, the coursework, and the writing of the doctoral proposal left little time for social life. The proposal had to be approved prior to my becoming qualified to take the final exams. Some of the courses were enlightening and crystallized the premise of my proposal; others honed my knowledge of the Elizabethan and Jacobean periods; and still others turned out to be achingly boring. No surprise there. While sitting around the seminar table, you could tell from the colour of the professor's notes the approximate date they had been scribbled. Faded in time like their tenured author, they gave off an autumnal yellowish whiff. On the whole, the calibre of the professors was intellectually outstanding, and their high quality was manifested in their wide breadth of knowledge. My former section instructor, James Boulger, a Romanticist, who boasted a delicate palate for fish, used to share his favourite dishes with me as well as his thinking. I appreciated his munificence on both counts. And there were my fellow students, doctoral aspirants, hard-working, stressed out, crouched in their library carrels, whom I liked to engage in conversation whenever physical and mental time allowed.

## An Immodest Proposal

These were spiritually and intellectually rewarding times. I was moving at a reasonable pace to meet the marked deadlines. While the relevant committee was considering my proposal, "Irrational Man in the Jacobean Drama and in the Theatre of the Absurd," I was getting ready for the final stretch. The proposal was an extension of my Masters thesis, to which Professor Fisch of Bar-Ilan had taken exception because of the chronological break between the two periods. At the back of my mind I had, therefore, a niggling doubt about the scholarly soundness of my dramatic concept. So when the chairman of the committee, Mr. Andrew Sable, asked me to "drop by in my office for a little chat," my doubts morphed into a constant haunt. Mindful not to hurt me, Sable chose his words carefully. "The committee appreciates your original ideas," the habitually ebullient Andy said, sounding rather grim, "but finds that the proposal needs more substantiation." He had more nice things to say about me that were of little consolation. Usually, I would go to David for advice, but this news was too shocking to share with him. I wanted first to digest it myself before broaching the subject with David. I rushed to the Ford Library, hoping to discover some kind of support for my thesis. As I pored over the drama magazines, Fischs's sentence "It's too big a leap," kept on echoing in my head. My doctoral project had been planned for three years. For the last two years, I had mulled over the affinities between the Jacobeans plays and the Absurdist plays. The productions I had seen in London had alerted me to their similarities. A switch of topics at this stage was tantamount to shunting railway tracks and directing the train to a different destination. I was mentally unable to do it, and even if I were, my scholarship was running out. I had suffered many setbacks over the years, and this one was particularly severe for several reasons. Living in the shadow of the swastika, I had had to take many winding roads, navigate shoals, evade hunters, and plead with evil-wishers, and consequently I was equipped to deal with danger. But this was a totally different situation. I did not face enemies. On the contrary, I was sure that each member of the committee wished me well and would be willing to help me, particularly to help me switch my topic. I met David for our customary evening walk, traditionally followed by a hefty portion of ice cream. I related to him my conversation with Sable. Though visibly disappointed, he was not as taken aback as I had expected him to be. "These things happen," he said calmly. "Let me take another look at the proposal tomorrow." He made an effort to hide his concern. That evening, we had no desire for ice cream

The library became my refuge. I worked out a research method focussing on the last ten years of any publication related even tenuously to the subject at hand. Later I flipped pages in a haze. Blurry-eyed and in a state of inertia, I pulled from the shelf a newly published book: "Tragedy and Melodrama: Version of Experiences," by Robert Heilman of Washington University, published in 1968. Following the routine, I first glanced at the table of contents then scanned the index, finally locating the indicated pages. Lo and behold, in front of me loomed words of redemption. Heilman identified common dramatic properties of the Jacobean Theatre and the Theatre of the Absurd:

> The world around us is naturally the final testing ground of a theory which endeavours to be tied to no particular world. That kind of theory makes it possible to juxtapose widely separated ages as a way of setting them off. Suppose, for instance, that we were to look at Jacobean drama in the light that each might shed on the other. It is imaginable that the decadence often imputed to the Jacobean theatre might lead us to see in the Jacobeans a richer, less specialized, more grounded drama of character than appears in the more conventional estimates. Whatever the conclusion, the juxtaposition should reveal indicative common grounds between the Jacobeans and us: the sense of the runaway motive of the centrifugal personality, of the freed destructiveness, the wide-ranging malice, the despair, the vision of nada.[16]

### Hosanna

A burst of energy tore through my inertia. "But, perhaps…I'm hallucinating…"

I walked like I was in a trance. The librarian with whom I had earlier shared my frustration looked at me as if I were an apparition. I rushed to David's office and from there to the lunch-room, where I found him deep in conversation and suspiciously eyeing a sandwich sitting in front of him.

---

[16] Robert Heilman, *Tragedy and Melodrama: Versions of Experience.* Seattle: University of Washington Press, 1968, p. 298.

David gave me a sideways glance, immediately noticed my agitation, and subsequently wound down his conversation. Showing him the redemptive page, I anxiously asked him whether this was real or a figment of my feverish imagination. David's eyes gave me the answer. I left copies of the title page and the relevant page in the letter-boxes of my committee in hopes that they would see them the same day

Academics obsessively check their mail numerous times a day, in expectation of a lucrative offer from a university, not unlike Wall Street investors who diligently watch the bobbing figures on the screen. Naturally anxious to see their reactions when reading the page, I found a vantage position from which I had a full view of the mail boxes. The first to come clattering down the stairs was Boulger, puffing on his favourite cigarillo. "No offer, Jim, just my two pages rendering your rejection null and void," I mouthed. And just as he was about to clamber back up the stairs, I came out of my hiding place. Throwing a quick glance at the two pages, he congratulated me. "Eli, you must've had a rough week," he said, referring to my eight-day suspense in limbo. My chowder-eating partner showed obvious signs of happiness.

Sable, the chairman's committee, had a late class. I knew the routine he followed: from class, to the department, to the mailbox, to his office, picking up his rucksack and finally going home. He made his way across the campus to his house, situated a block away. I encountered him as he made the turn to his street, and he greeted me cheerfully. "Fancy meeting you here. What an auspicious meeting, Mr. Pfefferkorn. I've just read the Heilman pages; I'll speak to my colleagues. Good job." All this he pronounced in the overlaid British accent that he had adopted during his studies in England and that he kept refreshing thanks to his frequent visits there. Of course, I had a question or two for him, but Sable seemed to be in a hurry for the high tea that was awaiting him and I did not think it politic to hold him back from his ritual.

This episode provides a classic lesson on the inherent restrictions put on the imagination in the academic grove. While creativity is encouraged, it must act within the perimeters of scholarship. Once outside the prescribed limits, its wings are clipped. My committee, friendly though it was, could not bring itself to approve a thesis that had no scholarly reference. I wish I had learned this lesson earlier in my endeavours. But now that the thesis was approved, I was free to go ahead. I had a year and a half left to finish the doctoral process, which entailed two preliminary exams in sequential order, the first an oral and the second a written — the success of one being contingent on the other. Sable handed me a list containing approximately fifty titles of books chosen by the committee, to which I was to add another fifty of my own choice. He told me that I should be familiar with all the titles. Observing my bemused expression, he added, "We don't expect you to quote from the works, just a survey knowledge." Gentle, soothing Sable, who viewed life from the comfort and security of a WASPish estate, oozed amiability.

In choosing my references, I was obviously guided by the subjects that I was familiar with. Marxism was high on the list; the Hebrew Bible and the New Testament and related literature took up some space as well. The seminar paper on Jesus that I had written for the University of Bar-Ilan opened up many opportunities for discussions, and at the time I was teaching an advanced undergraduate course on Biblical elements in seventeenth-century English poetry, a fact that gave me an edge over the committee. And of course, I adorned the list with some famous plays. Nor was I unacquainted with the titles chosen by the committee. Some texts required a close reading; others needed less focus or just skimming. At first glance, the list looked formidable, but in due course, it became manageable, though at times frustrating.

Even as I read the texts, I inquired into the experiences of doctoral candidates who had already taken the prelims. The stories abounded in anecdotes ranging from the comic to the melodramatic with touches of the mythical. One of the stories related to me secondhand was peculiar. The examinee, brilliant and apparently of a rather mentally precarious disposition, developed a stigmata on his palms just before being scheduled for the exam. While engaging him in the usual give and take discussion, one of the professors noticed a red trickle on his palm and consequently the conversation turned to religion and to religious poets. The rumour, as my informant related it to me, had it that the committee was seized with fear and trembling and prostrated itself before the stigmatee, who walked out of the room in a glow that slowly shaped itself into a halo. In response to my question as to what extent the story was factual, my informant flexed anthropologist muscles. "This is how folklore is made, truth sifted through the imagination," he said. What I gathered from my other informants was that the oral prelims were intended to test the examinees' breadth of knowledge and conversational skills outside their prospective specializations, while the written prelim was meant to probe the depth of his knowledge and analytical skills by focusing on one work.

This division of sensibilities bore a similarity to one suggested by Isaiah Berlin in *"The Hedgehog and the Fox."* According to Berlin's classification, writers, thinkers and, perhaps, human beings in general are divided between foxes and hedgehogs: the former branch out in multiple directions, pursue a wide range of interests, their vision searching for new horizons; the latter are unidirectional, focussed on one single thing, their views excluding

●

everything but it. To put it in a more current argot, it is the difference between a Renaissance man and a Geek. While reading Berlin's enlightening book, I vacillated between my Fox Being and my Hedgehog Being and finally settled for defining myself as a "hedgefox," a classification implicit in Berlin's thesis. I included *"The Hedgehog and the Fox"* in my reading list, hoping that it would provide an opening for the discussion during the prelim.

On a late Saturday morning, I waited in the Common Room of the department to be called in for my oral prelim. Usually I wore my glasses only for distance, but right now I put them on to dispel the blurry vision caused by my anxiety. I was ushered into the exam room. Sable, sitting at the head of the table, greeted me with his habitual chuckle: "Mr. Pfefferkorn, I've never seen you wearing glasses." This observation brought out grins around the table. Keeping up with the congenial mood, I responded in like terms: "Only for insights, Mr. Sable, only for insights." The grins turned into smiles, and David, who officiated as my advocate, wore an especially wide smile. To open, Sable wanted to know which title of the reading list had left the deepest impression on me.

"A good omen for the opening," I mused for a moment, before answering. "I find that Berlin's distinction between the fox and hedgehog provides a compass for recognizing different human characteristics," I answered in a reflexive tone before adding a qualifier, as expected of a doctoral candidate. "However, we can be a fox in one situation and a hedgehog in another, depending on the circumstance." This remark elicited a range of give and take encompassing poetry, Marxism and the Bible.

"Take for instance the prelims," I continued, assuming Fisch's tone and mannerism. "Right now I'm performing as a fox moving in different and opposing directions, but in my written prelim you expect me to perform as a hedgehog, focussing on the meaning of the text at hand." I looked around and asked a pregnant question: "So what am I?" Sable chuckled and declared me a "hedgefox," to the surprise of everyone. Indeed, it was a "tour de fox" dialogue, which ended with Sable's announcement that it was lunchtime.

I stepped out of the room confident that I had made it. After a short pause that left me little time to mentally review my performance, the door opened and I was ushered back in. Sable congratulated me and declared me an official doctoral candidate, though I still had to take a written exam. Following a Brown tradition, I was invited to a communal lunch to celebrate the occasion. During the meal, my hosts were engaged in an animated conversation about hockey and football. I was vastly relieved, for their digression allowed me to mentally review the thirty-minute test that I had been given.

My mind wandered to the predicament of that doctoral student who had developed stigmata on his palm during his oral prelims. Mine was an enjoyable experience, but it could just as easily have been nightmarish under different circumstances. If the composition of the examiners were different, for instance, or if they were the same but in a fencing mood, seeking touché, or so many other unimaginable reasons — this could have been a "stigmata" ordeal for me. I reluctantly concluded that I was lucky.

I say "reluctantly," because one has no control over luck; it acts in mysterious ways like an arbitrary god. It has its own dynamics, oftentimes wreaking havoc and sometimes causing good results. When asked, "How did you manage to survive?" the confounded Holocaust survivor usually resorts to the mystical magic "luck," or its counterpart "miracle." He or she doesn't have any other explanation. Life under the Nazi regime, particularly for a Jew, did not accord with the customary laws and social norms of society. Life in what is widely accepted as normal society is, I tend to believe, analogous to a poker game: the player has no control over the cards he is dealt, but once the cards are in his hands, it is up to him to make the best of them.

This kind of balance, admittedly precarious, between chance and autonomy did not exist in the swastika kingdom. There the dealt cards were marked with the SS skulls. There was no shuffling of cards. Whenever I perceive myself as being caught in a helpless situation, I have an atavistic reflex that conjures an image of a caged animal hurtling from one set of bars to the other. Next to physical deprivation, helplessness permeated the victim: the concentration camp inmate; the hunted cowering in a *malina,* or hideout; the latter-day *conversos* averting prying eyes — these targeted victims had no escape routes from helplessness. It is worthwhile repeating a description of this psychologically crushing feeling because of the plaintive questions that abound in different circles: "Why did they go like sheep to the slaughter?"

My spouse, an emotionally composed person, showed signs of eagerness that day as she watched me climb up the squeaking stairs with a bit of an affected swagger. Earlier I had phoned her from the restaurant and told her the good news, but she wanted a live report, which I was happy to oblige her with. Later, David and I met for our after-dinner walk and our ritual ice cream and apple pie dessert. I shared with him my reflections on how chance and autonomy play out in extreme situations and in normal society. A scholar of Puritan literature, David put it in terms of predestination and free will, giving the theological concept an existential perspective. We discussed choosing a play for my written exam — the next step in the doctoral process. I was a Hamlet devotee. Each production I saw yielded new nuances of meaning; each reading of the play opened new vistas. Hamlet's signature is procrastination. Driven to rationalize his reluctance to act, Hamlet comes up with multiple reasons for his inaction. Instead of drawing the sword as implicitly instructed by the King his father, he weaves words into a poetic tapestry, something he is good at and enjoys. At the time I was still in the repressive phase of recovery from my Holocaust experience and consequently did not realize that my fascination with the play harks back to a specific circumstance in the ghetto that involved denial in the form of rationalization. Only a decade later or so, after having been seasoned by experience and reflection, did it dawn on me that the shadows of the past had been following me into academia. Indeed, the Stratford Bard taps a wide range of sensibilities.

In 1942 in the Międzyzec Ghetto, as I've mentioned, Menachem and I had intermittently planned to escape from the ghetto into the forest. As the frequency of the deportations increased, so did the frequency of our planning discussions. The money and valuables that I had retrieved from the peasant would buy us two guns, our entry fees into a partisan unit. We had also mapped out an escape route. Each time we were about to implement the plan, new obstacles seemed to emerge. First it was the elements: in the fall, winter was approaching and the forest would be an inhospitable place; in the spring the roads were muddy. When summer came, the Red Army made a breakthrough on the front and would, we felt, soon liberate us. Why not wait out the enemy, we thought. We kept on rationalizing our delays until we got caught in the trap. Now I had chosen Hamlet without being conscious of the reasons for my choice.

In the interim, I "took it easy," an endearing phrase that made me think: what if the "it" were heavy; how could "it" be taken easily? Of course, my fellow students wanted a re-enactment of what went on behind the closed doors on that Saturday, and I readily obliged. After hours, over a few beers, I put on my thespian cap. Sable was easy to take on. He had idiosyncratic characteristics: body language, gait, speech patterns and distinctive chuckles. He was a cartoonist's delight, a lampoonist's dream. Boulger was more of a challenge. I could not quite get into his character; the smoky cough interrupting his laconic sentences was tough to mimic. But on the whole, it was a success from a repertoire point of view.

After passing the written exam, I found that the interim fun time was over. I was ready to work on my dissertation. What I needed, as David put it, was a creative advisor, preferably an expert in the field, a kind of scholar-cum-playwright, one who did not have a heavy teaching load and would have the time to speed up the process. This was indeed a tall order.

Among the intellectually diverse faculty, there was one person who came closest to meeting these criteria. A widely published poet and playwright who wrote numerous scholarly introductions to his translations from Spanish, notably Lorca, Edwin Honig seemed to be the right person.

"I don't do this," Honig responded to my question on whether he would be interested in being my advisor. Yes, he liked my article on Durrenmatt's *Old Lady*, yes, my dissertation topic "is intriguing, but the time factor is crucial." Pointing to the cluttered papers on his desk, he said in a somewhat resentful tone, "I've got to get these out soon." The graduate creative writing course that he taught was the bane of his existence. He suggested a number of people in the department capable of advising me. As I got up to leave, he must have noticed the morose look on my face. "Let me sleep on it. I'll let you know."

Edwin Honig was not your average professor of world literature. Except for his attire, the standard patch-elbowed jacket and crumpled corduroy pants, he stood out in his idiosyncrasies. He sported a dramatic shock of wavy hair and carried his tall body upright with a bounce. His marriage to a younger woman, Margot, who had borne him two girls, enhanced Honig's reputation. When I met him at the letterbox a few days later, he greeted me with a friendly "Hi there," and rather casually remarked, "I'll take it on." The decoded "it" sounded like a choir of guardian angels announcing the coming of the Messiah or the Second Coming, depending which crossing you believe in — that of the Red Sea or of the Golgotha. At that moment I had the two confused. "We'll meet soon, and meanwhile start working," he added laconically. But Honig was far from being laconic during our ensuing working meetings. We would meet in his office or at his home to discuss the chapter that he had returned to me earlier, its margins generously marked with comments, mostly constructive and occasionally sardonic. I preferred the meetings at his house.

After the formal part of the meeting was done, we would sit in the living room and go on randomly chatting about whatever topic came up. Margot joined us with cups of tea. My relationship with Honig evolved until we were on a first-name basis, one that resonated not just with comradeship in the Communist Politburo sense, but with an affinity that withstood the passage of time, as evidenced ten years later when he came on a scholarship to Israel. I wished I'd had more time to work out some pivotal concepts before committing them to paper, but time was running out. Edwin was having one of his plays staged in London, and he planned to attend some of the rehearsals. To add to the pressure, my scholarship was fast coming to an end, so I had to have the dissertation done.

Notwithstanding the time pressure, I enjoyed writing the dissertation. I felt great satisfaction in managing to synchronize meaning and sound in shaping a sentence and making it flow from the preceding one to the following. More even than my satisfaction in style, I benefited psychologically and intellectually from the writing process. In the course of writing, I discovered subliminal layers of consciousness that lay hidden under the debris of my past, which further clarified to me my intellectual pursuits, emblematically expressed in the title of my dissertation.

At Brown University, people did not ask one's whereabouts during the war years. It was not a topic of interest. As for myself, I neither evaded such conversations nor offered to talk about my experience. Only David and George, his co-conspirator buddy, were privy to my past, and they were not aware of the details. As my chapters kept appearing in his letterbox in rapid succession, Edwin became intrigued by the spiritual antecedents of the dissertation. He wanted to know whether it was an incubation process or an insight that I had had. "After all," he said, "it isn't every day that you come up with an idea of setting off dramatic genres three hundred years apart." We were sitting in his living room chatting in a relaxed atmosphere and sipping tea. I was waiting for the rain to stop so I could leave. Edwin, in turn, must also have been waiting for me to leave when he abruptly set loose the question. Truth to tell, I was not surprised by his curiosity. As it often happens with poets, Edwin had a clairvoyant's inward eye that piloted him to look into man's intricate being. While reading my chapters, he sensed an undercurrent of passion feeding my sensibilities. "I look at the human condition through the glass, darkly," I uttered, paraphrasing Corinthians, and went into a philosophical, rather long monologue. "Shocking as it may sound, the concentration camps demonstrate empirically that these mammoth human labs were essentially microcosms of the human species and of the world at large; the predatory behaviour of the inmates in the concentration camps manifested in verbal and physical violence was a distorted reflection of the plots hatched at the water cooler, conspired in the Common Room, planned in the Boardroom and occasionally pillow-talked in the bedroom.

"Of course, there are differences, vital in the inceptive meaning of the word: there, people literally used violence to survive; here, people metaphorically backstab each other to climb the hierarchical structure to a reserved parking spot and a key to the executive washroom. In the concentration camp the struggle of survival was brutally naked; in society at large, the promotional struggle is sophisticated and devious. Ultimately, one is survival — the other is greed- or ego-driven. But the essence that makes up the human species hardly changed." I was overcome by weariness, and that was noted by Edwin. He suggested that we "take it up next time."

That night, I tossed in my bed. In my conversation with Edwin, I had established an anthropological link between the behaviour of inmates in a concentration camp and that of people in the workplace. But how did this theory translate into a juxtaposition of the Jacobean Theatre with the Theatre of the Absurd? Though I did not explicitly or consciously deal with the Holocaust in my dissertation, I felt that my fascination with the severance between cause and effect, the rampant rush of impulses that percolated through my experience, trickled down to the dissertation. "Just as the concentration camps were a distilled reality of normal society," I mused, "so were the Jacobean Theatre and the Theatre of the Absurd prototypes of their respective cultural backgrounds and times. Both dramas were driven by a savage impulse, an impulse embedded in the human species; both are manifestations of unleashed irrational action." Back in Israel, I had discussed this topic with David, but it was more of a tangential kind of talk, more musing than analysis. At a later time I shared my cogitations with Edwin.

## Chomsky and I

While working on the dissertation, I intermittently wrote for *Haaretz*. Providence, Rhode Island, however, was hardly a hotbed of exciting news that would interest the Israeli reader. So when the MLA (Modern Language Association) held its annual meeting in New York, listing Noam Chomsky on the program as a speaker, I thought that this would be good material for an article. In addition, the MLA Conference would enable me to meet in person fellow academics with whom I'd corresponded over the years.

Chomsky had been in an adversarial relationship with Israel for some time now. He saw a bi-national state as a solution to the Israeli-Palestinian conflict, a vision scoffed at by the Israelis but embraced by the post-Zionist revisionists. At the conference, I kept my eyes open for him, but he was nowhere to be seen on the first or the second day of the conference. Still the MIT people promised that "Noam will arrive on the scheduled day of his lecture." The name "Noam," uttered in a tone of reverence, indicated the guru status he enjoyed. I realized that my chances for an interview were slim.

When the time came for his talk, Chomsky entered the stage and was greeted by a tumultuous welcome by a tightly packed house; they were hanging from the rafters, as the saying goes, though the rafters were invisible.

The audience enthusiastically responded to his condemnation of American Imperialism in general and specifically of the Vietnam War. My expectations that Chomsky would take on the Israeli territorial expansion and wrap it up with American territorial greed were disappointed. The word Israel was not invoked. If his stage entrance was tumultuous, his exit was thunderous. Left with no interview, I put together a short piece reviewing more the reaction of the audience to his speech than the words of the speaker. I laced the end of the article with a sardonic-lite comment reminding my readers that another Jew had already made his appearance on the third day and disappeared on the same day, heralding a paradigm shift in the history of mankind. To prevent any misunderstanding, I added that these must have been coincidental similarities. When I received the next weekly edition of *Haaretz* about a week later by mail (this was before the satellite age), it had about three disparaging letters about my article. One, by Professor Assa Kasher, was particular acerbic. In a letter I received shortly thereafter, Tammuz asked whether I would want to respond to my critics. He himself, though he thought that Chomsky's bi-national ideas were dated and naïve, felt that he should be given a platform for expressing them in the Hebrew press.

Tammuz's democratic impulse made me proud of Israel. After all, Chomsky fathered many anti-Israel groups in his pursuit of his bi-national views, consequently harming Israel's standing among the left, and yet Tammuz, a fervent patriot , was ready to allow him a voice in a major national newspaper. True, Tammuz harboured an ulterior motive: he wanted the "children to play before him" on the pages of the newspaper; it made good copy and would make him smile under his bushy moustache. But the primary motive, undoubtedly, was his belief in the free expression of the press. And this ameliorated my misgivings about the country that I was about to return to and my plan to join the faculty of Haifa University.

Undoubtedly, being part of the Israeli enterprise since its inception — experiencing its ingenuity, tapped from the Talmudic gene pool, in industry, agriculture, and most notably in the military — instilled in me an antidote to the helplessness that I had suffered back in the *anus mundi*.

I did not subscribe to the widely-held view that the State of Israel provided a safe haven for the Jews, but I believed in Israel's determination to stand up to its enemies. Helplessness was anathema to the Israeli ethos. I therefore drew emotional strength from my country's military achievements and especially its cultural accomplishments. The rejuvenation of the Hebrew language, an ancient culture brought into modernity, maintaining a vibrant democracy despite the volatile regional politics — all these and many other achievements aroused pride in me. At the same time I had serious reservations about Israel's policies and was repulsed by the haughty behaviour of the settlers in the occupied territories.

## From Providence to the Holy Land

On our return to Israel, I found a country that had gone through profound changes. In our three-year absence, between 1968 and 1971, it seemed as though the very landscape had assumed different contours. What struck me was the frenzied building that went on and on, covering the hills and the plains. A ride along the old Tel-Aviv-Haifa road revealed dotted spaces on both sides of the road. Housing construction fever raged in the occupied territories, where red-roofed houses sprang from the bare land. We bought a townhouse still in the early stages of construction on the far end of the western part of Mount Carmel in Haifa, a patch of land that had stood desolate for twenty years. The triumphant glow that consumed Israel in the wake of the Six-Day War had morphed into a national state of mind. The dire predictions made by people who kept a cool head had turned out to be true. For the first time in the twenty years of its existence, the country was split between Messianic visionaries and political realists; the one advocated a Greater Israel from the sea to the Jordan River, and the other called for trading land for peace. Unquestionably, Israeli politics had shifted to the right.

The "Land for Peace" swappers dominated the university faculties and to some measure the student population. Haifa University had a substantial number of Israeli Arab students and facilitated dialogue between them and their Jewish counterparts. I watched, fascinated by how these well-spoken and politically savvy Arab students were going through an identity change. They claimed to be part of the Palestinian people and advocated the establishment of a sovereign state in the occupied territories. In answer to my question about whether they would relocate to such a state, they firmly stated that this was an irrelevant question. Playing the devil's advocate, I questioned why the Palestinians did not demand sovereignty when Jordan ruled the West Bank and Egypt the Gaza strip. The answer I received indicated political maturity. National consciousness was seeded in 1948, with the Naqba, the Catastrophe (referring to the establishment of the Israeli State), and evolved over time, but it was the defeat of the Arab armies in 1967 that brought it to a head. The Israeli Arabs, in league with their compatriots in the occupied territories, were visibly transiting from the general designation "Arabs" to the specific "Palestinian" identity.

Sadly, the Israeli political elite ignored this process of identity evolvement. With the economy booming and immigration reaching its peak, the Israelis appeared complacent. What was dubbed as "The War of Attrition" in the South, with Egyptians and Israelis exchanging heavy fire, was much too far from the bustling cities to cause worries. In a newspaper interview, Moshe Dayan, the Defence Minister, boasted that "we have never had it so good." Arguments aimed at sobering up this triumphant feel-good tipsiness fell on deaf ears.

Indirectly I was also the beneficiary of the spoils of victory, so to speak. We lived in a town house on the Carmel; our household had two monthly incomes. Life was comfortable. The fact that I was part of a people that occupied territories whose population desired to rid itself of the occupier was an abstract irritant. But the abstract became concrete on encountering reality.

One day I boarded a bus that would take me from Jerusalem to a military base in the occupied territories for reserve duty. Most seats were taken by settlers, their knitted skullcaps the signature of their ideology, and gun-toting soldiers. I sat next to a young settler with a peach-fuzz face, who held an especially big gun between his thighs. Exactly at twelve noon the news came on. The first segment broadcast was a resolution passed by the High Court that a stretch of land confiscated by the government and transferred to a certain settlement was confiscated illegally. The settlers were given a short period of time to evacuate that piece of land. My seatmate winced at every sentence that came through the radio. I asked him what he thought of the decision. Looking me straight in the eye, he raised his gun skywards and pronounced: "There is only one judge and that's Hashem (God), and no one else." I questioned him how he knew that Hashem was displeased with the High Court's decision: "Orthodox judges, like Eilon and others, sit on that bench," I pointed out. He just held on to his mantra: "We know best." As I was riding the buses from one military base to another I heard the same rehearsed chant for three days: "It's ours, God gave us the land."

This absolute conviction of an intimate relationship between the Almighty and the faithful also had its humorous moments. On a seasonably hot and damp August morning my spouse and daughter got into the car and we drove up to Jerusalem. They had never visited the ultra-Orthodox bastion of Mea Shearim, whose name translates into Hundred Gates. According to tradition, Messiah will come walking through one of these gates (of course in the fullness of time), and the original founders of this enclave, who had immigrated to the Holy Land in the nineteenth century, wanted to be among the first to welcome him. Covered from top to toe, so as not to offend the local custom, my spouse and daughter entered the enclave, while I seated myself on a stony bench next to a bus stop. After having read the anti-Zionist pamphlets stuck on the wall behind me, and having exhausted all other means at my disposal to while away the time, I crossed the street to buy an afternoon tabloid. They did not carry any Zionist publications, the shopkeeper told me.

From the vantage position of my bench, I was observing this benighted human scenery with fascination. Towering over the milling crowd, a heavily-built Hassid lugging a suitcase was striding toward me. It was beyond my comprehension why wearing heavy black garments topped by a black hat in the heat of a summer day would hasten the Messiah's coming. In my former life, I had heard yearnings for the Messiah, and when he eventually appeared, it was in the form of tanks and other vehicles wearing red stars. The black-clad Hassid was wiping rivulets of sweat from his face when I approached him at the bus stop. At first, my inkling was to ask him about his attire, but then I thought he might take offence of such an inquiry. Instead I touched on an impersonal issue.

Speaking in Yiddish, I expressed my frustration at not being able to buy a Hebrew newspaper. "Why is it that you don't have Hebrew newspapers?" I asked gingerly.

"And why do we need newspapers?" he answered with a question.

"What about radios, no antennas here?" A knowing smile curved on his lips.

"And why do we need radios?"

I felt that I was losing the fencing match, but I still had one more medium left. "But what about television?" I pressed.

"And why do we need television?"

"Ah," I exclaimed in a touché tone, "How will you know when Messiah comes?"

"Foolish Jew," he answered in condescending pity, "will the editor know before me when the Messiah comes?" The retort came like a rapier's thrust. The bus pulled up to the curb, and he got into it. Faith had trumped technology.

I began suffering from anxieties that would not let up. It was as if an apprehensive condition had been grafted onto me. Usually I would have had to delve into the depths of my psyche to find the cause for the distress. Not this time. I was teaching drama and English literature while my scholarly pursuits took me in the direction of Holocaust research. To satisfy my dean, I still published some articles on drama and poetry, but my mind was increasingly occupied with the events of those dark days. In my doctoral dissertation,

I had established links between the Jacobean drama and modern drama, notably the Theatre of the Absurd. Now I tried to show how certain patterns of the persecutors' as well as the inmates' behaviour bear resemblances to human behaviour in normative society, behaviour that found expressions in contemporary theatre, as a point of reference to evil. The burgher turned into a scheduler of cattle car trains headed for slavery or gas chambers; the policeman into the *Kommandant* of a concentration camp; the lawyer a collaborator with the prosecution, the doctor an experimenter on live human beings; the scholars of various disciplines providers of rationales of Aryan superiority with the clergyman's blessing — and all were acting in unison to the evocative speeches of the *Führer*. Even the dog, the proverbial friend of man, was trained to bare its fangs at the victim upon hearing "*Jude*."

Once these were law-abiding citizens and Scripture observers, but they seamlessly morphed into torturers and subsequently killers. The suspension of the human sensibilities of the S.S. directly affected the behaviour of the *prominante*, who imitated their masters. The campgrounds became a Darwinian habitat — "Nature, red in tooth and claw," to quote Tennyson — and its inmate population lay in wait to prey on the weak. This unleashed evil in man, dramatized in refined manifestations, percolated to the stage. In my intellectual pursuit, intended to show the liquidity of human nature shaped by circumstances and how it was transmigrated to drama, I thought that wedding the two would satisfy my dramaturgical impulse as well as my quest to understand even just an inkling of the fickleness of human nature. After all, I mused, academics dealing in drama are in abundance, but there were few, if any, who could view the theatre through the prism of extreme situations. I would bring to the academic discourse a double perspective of the human condition in extreme situations.

In the course of my research, I was emotionally drawn further into Holocaust materials. It was not a wise career move, and was one that I occasionally came to regret. David was privy to my dilemmas, but, like me, he could not resolve my conflict.

### The Yom Kippur War

This was the second Israeli war that I sat out in the rear, serving in the reserves. I had been disqualified from serving in the preceding one, the Six Day War, because I was not up to snuff technologically due to my absence from the country; now I served in what was named "The Education and Culture" unit, hardly fit for fighting in the desert. The news from the front was sketchy, brought back by the wounded soldiers. Ominous news from the front made its rounds on the beaches and coffee shops, but we learned about the Israeli Defence Force setbacks in the opening days of the war only after wounded soldiers began returning from the battlefield. As soon as the war ended, I was called up for duty and sent up North, where fierce battles had taken place. What struck me was the change of mood among the officer corps. Gone was the hubristic swagger of invincibility.

They had battled the Syrian tanks rumbling down the Golan slopes to the edge of the Bnot Ya'akov Bridge, heading for the Israeli cities. Something stirred inside them, perhaps a realization of the precariousness of the Jewish State. I had been to Israeli military bases numerous times but never encountered such a sense of historical maturity among the high-ranking officers as in the wake of the Yom Kippur War. Soon this awakening translated itself into a national awareness that viewed the *Shoah* in a new perspective. The media, the arts, the literati — all embraced the *Shoah* with a passion. Most importantly, the high school system began developing curricula and training teachers. Observing the eagerness that swept the country, Meir Wieseltier, an acerbic poet, commented, "Auschwitz, I heard that you're in style. Nice men talk about you with respect."

Undoubtedly the *Shoah* was causing a buzz in the country. Now it was easier to be Elie Wiesel's "champion," as the literati dubbed me, and pursuing the Holocaust subject was no longer looked down upon. With a grant obtained from the Strochlitz Foundation, I hired bi-lingual and sometimes tri-lingual students to research the archives, identifying diaries written by children.

Writing under siege and immediately after liberation, these young authors, ranging in age from their early to late teens, put down in excruciating details their encounter with evil. Surprisingly, there is hardly any self-pity in their accounts, only descriptions limned in indelible images. T.S. Eliot would have defined them as objective correlatives. "Mother Live for Me" is a story told by a girl in an orphanage in post-war Poland, recounting how she and her Mum trudged from village to village to seek shelter, and when all attempts failed, the mother took her in her arms and walked towards the river: "No, no," the girl pleaded, "Mum live for me." A detailed diary written by an elementary-school Czech girl over a period of two years recounts a series of humiliations. In the course of these two years, she describes the officially sanctioned edicts and notes how deportation orders increasingly slice away Jewish homes. She waves final goodbyes to her friends as they are deported, and at the end she was being waved to by a remaining friend on her way to Terezin. The last entry of the diary, which began March 15, 1939, is dated December 8, 1941.

Among the numerous singular childrens' writings, one that stands out in its uniqueness is "A Jewish Grave." Structuring it as a film script, the author, high school student S. Dratwa, predicts that after the war, "…investors and profiteers…. will make a film about the suffering of the Jews," which he describes in a series of pictorial presentations. The versed script ends with the following stanza:

> When this film grows popular
> the public will call it "A Jewish Grave."
> It will be shown in America,
> England and Scotland.
> And, wrapt in emotion,
> Quivering with emotions,
> Everyone will think:
> "The film is fabulous;
> The scenes are wonderful,
> But nothing is true.
> They are only tales
> Drawn from a grotesque land.

It isn't that the witnessing authors writing under siege did not often express premonitions that their stories would be taken as figments of their anguished imagination after the war, but that those who did so were mature people, some of them seasoned authors. What makes Dratwa's writing so extraordinary is that he was just a high schooler when he constructed a script, shaped in style and structure, fit to be filmed, and imagined the reaction of the film's audience.

In the course of researching Holocaust archival materials, I had managed to find a modus operandi that enabled me to view the materials from a time perspective without losing the emotional immediacy of the moment. But this distant proximity, to use an oxymoron, deserted me on reading the children's writings. I obsessively identified with the young authors to the extent that I assumed their personae. It was an unwilling mental exercise in re-imagining.

Teaching the Holocaust had its own difficulties. While teaching the subject, I tried to bring my class as close as humanly possible to the realities of the events, without exposing the students to my philosophical views about the dark side of human nature. Wary that my pessimistic views might be attributed to my past ordeals, I avoided mentioning it unless directly asked. Not all survivors seemed to share my bleak views. I invited a fellow survivor my age to give a talk to my class of overseas programme students at Tel-Aviv University.

An accomplished architect, actively involved in promoting Holocaust awareness in his adopted U.K., Romek presented his philosophy to the class. It was a "gather ye rosebuds while ye may" theme guided by the operative phrase "to look forward." All the while, I was wondering whether his sunny view of life was a self-delusional product or whether he was giving voice to his convictions. My fellow survivor loved humanity. Later, over coffee, we talked about our friends back in London and in other countries. I was tempted to probe his pronounced convictions, but decided it would be gauche to upset him.

In the course of my research in the archives I met young Germans who came as volunteers to work in the archives; others came to do their graduate work. These were for the most part the first post-war generation; some were children during the Nazi period, and were humorously referred to as "the sandwich generation." In conversation, they referred to the war generation as "them," implying a break with the recent past without disowning the Fatherland; they distanced themselves from their families without renouncing them. Making conversation with them came easily to me.

My interlocutors referred to the Allies not as "liberators" but as occupiers. They recognized that the Nazi party was democratically elected to power and that by and large their parents either supported or tolerated the Nazi regime. Hence the Allies did not liberate them, but rather occupied the country. This canard of being liberated by the Allies travelled across the Atlantic to meet political exigencies during the cold war. But these young people looked history straight in the eye, ready to carry the weight of responsibility that their ancestors burdened them with. They endeared themselves to me. At the time, I had no idea to what extent they were representative of their generation.

About two decades earlier, I had come across German students in London and Edinburgh, during my studies of linguistics. But our exchanges were limited to professional argot. It was not animosity that made me avoid social contacts with the German students; rather I feared that such contacts might make me revisit the dark past — exclusively reserved for nights — and I was not ready for that yet. With the passage of time, notably after having written my dissertation, which prompted me to get reengaged with the world of the grotesque, I was eager to establish a dialogue with the young Germans. It turned out that they were as eager to talk as I was.

By now, I recognized evil as an intrinsic part of human nature manifested in ripe circumstances. The same young men and women who had come to Israel to make amends for the sins of their fathers, mothers and grandparents might have become participants in the Final Solution, had they been born three decades earlier. And had Germany triumphed, they would have been part of the Master Race, lording it over the Slavs in the East. For that matter, I myself could have become an S.S. trooper had I been born into the Aryan race at the propitious time. The paradigmatic Cain and Abel story illustrates the roles randomly assigned to us, which we play out in life. Had Cain been the shepherd and Abel the tiller of the soil, then Abel would have been the exiled murderer and Cain the victim. Whatever resentments I harboured against the German war generation, I did not visit them upon their children. Jeremiah, among other Hebrew prophets, pronounces that in the future, "everyone will die for his own sins; whoever eats sour grapes — his own teeth will be set on edge."

## Touching the Past with Dieter

It was in this state of mind that I was invited to attend a conference on the "Quantum Residue of a Polity: Israel and the Holocaust," sponsored by ISPP, scheduled to take place in Mannheim, Germany, in 1981. There was a rich menu of topics, some of more interest than others. My eye was caught by one entitled "Compliance and Oblivion," given by Dieter D. Hartmann. It was the first part of the title, "Compliance," that intrigued me. There was always something in me that resisted compliance in its different variations. During my two years of concentration camp sojourns, I stifled that "something." In those brutally-ruled places there was no margin for defying the rules. The only way an inmate could thumb his nose at the tormenters was to fling himself at the electrified wires. The SS did not take kindly to such daring. Masters of Life and Death, they regarded suicide as an act of disobedience that incurred punishment of the entire camp. Over the years after liberation I adapted to the norms of Civilization, but my native aversion to conformity did not abate. It actually evolved into an article of faith. I believed that blind obedience to Powers — divine, earthly and other kinds — if not questioned, challenged and, if necessary, defied, threatened my human dignity. I was, therefore, from the beginning favourably disposed towards the topic and its author.

The paper analysed the range of reactions of the German people to the persecution of their Jewish neighbours. After having cited an array of scholarly sources on the subject, Hartmann noted, "More often than not, Germans stood by all the suffering they saw." Forestalling an excuse by the apologists that bystanders were emotionally dysfunctional because of fear, he asserted, "People in general were no sadists. But most of them proved unable to be really moved by the victims' fate. Compassion was beyond many Germans' reach." Hartmann's assertions were largely drawn from the Nazi trials, which he had thoroughly researched.

As the Conference was winding down, I ran into Dieter in the hotel lobby. After some courtesy exchanges, he offered to take me on a tour to the towns and villages along the Neckar River, home to many Jewish communities in the pre-Nazi era. In the Middle Ages the river was used to carry rafts from the Black Forest to the Rhine.

The following morning I and another Conference participant got into Dieter's car and we set out to the Baden-Wurtt Emberg region. Dieter's familiarity with the area was obvious. He walked us through the villages and towns, pointing out the painted-over *Mezzuzot* on the doorframes of the houses, an indication of former Jewish residency. He knew the exact places of the synagogues, now converted into barns or other facilities, and the location of the *Mikvah*.

For Dieter this was not merely a guided tour into recent history. Rather, it was a mourner's visit to a cemetery that held in its tombs the destruction of a civilization. Among the myriad images that filtered into my consciousness that day, there was one moment that stands out. As we were walking toward the car, I heard songs coming out of a beer hall. I was curious to see the people in the beer hall and suggested that we enter the place just for a few seconds. Dieter refused, but I went in nonetheless. I saw flushed middle-aged men and a scattering of women sitting at tables, drinking beer from tall glasses and giving full throated voice to their songs. I had heard these songs before and seen these faces before. When I came out, I noticed Dieter with our companion standing quite a distance from the beer hall. "I never go into these places," Dieter said, accentuating each word. "They brought the Nazis to power." He wore his distaste for Nazism in its multiple manifestations on his sleeve. He was for real and he put his money — literally — where his mouth was.

Later, when Sarah and I met Dieter in Tübingen, he took us on a tour of old Jewish cemeteries. I watched him in fascination: how he put on a *Kippa* and, as we walked through the rows of graves, placed pebbles on the headstones while reading the Hebrew inscriptions. He was instrumental in buying a barn that used to be a synagogue and converting it into a local museum. Though we come from two diametrically different life-experiences, Dieter and I seemed to look at humanity through the glass darkly. Our regular correspondence bears out this view.

A telephone message from Washington awaited me on my return home. A Ms. Lark of the Education Department would like to talk to me, and asked that I call her collect. Ms. Lark came right to the point. Would I be interested in coming to Washington on a Fullbright-Hayes scholarship to develop Holocaust curricula? Forestalling my expected questions, she hastily added that the scholarship vacancy occurred because of a sudden cancellation. She would not tell me who recommended me, nor the name of the person I would be replacing. "The situation needs a quick resolution, otherwise we lose the scholarship," she added in her lilting southern accent. I had three days to make up my mind. Even before consulting my family, I called my lawyer and the University. There were some legal issues to be sorted out before replying to Ms. Lark.

## Pfefferkorn versus the State of Israel

These legalities involved my daughter, who was disabled and was therefore entitled to a fuel subsidy from the government. As oil prices spiralled upward, her grant remained at the same level. I wrote a most polite letter to Mr. Abbulafia, the CEO of the Ministry of Finance, who had jurisdiction over this matter. In the letter I requested to know why the subsidy was not being adjusted to match the current oil prices. As expected, I received no reply. A follow-up registered letter that could be best described as assertively polite — leaning more to the assertive — was likewise ignored.

I called the Ministry's office requesting to talk to Mr. Abbulafia and was put through to his secretary-cum-assistant. "Yes, we've got your letters, Dr. Pfefferkorn," she said in a rather surly tone. "But we're swamped here." Talking to Mr. Abbulafia was out of the question; "he is out of the country." My subsequent attempts to get Mr. Abbulafia's attention also failed. In one of my numerous calls, just about when the telephone conversation hit its last syllables, "… lafia," an idea struck me. "If this thing doesn't get resolved by the end of this week, I'm going to file a Nisi Order grievance," I stated in a determined voice, citing a legal clause I knew of whereby a citizen can sue the government or its agencies directly.

This statement met with the aforementioned secretary-cum-assistant's drawn-out ridicule. "Dr. Pfefferkorn, I've been to this movie many times; it's not serious." She was right. I was not serious. People did not go through that hassle for a mere 1,000 Shekalim. But later, riding on the train home from Tel-Aviv, I mused: why not make it serious? Why not take on this impenetrable bureaucracy? The advantage of a Nisi Order grievance was that it spared the complainant going through a cumbersome judicial process; it allows direct access to the High Court, if only after an initial lower court hearing.

But to pull this off, I needed a smart lawyer, one who adhered to principles and who would take the case on a pro bono basis. This was a tall order. I mentally shuffled through my list of lawyers. Each one had one of the required attributes, but only one attorney possessed all three. This was my friend, Marcel Kedem, a man who wore his principles — some of them idiosyncratic — on his sleeve. He had been practicing law for a number of years, but had never yet appealed to the High Court. I broached the subject with him. Yes, he would do it, prepare the writ pro bono, but I had to do the research and if the application was accepted I would have to appear at the court hearings in person. He gave me a list of legal books to look up. The following morning I was in the library hunting precedents. After the day's search, I'd come to his office and he would go over the list, sprinkling the margins with lawyerly comments. This routine went on for a week, until my findings satisfied Marcel's rigorous legal criteria. When my writ was accepted, we drove up to Jerusalem on the scheduled date. I was all dressed up for the occasion.

The court panel was made up of three honourable judges. His Honour, Judge Susman, presiding, sat in the middle, and on his right and left sat two other judges. One of the two judges appeared to be catnapping, eyes half shut, the slit widening and narrowing intermittently; the other was fussing with his fingers and hardly listening to the procedure. If memory serves, in my entire fifteen minute court appearance, these two judges did not ask a single question or make a single comment.

Judge Susman began by congratulating the author of the writ. I pointed to Marcel who stood up and bowed slightly. This was quite a feather in his legal cap, and in his first High Court appeal, too! As coached earlier by Marcel, I answered the Judge's questions point by point, without elaborate trailers. "This is not a university seminar," Marcel had cautioned me. The Nisi Order became absolute and Judge Susman ordered the government to respond to my grievance within thirty days.

We stayed over in Jerusalem to spend time with friends and regale them with stories of our court experience and returned to Haifa the following morning. No sooner had I entered the house than the telephone rang. The secretary-cum-assistant was on the phone, voice dripping milk and honey. Mr. Abbulafia "wants to talk to you." My unrequited pen pal had finally succumbed to my doggishness — or was it the Nisi Order that did it? The following exchange ensued:

Abbulafia: Dr. Pfefferkorn, if there were many like you, we'd move this country forward.

Pfefferkorn: More like me, and fewer like you, perhaps.

Abbulafia: (amused) You do me wrong. Believe me. I haven't seen any of your letters till yesterday.

Pfefferkorn: You had better change your staff.

Abbulafia: Dr. Pfefferkorn, come to my office on Sunday morning, and over a cup of coffee we'll settle the matter.

Pfefferkorn: Meaning?

Abbulafia: 1,100 Shekalim that's coming to you.

Pfefferkorn: What about my lawyer's fees?

Abbulafia: I'll tell you straight. My lawyers tell me that you're going to lose the case. The reason I'm offering you a deal is that I want to avoid the press. It's our reputation.

He delivered his reasoning in a Sephardic pronunciation, enunciating every vowel, music to my ears. I was envious of his Hebrew enunciation and marvelled at his honesty.

Abbulafia's dire prediction turned out to be accurate. As the honourable presiding judge, Haim Cohen, put it at the full-fledged court panel: "The Knesset is a sovereign entity and its committees have sovereignty to fashion policy." But I had a reward of another sort. On the door of the room where the court hearings were held hung a note printed in large letters: "Pfefferkorn Versus the Government of Israel." That alone was worth the price of admission, for as is clear from my history, opposing authority comes much more naturally than bowing to it.

The court's ruling was a mixed blessing of defeat and triumph. It had been a long time, a very long time, since I could stand up to the arrogance of power. Though the court's ruling went against me, ultimately I was the winner. Sixty years earlier, I had been unshod of human dignity, and marked as a target, with open season declared. I walked out of the Terezin ghetto on that last beautiful morning and took a silent vow to never again submit to the arrogance of power. It's a vow which at times was costly to keep.

In any case, now that this matter had been settled, we were free to travel. Upon our arrival in the States, I was assigned to the Board of Jewish Education (BJE) to develop a Holocaust curriculum for the Greater Washington area, as well as to give occasional talks on the subject. I had scant experience working in this field and had to start from scratch. Developing a Holocaust curriculum carried some formidable challenges, as I found out. The foremost was to find a way to teach the horrors of those times without traumatizing the high school students. The task at hand was to introduce the young student to an experience that was outside the pale of human conduct, or to put it differently, to make the strange familiar. Kay Ackman, an activist member of what's known as the Second Generation, the children of Holocaust survivors, helped me overcome these pedagogic hurdles and bring the curriculum to publication.

Even as I was putting the finishing touches on the curriculum, I joined the staff at the U.S. Holocaust Council, in the beginning as a part-time consultant and later as a full-time director of research. The Council was mandated by Congress and the President to build a Memorial for the victims of the Holocaust. No sooner had the ink dried on the paper than two vital issues arose: the definition of a Holocaust victim and the nature of the Memorial. The Polish Congress's representatives on the Council called for memorializing three million Polish victims next to the six million Jews. Another figure bandied around was eleven million victims killed in the occupied territories. This would include the Ukrainians, allies of Nazi Germany, whose sons served in the war and many of whom took part in ghetto deportations and served guard duty in concentration camps. What all this meant was divesting the Holocaust of its uniqueness.

I was sitting against the wall, fascinated by the debate at the Council meetings, which were at times charged with tension, and imagining addressing the Council: "Back then, hidden in the shadows from the prying eyes of my enemies, both German and Polish, I saw no one seeking victimization; now I am witnessing a victim rush. Then, some of my Polish fellow citizens would have bartered me to the Nazis for a kilo of sugar or other commodities, even though they did not hate me." After the war, many of them perpetrated pogroms on Jewish survivors. Now the Polish representatives were seeking moral equivalence to the hunted Jews. It is not that I belittle the Polish people's suffering at the hands of the Nazis, who relegated them to slavery in their vast empire, but they were not assigned to the gas chamber as we were.

There were plenty of dramatic moments during these discussions, but there is one that stands out. An Auschwitz survivor, Sigmund Strochlitz, told the Council about the discriminatory measures taken against the Jewish students at the Kraków Jagelski University he had attended before the war. One infamous decree prohibited Jewish students from sitting down during the lectures; they had to stand on their feet at all times. I could not resist a sardonic smirk at this recollection of the kind, brotherly feelings of our supposed fellow victims.

The person who led the charge against diluting the singularity of Jewish survivorship was Elie Wiesel. The presidential appointment to chair the Council granted him the prestige and his Auschwitz internment gave him the moral voice to uphold the distinctive Jewish character of survivorship, notwithstanding the political pressures that came from the White House. Yet, mindful of the Nazis' genocidal ramifications, he defined the "Holocaust [as] a uniquely Jewish event that has Universal implications."

In this struggle to preserve the uniqueness of the Holocaust as different from genocide, Wiesel drew moral and emotional strength from the community of survivors and the unanimous support of the survivors on the Council. He gave them a voice and a vocabulary, articulating the purpose of their suffering. The theme that wove the multifaceted narrative strands into a survivorship tapestry was Remembrance. It ran through the entirety of Jewish history, from the wanderings in the desert to the destruction of the Second Temple to the Diaspora, bursting forth in the aftermath of the Holocaust. Riding in a car with Wiesel to Brooklyn, I asked him what the defining moment of the post-Holocaust era was. *Zicharon*, he replied spontaneously. We spoke in Hebrew and the word *Zicharon*, remembrance, came out as if chiselled in a Judean rock.

Sigmund Strochlitz and Miles Lerman, both surivors, functioned as Wiesel's operative arms in Washington. They were inseparable, joined by their survivors' experience and the Chairman's imprimatur, and were dubbed Wiesel's lieutenants. An unusual relationship evolved between Wiesel and Strochlitz, akin to that of father and son. Respectful of his older friend, Wiesel lent Strochlitz an eager ear and vested in him important responsibilities. In its first phase of existence, the Council primarily focussed on raising Holocaust awareness countrywide. Strochlitz chaired the Days of Remembrance committee, which was charged with implementing an annual memorial for the Holocaust victims in April. While Days of Remembrance were annually held in each state, their centrepiece was observed at Congress.

Lerman was in charge of organizing international conferences, notably the Liberators Conference that honoured the soldiers of East and West for their roles in the liberations of the concentration camps and the Righteous Among the Nations who rescued Jews during the war. These Conferences were covered by the mass media and consequently helped to bring the Holocaust to the forefront of American consciousness. The initial stage of the U.S. Holocaust Council can best be described as "Consciousness Awakening."

Even as the Remembrance took root in American awareness, the Council was seeking ways to translate Memory into visual artefacts. Wiesel wanted the visitor to the museum to come out two hundred years older; he spoke of a flaming temple that consumed time and space. How does one transfer into a visual object a mother's silent sob at the sight of her newborn baby being choked during an *aktion* so as not to betray the family hideout to the Nazi hunters? What visual magic can capture a self-induced anaesthetic state of mind while looking into a pistol's barrel? What words can describe the ceaseless clawing in your entrails, the cruising acid seeking food, the icy wind swishing into your very bones, the scorching asphalt under your feet on the Death March? Is there a designer in existence who could transcend experience to encompass that which was beyond experience?

The search for museum designers went into full gear. My work at the Council in the position of chief researcher directly involved me in the search. The working relationship between Wiesel and me evolved into friendship, and thanks to it I was often privy to privileged deliberations. We commissioned designer proposals from coast to coast as well as from Israel and France. Israel Gutman, a history professor at the Hebrew University, who combined first-hand experience in the 1943 Warsaw Ghetto Uprising with Holocaust scholarship, headed a newly-founded Content Committee of experts in charge of researching documents, photos and artefacts. What was missing from the Council's activities, however, was discharging its *raison d'etre*, namely erecting a museum.

The Council was lagging behind in fulfilling its Congressional mandate. Fundraising was slow and the actual work on planning the museum was not making much headway. The entire project seemed to hang in limbo. Absent from the impressive body that made up the Council were developers who had actual building experience and would translate the survivors' vision, poetically articulated by Wiesel, into bricks and mortar. Strochlitz and Lerman, working in tandem, discovered such a person.

A well-connected Washington mall developer with prodigious building experience eagerly agreed to undertake the enterprise. Exuding charm matched with a resolve that projected through his steely eyes, Sonny Abramson impressed Wiesel. "Even though he [Abramson] is not a member of the Council" writes Wiesel in his autobiography, *And the Sea is Never Full*, "he offers his total support... He says he wants nothing, he simply has faith in us and in our mission." To move the project from its stasis, a Museum Development Committee was formed to advise the Council on how to proceed with planning the Museum. Abramson invited Harvey Meyerhoff, also a developer, to join him in the Museum Development Committee. Like Abramson, Meyerhoff was blessed with worldly largess and connections, but he lacked the charm, persuasive skills and personality presence of the former. These lacks he made up for by strutting his stuff, as expressed in his mantra: "Let's move forward." And when he encountered opposition to his "move forward" slogan, he would throw his weight around in the kind of haughtiness associated with people who rode roughshod over opposition. Jointly, the two developers became at once the engines of the project and the cause of a friction that eventually changed the Council's character.

Eli Wiesel seems to have shared Lerman's and Strochlitz's enthusiasm for Abramson. "If we tell him what to do he will take care of everything having to do with renovation," Wiesel said, paraphrasing Abramson's promise in reference to the building on the Mall marked for housing the Holocaust Museum. But when the renovation of the old Accounting Building was deemed to be impossible and it had to be demolished, Abramson's role expanded from that of mere renovator. He argued that the Museum Development Committee would not be able to do its job without assuming the exclusive responsibility of shaping the exterior of the museum, which meant its architectural design. The interior designs, the exhibits, would remain the prerogative of the Content Committee, which would be manned by survivors and chaired by Sigmund Strochlitz. This division of responsibilities, on the face of it, was a reasonable compromise, but alas, not workable in museological terms. Building a museum, as is widely known, requires an organic link between form and function, namely between the exterior and the interior. Abramson and Meyerhoff, though not museologists, seized on this basic truism and pressed the Council to grant them full responsibility for both the interior and exterior designs.

## The Latter-Day Hellenists

From my vantage point on the Content Committee as it was preparing the blueprint for the exhibit designs, I watched in trepidation as Abramson and Meyerhoff encroached on the Council's purview. In person and in numerous memos, I kept Wiesel abreast of the news about the raiding of the Council. The shift from an appended entity to the Council to the sole decision-maker was illegal. The developers proposed a change to the bylaws that governed the Council to give their newly formed committee legitimacy. I was not the only one who saw the writing on the wall. In a memo to Wiesel dated October 15,1985, Sharon Freed, the Council's General Counsel, advised Wiesel to reject Abramson's and Meyerhoff's proposal to amend the bylaws "because this would have the effect of granting total autonomy and power to the

Museum Development Committee without the necessary supervision legally required by the Council." Silver Stuart, a renowned designer whom Wiesel had hired to design the building's interior, panned Abramson's architectural model in a letter as a "mediocre building." In the same letter of May 16, 1986, Silver put a rhetorical question to Wiesel: "Is he [Abramson] to impose on the future what one individual with no particular aesthetic, historic, or cultural background thinks is the proper Memorial?" The extent to which Abramson and his retinue cast their plutocratic shadow on the enterprise is evident in the letter's P.S.: "This is intended for your own eyes only. Please destroy." Silver feared that his contract was at risk should Abramson get hold of the letter.

In this antagonistic environment, in which the balance of power was increasingly listing toward the Museum Committee made up of developers not appointed by the President, what position did the survivors take? And most notably, how did the Council's Chairman react to the naked grab of the decision-making powers? The behaviour of the survivors provided a mother lode of information on the post-Holocaust survivorship mentality; an entire psychological morphology surfaced in those days of turmoil.

The survivors on the Council had made it in America. They were successful businessmen, active in their respective communities; their children were professionals. Yet for all their achievements, they felt alienated. Society turned a deaf ear to their story. They saw in the building of the Museum in the nation's capitol an acknowledgement of their suffering; their harrowing experience shown in a series of exhibits would receive recognition on a national scale. It took a long while for the survivors to come to a sense of self-worth, to come into their own. Elie Wiesel led them to believe that by preserving memory, they would redeem the dead and give meaning to survivorship. His word became an eleventh commandment that they would follow to the end of time.

Abramson detected the survivors' vulnerabilities and exploited them to the hilt. He had a hunter's eye for people's Achilles heels and released his arrows at the marked target. And they hit home. He spoke directly to the survivors' anxieties by letting it be known that unless the Council accepted the conditions put forward by the Museum Development Committee hook, line and sinker, the developers would pull out of the project. Against the developers' assertion that, "We've made it here, we know America," the survivors countered, "We were there and we know what it was like." On one memorable occasion, at a Content Committee meeting, Abramson addressed the survivors, stating: "We've building experience and we've a sense of America." His self-assured tone, which verged on hubris, enraged me, but

I kept my rage hidden. Still, I could not let him get away with this verbal step-strutting. "Mr. Abramson," I asked ever so calmly, "why do you think that my concentration camp experience, education and aesthetic sensitivity are less valuable than yours?" Dynamite-packed silence pervaded the room. No one dared to talk like that to Abramson. Some of the survivors at the conference table went into shock. I could read on their faces what was crossing their minds: "The Museum redemption has been put at risk by Pfefferkorn."

As soon as the meeting ended, my fellow survivors pulled me aside and spoke to me bluntly. "It is not your business to question Abramson," they said angrily. "Elie protects our Birthright; just follow his instructions." They were ready to sacrifice me on the altar of Memory. Obviously, Abramson injected paranoia into their hearts and they acted on it.

By now Wiesel was disabused of his initial idea of the developers' intentions. He did not, however, invoke his Chairmanship authority and put a halt to their colossal ambitions, fearing that they would quit if he acted. His fears were well founded. Karl Kaufman, an architect resident in Abramson's Tower Construction Company, drew a sketch design of the museum, which was presented to the Fine Arts Commission. The Commissioners roundly panned it, as did the Washington Post architectural critic. Voicing the sentiments of his fellow panellists, one Commissioner called the design akin to a monument dedicated to the perpetrators. The Fine Arts Commission Chairman saw the design and was astounded. "…The sheer massiveness of the elements… tends to an inhuman scale and an overstated strength."

I looked at Kaufman's design sketch through the prism of the "Chairman's Guidelines," authored by Wiesel with my assistance. I was astounded. I experienced a moment of suspended disbelief. The design sketch was an imposing building exuding power and self-assurance, the very negation of Wiesel's vision of the Museum as stated in the Guidelines: "I see a building at once arousing total despair and infinite hope, ultimate vulnerability and resolute firmness." Wiesel's vision was a delicate point counter-point minuet, an intimation of the human condition at the edge of existence. By contrast, Kaufman's design was worthy of Albert Speer's sketches of Hitler's visions of a post-war triumphant Berlin, imperious in its expanse and ostentatious in its façade.

Wiesel's vision, structured in syntactical opposites, expressed "…the frightful fragility and the resilient strength" of the concentration camp inmates, clashing with the solid mass of brick and mortar. When he saw this sketch, Wiesel openly distanced himself from the design, his sensibility offended. "Unfortunately, the present design," he asserted, "does not meet the historic and human values, nor the artistic requirements, inherent in this awesome event." Pulling no punches, he stated "that it is the wrong design. But for a variety of reasons we must accept it."

Abramson was not amused. He threatened that unless Wiesel's pejorative comments were removed, the developers and he would pull out of the project. Sadly, the threat hit home. Five days later a three-page corrective was sent to the Council members and other recipients of the original. "It was Albert Abramson," writes Wiesel, "who won the race against time and was successful." Lavishing further praises on Abramson and his chosen team of experts, he predicted that the model would be approved by the Council — after having been approved earlier by its executive committee and other regulatory committees.

Notwithstanding the deep friendship I felt for Elie Wiesel, for whom I had sparred with many adversaries both in Israel and in the United States; notwithstanding my dedication to our shared cause, something inside me moved, something I could not articulate — except the sensation of pain. In retrospect, I realize that this was the first sign of a fissure between Elie and me.

## Imitatio Dei

The Bible postulates that we are made in the Creator's image, and we, I extrapolate, in turn create images in our own image. But in the long chain of *Imitatio Dei*, imitating God's creation, the mimicked copies become somewhat fuzzy, eventually bearing little resemblance to the original image. Likewise, the Kaufman design, modified by Feingold, another designer, and made in Abramson's image, was a distorted copy of the original as stated in the "Chairman's Guides." What the design was lacking was an evocation of the brittle nature of civilization and the ease with which it could come apart.

In a stifled room at the offices of the U.S. Holocaust Memorial Council, the Council met in full session on April18th,1985, in the presence of the Museum Development Committee. Two building proposals were presented. The first was a three-dimensional design created by Zalman Enav, commissioned by Wiesel. A well-regarded Israeli architect, Enav had earlier shown the model to Wiesel and Marion, his spouse, at their home in Manhattan. Both were taken with it. Wiesel found it "sober, modest," as he put in his autobiography.

I vividly remember the scene. Enav came into the room greeted by faces expressing impatience, a kind of "get on with it." They looked on the hung-up sketches and building design with the edginess of car drivers waiting for the traffic light to change. No questions were asked. Some of the Councillors' faces showed discomfort, others signaled a palpable message of irritation. Abramson and his entourage sat self-assured about the outcome. Enav's model was far closer to Wiesel's vision as crafted in the "Chairman's Guide." It was a model that intimated the fragility of the human spirit and shades of Jewishness that should have pleased the Jewish consciousness of the survivors. But this was not to be.

Wiesel stood, chin cupped in palm, and looked on as Enav was taking down the sketches. He did not utter a single word. Against my better judgement, I broke ranks with my fellow survivors and crossed the forbidden line in an open act of solidarity with Enav and in defiance of the developers, as well as Elie Wiesel.

Whether they had spent the Holocaust in a concentration camp, masquerading as Christians, or in hideouts, the survivors around the table were veterans of alienation; they had experienced banishment, loneliness and dehumanization. One would have expected that these painful memories would emerge to guide them in these trying circumstances, when human dignity was at stake. Wiesel had advocated that the ordeals experienced by the survivors made them attuned to human suffering. Contrary to Wiesel's views, suffering is not necessarily a morally refining agent that turns apathy into compassion, greed into generosity, meanness into graciousness and ambition into humility. With few exceptions, the good did not become better and the bad might have become worse. I met survivors who brought with them Darwinian survival rawness to post-Holocaust life; and survivors whose suffering made them sensitive to that of others. Basically, when facing a dilemma, when a moral choice had to be made, the survivors' past ordeals do not factor into the equation. The choice is determined by their perceived exigency and driven by impulses of the self. Those survivors who sat around the table had one thing in mind: the Memorial Museum — and only Abramson could deliver it. This belief they held to, even at the cost of Enav's human dignity. And how did Wiesel, the shield of human dignity, react to the stripping bare of Enav's? He stood there, a reporter on an assignment, taking mental notes for a newspaper article.

A document dated April 18, 1985, prepared by Marion Craig, Wiesel's assistant, describes Enav's presentation in three lines. Abramson's sponsored model, the one which reminds Wiesel of "a glorified supermarket," was discussed and unanimously approved. Wiesel mentions that the vote was taken "while he was out of the room giving an interview on television." It is surprising that the model intended to become a Memorial Museum on the Mall, a Remembrance site for future generations, was voted on in its Chairman's absence. In an interview I conducted with Enav in his Tel-Aviv office in 1988, he painfully recalled that day when he presented his model and "no one spoke a word. But what most astonished me is that Elie didn't say a word, he didn't promote his own concept." Is it far-fetched to assume that his walkout to the interview was not coincidental?

## The Bitburg Offence to Memory

On April 11, 1985, the White House announced that President Reagan was planning a trip to Germany to lay a wreath at the Bitburg military cemetery. The visit would be made, declared the White House, "in a spirit of forty years of peace, in a spirit of economic and military compatibility."

Even as the Council convened in New York on April 15th to craft a response to the White House announcement, a shattering story broke. The media reported that the Bitburg cemetery contained about 30 graves of Waffen S.S. soldiers. During the Council's debate in New York and three days later in Washington, I watched from the sidelines as a human drama unfolded. Genuine passion, typical Washingtonian politicking, and self-serving egotism, all wrapped up in solemn speeches and sprinkled with vows of faithfulness to the dead and the living, filled the airless room. Yet the Council voted down a resignation proposal spearheaded by Sigmund Strochlitz and McAfee Brown. The majority of the survivors voted against resignation. Their vote foreshadowed things to come.

By now, I had worked closely with Wiesel for about seven years, spent time with him in conversation on a variety of subjects, read his works, listened to his speeches, and believed that I had a good grasp of his personality. Though not a naturally forthcoming person, he nevertheless shared his thinking and moods with me. The fact that we talked in Hebrew made intimacy easier to come by. But every so often I was taken aback by some of his actions. His egregious absence from the vote over the choice of the model bewildered me, and his ambivalent stand on the resignation proposal left me bemused.

Wiesel had not taken a firm position concerning the resignation issue. Raul Hilberg, an impeccable chronicler, took notes at the meeting and remarked that "Elie was not ready to resign." Indeed, the minutes of the meeting corroborate Hilberg's observation. Wiesel called for a battle with the powers that be. "I will turn it around — resignation wouldn't be enough, and therefore we decide to accept the call to battle." The battle cry met with applause. The Council's majority and the majority of the survivors were determined to stay, and it is for this reason that Wiesel claimed that he did not want to sway the Council to resign.

Wiesel enjoyed enormous moral prestige not only among the members of the Council but among the public at large and the mass media, which supported his efforts to persuade the President to cancel his visit to Bitburg. On April 19th, 1985, he was accorded the Congressional Medal in the presence of the President and other political notables in Roosevelt's room at the White House. In the full glare of international television, he spoke truth to power, calling on the President not to go to Bitburg. "Tell us now that you will not go there: *that* place is not your place. Your place is with the *victims* of the S.S."

It was a speech that reverberated in the mass media in the States as well as in Europe. On May 13th, the President's visit to the Bitburg cemetery was followed by a visit to Bergen-Belsen, a former concentration camp.

Around that time, I accidentally met Abramson, who was moved by Wiesel's appearance. "I could not make such a speech, even if they put me away for years," Abramson admitted, adding, "But buildings are my trade." I wondered whether he was trying to use me as a conduit to convey this message to Wiesel. Despite the Council's reluctance to resign, Wiesel could still have swayed its members to change their minds. He is charismatic and smooth: I saw him once appear before a Senate committee and witnessed how these speech-weary senators became alive listening to his melodious voice.

Wiesel's later resignation from the Council's Chair in 1986 did not surprise me. What surprised me was the timing. A recent recipient of the Nobel Prize, his tenure of chairmanship renewed by the White House, he enjoyed tremendous prestige internationally and was therefore well positioned to take on the developers. He chose, however, to submit his resignation. The resignation was guided by granite realism. This enterprise needed a person with CEO skills that he lacked, Wiesel asserted in a rather sombre voice; the time had come to hand over the enterprise to the developers.

In the wake of Bud Meyerhoff's appointment to succeed Wiesel, the process of the survivors' marginalization began. It was not, I admit, done in Bolshevik elimination style; rather it was in a distinctively Washington style that the key positions on the content committee were reshuffled. Up to this point it had been widely accepted that the architecture of the Museum building would be the sole province of the developers and the interior design would be the responsibility of the Content Committee, chaired by Strochlitz. But the developers had some other ideas in mind.

Influenced by Wiesel's recurrent theme extolling suffering as an agent of moral refinement, and thanks to my own naiveté, I tried to rally the survivors around the Pledge of Remembrance taken at the Western Wall in 1981. I put together a document titled "The Survivors' Credo" which invoked the survivors' commitment to the memory of the victims and urged them to ensure that "we have a decisive function in shaping the exhibits and the other content components of the Museum." To the best of my recollection, the only Council member who responded to my missive was Sigmund Strochlitz. By then, stripped of his status by the developers because of his opposing stand to them, he commended my efforts but expressed doubt regarding their success. "Eli," he said, in a grave voice, "what you're doing is admirable but fruitless: the King's dead, long live the king." He spoke to my fears and yet I would not give up.

I must have made countless calls to survivors and other Council members sympathetic to the survivors' cause. One of the first was James Freed. A senior partner in the renowned I.M. Pei architecture office, Freed was a German refugee who had been only a few cattle cars away from Auschwitz. Wiesel retained him to design the Museum's architecture. At Wiesel's suggestion I had earlier met him in his office and elaborated on the survivors' vision. His questions, like laser beams, hit the core issues. Now I appealed to him to help protect the rightful places of the survivors on the Council's committees. In his letter to me of February 26, 1987, he regrets that the survivors were standing on the sidelines. "It would be very sad if the survivors, who, after all, are the only first-hand witnesses to the tragedy, felt disengaged in the process of making the museum and its exhibits, as you seem to indicate." The truth of the matter was that survivors did not choose to be disengaged; they were being methodically disengaged.

The way the survivors reacted to this momentous slide of their positions provided a study of human nature. Most survivors on the Council resigned themselves to a passive presence; they settled for being listened to without being heard. A minority hailed the new rulers as the carriers of their legacy to the Mall — their ardent desire to see the Museum, to tell their stories and give purpose to their sufferings. Miles Lerman, a one-time Wiesel loyalist and a close friend of Strochlitz, told me, "For us, survivors, content goes to the very heart; it's a burning issue with us." Encouraged by these words, I thought I had found an ally to ensure the rightful place for the survivors on the Content Committee. We arranged a meeting in New Jersey. A few minutes into the conversation, I realized that he had switched allegiances. Between our last telephone conversation and this meeting, his pronouns had shifted. Whereas in the telephone conversation it was "we survivors," now he had shifted to, "The most I can get for *you* are a few spots on the Content Committee." And to dramatize his new alliance, he grabbed the ashtray from the table, lifted it to the level of his mouth, and said, "If Elie tells Sigmund that this is Cholent, he'll eat it. I'm a realist."

On the train back to Washington, I took stock of the situation. The survivors had relinquished their birthright, as Miles used to call it before switching allegiances. From the very beginning my attempt to rally the survivors was doomed; I had been tilting at windmills. My own position on the staff was in jeopardy. My survivor friends on the Council left or were made to leave; and those who stayed behind lost their voices.

I was alone.

## The Water Cooler Metaphor

Flush with victory upon his appointment to the Council's Chair, Meyerhoff convened a meeting of the Council staff, followed by a meeting of the Content Committee and its staff. It was apparent that he had come loaded for bear. He started off by laying out his streamlining policy, triumphantly declaring "an end to waste." When I asked in the most civil voice I could muster if he would point out the waste, he lit into me with a passionate intensity usually reserved for hunting game. Around the table sat the survivors, wrapped in silence, the latest crossovers to the new regime. Later, when I joined the line at the buffet, the survivors gave me a wide berth and staff members who only weeks ago had sought my council and had sweet words for me navigated away from me. I became an untouchable, a sad evocation of those dark days when contact with a *Muselmann* was a death omen. Now, I morphed into a latter-day *Muselmann*. In the washroom, Miles was visibly uncomfortable with what had just happened and said, "We, the survivors, must settle for less now," referring to our influence on the Council. Ben Meed, another survivor — an earlier crossover — cautioned me to "be more careful."

But I was not the only survivor purged from the Council. Sigmund Strochlitz, who had dedicated his life to the cause of Remembrance, was excluded from the newly-appointed executive committee and "...not one survivor rallied to his support," remarked Wiesel in *And the Sea is Never Full*. "A comrade, a colleague had been humiliated, and they all looked away. The same was true for Pfefferkorn." He then asks a soberly shocking question, indicating a dark view of the survivors and by extension of human nature. "How can these people labour for remembrance of the past," Wiesel wonders, "when they flout the dignity of the living people?"

An astonishing query coming from a man who merely a couple of months earlier had exalted the survivors as paragons of compassion, and then stood by in silence when Enav's human dignity was left hanging. And he answers his own rhetorical question: "But then I expect too much of them. They are human, hence capable of anything. Just as everyone else."[17]

## In Image and Word

"One picture is worth a thousand words," perceptively remarked Frederick R. Barnard in 1927. This observation was intended to point out the advantage of the visual over the verbal in advertisements. The advertisement mavens on Madison Avenue must have known this all along, though to make sure, they accentuated the picture with a label. Indeed, a pictorial design makes an impact that a string of words by itself, no matter how effectively formulated, could hardly achieve. The following is an illustration of the way an image underlined by words is likely to affect the viewer.

A picture of an orange tree on whose branches hang ripe oranges spouting a flow of juice, set against the background of a scorching midday sun in the desert, can stimulate thirst. In the Israeli context, an added text which says, "You don't need Moses's staff to strike juice," might stir an urge to slake that thirst. But would a pictorial device of comparable effectiveness put on view in a museum, showing atrocities, trigger an emotional response as strong as that of the orange display? I would like to use the Holocaust Museum in Washington to illustrate my thinking.

I'm indebted to Mrs. Lola Berliner, a survivor, who, after visiting the Washington Museum, raised the problematic issue of transmitting experiences engendered in extreme situations. Our conversation has added to my considerations. Visualize a single tin spoon leaning on a dented tin mess kit, and beside it a text describing the object: "These were the utensils used by a concentration camp inmate, without which he could not last the day." In the orange advertisement image, the perceived palpability of the artefact is within the Israeli experience. By contrast, the tin mess kit image, though

---

[17]  Elie Wiesel, *And the Sea is Never Full: Memoirs, 1969-*. New York: Alfred A. Knopf, 1971, P. 247.

accurately described by the text, misses the quintessence of the story beyond the displayed object. The human experience enfolded in the spoon and the mess kit is outside the viewer's experiential range, similar to a motorist driving on an unfamiliar route whose visual view of the road is limited by a hidden curve. What the viewer sees in the photo is just the foreground, but the atmospheric environment, the making of the photo, is beyond the viewer's reach. Admittedly, we have the capacity to relate to death without having died, because it is a vicariously human experience.

Elie Wiesel envisioned the museum as a flaming temple that changes the visitor's total being. He saw in his mind's eye an exhibit projecting fear and trembling in a moment of time. But this moment in time is not replicable. I will try to make my point by a scenario drawn from my own experience.

A museum visitor comes across a photograph of me: the label beside the photo says: "A fifteen-year-old new arrival in the Majdanek concentration camp stands on the 'selection,' about to be dispatched either to the gas chamber or to slavery." The photo is authentic, the description accurate, and yet they do not convey the moment, my self-induced void of feeling as the baton points at me, assigning the boy in the image to his fate. A picture may be worth a thousand words, sharpened by a write-up, only when it recalls the familiar steeped in a common experience. This is precisely where we, the survivors, guided by Wiesel, erred in our controversy with the developers.

A Holocaust museum by its very nature is designed to afford a fleeting moment of dread that will not stay with the visitor unless he faces an emotional crisis that casts his mind back to the exhibits. The exhibits are not meant to invoke the imagination nor encourage memory unless they evoke the familiar.

Ironically, due to their lack of historical imagination, the developers intuited that the story told in the exhibits should be fashioned in a style that relates to American sensibilities, neither exceeding the range of human experience nor making undue demands on the visitor's imagination. When Sonny Abramson pronounced his aphorism, "We've made it here, we know America," he was right, but the survivors' response, "We were there and we know what it was like," begs the question: "How do you transmit this experiential knowledge to a Midwest museum audience, for example?"

The Washington Holocaust Museum, shaped according to a mental déjà vu, testifies to this with its enormous success. The snaking lines of people around the building waiting to enter the museum, people who come from all walks of life and regions, are visibly moved by the exhibits; their human commonality is offended at the sight of arbitrary suffering inflicted on human beings by their fellow human beings.

The visitors come out of the Museum knowing *about* the Holocaust, but will never know *it*, which is the sole domain of the survivor. Man does not live on pain alone; or, as the Yiddish saying has it, too many tears are not good for you. One should also note that the politicians on the Hill are pleased with what their constituents tell them back home: they were moved by what they saw in the Museum.

In retrospect, my retort to Sonny Abramson that my historical knowledge and life-experience carried as much weight as his worldly wisdom was, while basically right, misplaced within the American context. Had the Museum been shaped to match the pristine vision advocated by Wiesel and his spiritual kin, it would have been a hallowed temple of Memory, but, I am afraid, not transmittable.

### The Life of Pi

The psychological impossibility of conveying an experience outside the realm of normal human behaviour is convincingly illustrated in a Booker Prize novel, *The Life of Pi*, by Yann Martel. The author, describes the shipwreck of the *Tsimtsum* on the high Pacific sea. Pi's family, the owners of a zoo, were shipping its animals from India to Canada. They went down with most of their animals when the ship sank. The only human survivor is the sixteen-year-old Pi, who finds himself sharing the lifeboat with a hyena, an orang-utan, a wounded zebra and a 450-pound Bengal tiger. The tiger, named Richard Parker, satisfies his enormous appetite by devouring his former jungle mates. Finally, the only two passengers left adrift on the lifeboat are Pi and the tiger, sharing an uneasy co-existence. Ironically, the survival of the human and the animal depends on mutual accommodation. Isaiah's prophecy virtually comes true: man and tiger dwell together. Resolved and infinitely ingenious, Pi faces the ferocity of nature both inside and outside the lifeboat. He hooks fish; nets turtles to feed the beast and himself; discovers emergency water cans to slake his own thirst and his companion's. The tiger, for its part, refrains from eating the boy. After seven months of drifting on whimsical currents, the lifeboat mercifully reaches the Mexican shores.

Since *Tsimtsum* is registered with a Japanese company, two agents of the Japanese Ministry of Transport are assigned to investigate the cause of the shipwreck. After initially getting lost, they finally arrive at Pi's location. The two government officials bear the names of Tomohiro Okamoto and Atsuro

Chiba. Their absurd-sounding names add a further ironic touch to a situation fraught with irony, worthy of Eugene Ionesco's "Rhinoceros." Lying in bed and stuffing himself with cookies supplied by his two guests, apparently to humour him, Pi narrates his ordeals on sea. But the two investigators question the truth of the survivor's story. "We don't believe your story, Mr. Patel," says Mr. Okamoto bluntly, calling him by his family name. "The tiger is an incredibly dangerous wild animal. How could you survive in a lifeboat with one?" As they keep on probing the veracity of each described vignette, each narrated episode meets with their outspoken incredulity. Pi's story is off their imaginative spectrum, a daring defiance to their empirical knowledge. They "would like to know what really happened." To which Pi asks whether "you want another story?"

"Uhh… no," they purr, "but we would like to know what really happened." They insist, "We don't want any invention. We want the 'straight facts' as you say in English." And Pi complies.

Amused by their lack of imagination, he tells them the story of the shipwreck from another perspective. He draws from the original the basic elements, the bricks and mortar, so to speak, and shapes the story with a new architectural facade. Drawing on his narrative skills, he tells them a story that corresponds to human reality as they know it.

In his refitted story, Pi replaces the animal lifeboat passengers in the original story with four humans: Mother, the ship's cook, a wounded sailor and himself. A struggle over food ensues after the cook steals the food and water supplies; the cook, who would stop at nothing to survive, practices cannibalism. Indeed he is what has become known in concentration camp literature as a rapacious survivor. The cook's naked brutality offends Mother's human dignity, and she makes no bones about it. Eventually, Pi knifes the cook to death as an act of revenge for killing his Mother.

On finishing the story, Pi wants to know whether this story is better. "So tell me, since it makes no factual difference to you and you can't prove the question either way, which story do you prefer? Which is the better story — the story with animals or the story without animals?"[18] The refurbished story sounds plausible to Okamoto's and Chiba's ears. Human strife and revenge are familiar to them. The sentiments have credence.

*The Life of Pi* throws light on the inherent complexity involved in telling the story about the Holocaust, whether in image or in word; and the last chapters of the novel partially explained the difficulties I had (and still have)

---

[18]  Yann Martel, *Life of Pi*. Toronto: Vintage Canada, 2002, p. 352.

in articulating my own experience — even to people whom I considered vicarious survivors. On the first walk I had taken with Jonathan on Hampstead Heath, he gingerly phrased his questions so as not to be intrusive, careful not to tear my thinly-filmed wounds. My limited English vocabulary, at the time lagging behind the complexity of the narrative, frustrated my efforts. Later, on our subsequent walks, I cautiously revealed episodes of my endurance that merged into the apocalyptic vision of the Holocaust which he harboured.

With David, the telling was much easier. He had the historical knowledge and sought confirmation from Memory to construct for himself a virtual Holocaust world. By then my vocabulary was well honed, making transmission easier. I found in David an eager listener. The reason that I withheld my ordeals from my family and friends was that I wanted to be treated as an ordinary person and to be judged on my own merits and demerits. When teaching the Holocaust, I tiptoed around my personal life if it happened to come up. My emotional equilibrium was holding out, only occasionally being upset. One of the upsets caught me totally by surprise.

## My Secret Garden

I taught two courses at Tel-Aviv University in the Overseas Programme: a Holocaust course, titled "The Land of the Grotesque," and the other, on the Theatre of the Absurd, titled "Language Dissonance in Pinter's Plays." Applying my tried-out objective correlative teaching method, which allowed me perspective, I tried to initiate my class into the paradoxical realities of living under siege. A seriously-inclined student of mine who must have spent more time in the library than on the sprawling campus lawns came into my office after class. His face sombre, his body language showing distress, Kevin was groping for words. "I've a question and I don't know how to put it," he stuttered. Trailing behind his opening sentence came, "Dr. Pfefferkorn."

I tried to ease his concern by expressing my response with Pinteresque humour, saying that I wore many caps, among them one reserved for emergencies. Indeed, he looked like a patient in need of immediate attention. My first thought was that he'd gotten a girl pregnant and he sought my advice. "I've come across your article on Abba Kovner," he said, "and at one point it implies that you're a Holocaust survivor." Indeed, a pregnant statement, but thankfully not the one I'd dreaded. Yes, I recalled making such an oblique reference. "So?" I uttered in an affected tone in anticipation of the next sentence. It came in a tone of bemusement pigmented with a sulk.

"But you've never mentioned it in class." I motioned him to sit. This would be a tasking session for both of us. Now it was my turn to seek the appropriate words. After a couple of significant shuffles in my seat, I explained this covert part of my pedagogical conduct. "Sharing my teenaged ordeals in a class situation might erect a partition between you and me." I paused. Kevin sat still and alert. "'He was there, so how can I question him? I might hurt him, offend him' you would be whispering in awe." I spoke slowly and deliberately. "And this might put an end to the class discourse which is the basis of good teaching." I then told him about my clash with the black students when I was a teaching assistant at Brown University and how I lashed out at them for making the slavery of their ancestors a launching pad from which to assault my racial whiteness. In my outrage, I had not evoked the Holocaust or my survivorship. "Each one of us has a secret garden hidden from prying eyes, let alone trespassers. Mine is the Shoa experience."

He listened eagerly to what I was saying. Underlying Kevin's hurt was the fact that I'd failed to be forthcoming with the class when teaching such an emotionally charged subject. From his perspective, the hurt feeling was not groundless. It was Friday afternoon and I wanted to get back home to Haifa to avoid the weekend rush hour. "Kevin," I said, "the class meets next week; I'll present this issue, but you must promise me not to mention the subject of our conversation." He proved to be as good as his word.

When I met the class the following week, I elaborated on what I had earlier told Kevin. I had planned to take the class to the Carmelite Monastery on the Carmel in the last leg of the course. But in the light of the recent skeleton discovery, as I called it, I moved up the date of the trip. The purpose of it was to meet Brother Daniel, whose original name was Rufeisen.

Brother Daniel was an intriguing personality. In 1941 or thereabouts he had obtained forged identity papers indicating that he was a *Volksdeutscher* whose ancestors had immigrated to Russia in the Middle Ages. His bilingual skills and intimate knowledge of the local culture were invaluable assets to the Gestapo and the police. Employed as a translator by the police, he had access to secret information concerning the ghetto and other plans. He managed to establish contact with an underground cell in the ghetto and funneled that information to it. His activities were uncovered and he was duly arrested. During one of the interrogations, he managed to escape and found refuge in a convent, where he converted to Catholicism and eventually took vows.

Because of his ardent Zionist convictions and his desire to be nearer to family members who lived in Israel, Brother Daniel requested to be placed in the Carmelite Monastery in Haifa. On his arrival, he applied for Israeli citizenship under The Law of Return, which bestows automatic citizenship on immigrants of the Jewish faith. Daniel's faith was, however, Christian, and so he did not qualify. He argued that he was Jewish by nationality and Christian by religion, but Judaism does not recognize such a division. He appealed to the High Court, which upheld the Government's decision. His was a journey, I thought, that would interest my students.

Brother Daniel freely talked about his Via Dolorosa journey and openly carried the Cross. A natural raconteur who carried his past over into the present with emotional immediacy, he engaged his listeners with exciting stories about his journey from Jerusalem to Rome, both of which he held sacred.

## Speak No Evil of Man: He, Himself, is Testimony to It

By the time I came into my own academically, I was pulled by two opposite impulses. I was drawn to teaching drama and to teaching the Holocaust. The transformation of words into stage dynamics fascinated me; the actors' ability to beguile time enchanted me. Shakespeare's view that the whole world was a stage held me in a strong grip. And there was this underlying past, heavily weighing on me, that would not go away and persistently demanded my attention. In the course of time I realized that the pursuit of the Jacobean and the Absurdist plays were not moving in opposite directions. Rather, these plays navigated me to examine the dark side of humanity that occupied much of my mental time.

Or perhaps it was the other way round: my bleak view of humanity drew me to these plays — a happy junction of sentiments. My experience watching the stage from the comfort of the theatre seat differed vastly from being the one standing on the roll call grounds. Accordingly, describing my singular ordeals under siege necessitated using a language corresponding to their singularity.

While describing the rampant evil in the Jacobean plays and the incoherence of the Theatre of the Absurd, I can draw from the extant wealth of critical language; there is no corresponding extant language, however, to express my experience. My attempts to give it voice raise aesthetic and epistemological problems. I look for a verbal construct made up of coherent syntactical structures that will convey the incoherent camp existence; distil the real from the surreal and yet make the latter palpable; stir the readers' emotional depth with an underpinning intellectual statement.

Ultimately, what I try to do is to pull my prospective readers' knowledge a notch up, from "knowing of it" to "knowing about it." My pedagogic aim has been to achieve the opposite effect from the one produced by the widely acclaimed film "Life is Beautiful," directed by Roberto Benigni. In this film, the director revamps the incredible nightmarish quasi-life endured by the concentration camp inmates into a dreamlike spectacle, its characters choreographed in slow-motion movements veiled in a gauze-like screen. Unlike the museum developers, Benigni had a creative imagination, but like them he was wanting in historical consciousness. And like the developers, he tailored his product to meet the sensibilities of those who only "know of the Holocaust." These aesthetics, undoubtedly, made the audience watching the film find it tolerable, but they came at the cost of authenticity.

Even as I watched "Life is Beautiful," I recalled the last stretch of the "Death March," amidst the final sputtering of the Nazi destruction machine. As our long column was slouching toward the east, a small ghostly-looking column emerged from behind the curve, shuffling towards the west. We passed alongside each other without so much as questioning its senselessness: a quintessential picture of the Apocalypse.

In reminiscing, I try to recreate my response to this apocalyptic moment in its native being and transmit it darkly, bearing in mind the volume of my readers' mental receptivity. To put it succinctly: I touch Memory at its rawness and aim at bringing it closer to the readers' own experience.

For decades I could not find my voice and modulate it to a pitch audible to the uninitiated. But even after having found my voice, I was reluctant to talk to large audiences. I was apprehensive lest rehashing the story, even in its multiple versions and from different perspectives, might dilute the essence of the story, make fuzzy its primary impressions, and result in blunting its momentous import. This I much feared. Admittedly, there are survivors who raise the spectre of a selection as if with a magic wand and can repeat stories with revelatory excitement. I have neither the magic nor the wand to conjure the scene as if the audience lived it. And yet the tale must be told and told by the survivors before they are gathered up to their sixty-years-postponed appointment. Many a time I've wondered what spurred me to take up this endeavour to record my war experience. I am not the Coleridge Ancient-Mariner type, driven by an urge to tell the tale of horror; nor do I believe in the overly optimistic "Never Again" slogan. So why bear witness? I can only reflect on these questions and speculate on their answers.

Ironically enough, it was the Jacobean Theatre and the Theatre of the Absurd that prompted me to take a scholarly interest in the Holocaust. The motiveless malignance underlined by cognitive dissonance in the Jacobean plays and the severance between cause and effect in the plays of the Absurd linked the two theatrical genres and both, in turn, established a link with the Holocaust. Undeniably, the stage on which the characters displayed their evil and the concentration camp grounds on which evil manifested itself were vastly different from each other, but the inherent human malediction was essentially the same. Both the grounds and the stages created the environment by which human nature was tested in extreme situations. Since I was a test case in one and an observer in the other, I believed that I would have better access to the dark impulses of human behaviour.

I was therefore well positioned to transmit knowledge of the lurking evil in Man through the prism of a witness and an observer. At the start of my pursuit, I thought that I could testify with impartiality. After a decade of academic training, I believed that I would use my academic discipline and be able to handle the survivors' accounts and other related materials dispassionately. But once I touched Memory, it stirred images from their dormant nocturnal reveries. Though in imparting my story I've encountered numerous difficulties, I have tried to narrow the gap between recall of the inceptive moment and its narration.

When the Holocaust emerged from obscurity and began making its cultural marks on both sides of the Atlantic in the early seventies, an array of pretenders claimed kinship with it. Institutions, organizations and individuals rushed to lay claims to its legacy. Some even jockeyed to assume the position of survivorship, though they could hardly tell the difference between the sweet smell of incense and the noxious odour of gas. "We are all survivors" ran the mantra. The legitimate heirs to the Holocaust were the Jewish people who spoke for the victims, but Christianity also claimed moral and spiritual kinship to them.

Both Catholic and Protestant theologians put forward sophisticated arguments to stake their claims. They took the suffering of the Jews at the hands of the Nazis as a Second Crossing, the re-enactment of the Suffering Servant, *Eved Adonai,* and assumed the Redemption would ensue. Franklin H. Littell, a Protestant Minister and scholar, put forth this theory in the title of his book: *The Crucifixion of the Jews.* The book's title alludes to the similarities between the Golgotha Cross and the Auschwitz Gallows. In the spirit of the Christian *Figura* tradition, Jurgen Moltman, a celebrated Tübingen theologian, asserts that the Golgotha Crucifixion points to the Auschwitz Gallows, a continuum in the unfolding of the Suffering Servant story. Referring to Elie Wiesel's *Night,* which describes a public hanging at Auschwitz, Moltman suggests, "God himself hung on the gallows," adding that "like the Cross of Christ, Auschwitz is in God himself. Even Auschwitz is taken up into the grief of the Father, the surrender of the Son and the Power of the Spirit."[19]

Less dramatic but no less emphatic, Cardinal John O'Connor follows the Figural interpretation of the Bible. On his visit to the Holy Land in 1987, the Cardinal mused aloud, "It might well be that the Holocaust may be an enormous gift that Judaism has given to the world." What the Jewish suffering taught the world, the Cardinal continued, was "the sacredness of dignity of every human person."[20] An ambiguously suffused evocation of the Suffering Servant ideology is manifested in an excellent Czech film *United we Fall*, in which a character named Joseph finds refuge with a Christian family in the bosom of a Maria-like character. An egregious attempt at appropriating the Holocaust was demonstrated in the outer environment of Auschwitz, where Carmelite nuns planted crosses around the camp.

What particularly concerns me, and the reason I have inserted this bit of theology into the memoir, is the question of how my ordeals fit into this theological configuration? Does it make my memories easier to bear? Can it console me for the loss of my family and classmates? And what about the loss of my youth: the laughs with the boys; the mischievous pranks played on the girls; the provocative questions put to the teachers? All these youthful thrills cruelly cut and left fragmented, emerging in the twitching hours of the night — what of them? At an intellectual level, in what way does the Suffering Servant theory help me to sort out my internal turmoil?

Jewish theologians have offered a variety of answers to these queries. Best described as the "Cyclical School," one points out the alternating phases of building followed by destruction in the course of the tortuous Jewish history, ultimately ending with the establishment of a Jewish State in1948. Israel, according to this theory, is the Divine reward for the long-lasting suffering which climaxed in the Holocaust. And then there is the Universal explanation of God's working in mysterious ways — ways out of bounds to mortals. But the theory known by the name of "God's Face Concealment," *Hester Panim*, is the most intriguing. It posits that God removes His protection from the chosen people because of their straying

---

[19]  Jurgen Moltman, *The Crucified God*. London: SCM Press, 1974, p. 278.

[20]  The New Yorker, March 30, 1987.

from the Torah to cavort with strange gods. By contrast, when abiding by God's ways, the Israelites enjoy God's protective shield. Evidently unsettled with this tit-for-tat premise, Zvi Kolitz, the author of *Yossele Rakover Speaks to God*, tweaks the text, a tweak worth quoting in full:

> God has veiled His countenance from the world, and
> thus delivered mankind over to its most savage impulses.
> And unfortunately, when the power of the impulse dominates
> the world, it is quite natural that the first victims should be those
> who embody the divine and the pure.[21]

This is hardly a comforting explanation for the survivors. What it suggests is that purity incurs punishment — an idea that harks back to the God-Satan wager in *The Book of Job*.

## The Lost Generation

Abba Kovner, who became the ultimate bard of the *Shoa*, captures the moment when the survivors emerged from under the siege. Attuned to his fellow-survivor's psyche, he encapsulates it in a metaphor:

> As in a flood dammed too late
> they will come, come to the shore
> their hearts full of pity, to set
> the survivors with swollen feet
> in the book of chronicles,
> to extend a brother's hand!
> And they gave them a hand
> In spite of their ugly smell,
> And before heart and reason could separate
> They cried,
> and applauded them.
> As in a melodrama that ended:
> the characters
> are asked
> to step before the curtains! (My Little Sister)

Indeed, we were met with wonderment mixed with compassion, but even before the wonderment could settle in, compassion vanished; the sentimental

---

[21] Zvi Kolitz, *Yossele Rakover Speaks to God*. New Jersey: KTAV Publishing House, Inc., p. 17.

*tableau vivant* came to an end. From New York to Paris to Tel-Aviv, we were gently prodded to merge into the mainstream: Look forward; move on; be like us. These slogans cut across countries and cities where the survivors came to build homes and find peace of mind. On reading the memoirs written by survivors, one wonders why our well-meaning well-wishers wanted us out of sight.

Arthur Herzberg, a prominent Jewish leader and the rabbi of Englewood Cliff Temple in New Jersey, related the following anecdote at the Holocaust Museum in Washington about the time he had, in 1961, invited Elie Wiesel to give a talk about *Night* at his Temple. "Thousands of Jews lived in Englewood in 1961, but only eighteen people showed up," the rabbi told his audience. After Wiesel finished his talk and the sparse audience left, an odd few of people lingered in the corner. Finally they approached him, "I was there too," said one, *sotto voce*. "And I was there too," whispered another. The survivors, like the Marranos, were closeted in their identities, for their stories sounded incredible.

A glance at the mental make-up of the American Jewish community reveals that at the time it suffered from a lack of self-assertiveness. The survivors' very presence unsettled their belief in the lofty image of God's paragon creation — Man. They could not countenance evil on the scale represented by the survivors — not even in silence. It was not malice. Rather, it was fear of losing faith in the very tenets of the Judeo-Christian culture that shaped their consciousness and made them who they were.

At the time Wiesel wrote his seminal essay "A Plea for the Survivors," entreating his American fellow Jews to show sympathy to their brethren, I lived in Israel. If in the States the survivors' presence disturbed the socio-psychological state of mind of the Jewish community, in Israel the survivors upset the Zionist self-assertive spirit. Perceived as meek for not resisting their mortal enemy, the survivors were looked down upon. The thrust of Israeli civic society and its governmental institutions was to absorb the survivors into Israeliness. The slogan, "Be like us, act like us," was persistent. The government did not recognize the survivors' need for healing time before immersing themselves in the Israeli culture and ethos. The Israelis gave no quarter. At the time, I was reviewing books and theatre for the *Haaretz* Literary Supplement. Thursday, the last day of the submissions, the columnists crowded into the small editorial office. A lot of bantering went on, invectives were bandied around, and the lion's share of them was portioned out to the author-survivors. At times the banter took on a bantering tone, at other times it turned nasty.

I stood there and kept silent.

The legacy that we are leaving behind is ambiguous. We've borne witness to the inherent evil of humanity and its consequences when unhinged from civil constraints, but our testimony has hardly affected human nature. At most, it afforded a new look into its tortuous complexity. Cain's feigned innocence — "Am I my brother's keeper?" — has echoed through history and still reverberates in our own times.

The very last sentence put down by Chaim Kaplan, the author of *The Scroll of Agony* — *The Warsaw Ghetto Diary*, reads: "When my life ends, what will become of my Diary?" And when mine ends, will my memoir survive to keep on telling the story? And has it been worth it?

# Index

CPSIA information can be obtained at www.ICGtesting.com
Printed in the USA
LVOW111031250912

300204LV00003B/1/P

9 781618 111579